Fortu... ...rs, and just kept right on travel... ...bouts as a freelance illustrator and children's book author. She has recently turned her attention to more adult themes of travel, food and men – her three greatest passions in life. *Men on the Menu* is her debut memoir.

Bambi lives in the leafy inner suburbs of Melbourne, where she enjoys hanging out in cafés, going to just about every movie that's showing (including a zombie film by mistake), experimenting on her friends with new recipes and being a passionate advocate for animal welfare.

She currently has no husband, or children, but is thinking of adopting a three-legged dog.

See more of Bambi's amazing odyssey researching *Men on the Menu* at www.pinterest.com/bambi1183/ and learn more at www.bambismyth.com.au.

BAMBI SMYTH

Men on the Menu

BLINK
bringing you closer

Published by Blink Publishing
107-109 The Plaza,
535 King's Road,
Chelsea Harbour,
London, SW10 0SZ

www.blinkpublishing.co.uk

facebook.com/blinkpublishing
twitter.com/blinkpublishing

978-1-910536-01-8

A CIP catalogue of this book is available from the British Library.

Printed and bound by Clays Ltd, St Ives Plc

1 3 5 7 9 10 8 6 4 2

Text copyright © Bambi Smyth, 2014
First published 2014 by The Five Mile Press

Papers used by Blink Publishing are natural, recyclable products made
from wood grown in sustainable forests. The manufacturing processes
conform to the environmental regulations of the country of origin.

Blink Publishing is an imprint of the Bonnier Publishing Group
www.bonnierpublishing.co.uk

To my sister Bonnie, who provided 'sage'
advice along the way,
To my Dad, for teaching me the difference
between filet mignon and chump chops,
To all the seventy-five men who let me nibble at them,
And to my Mum – I'm sorry about the spicy bits!

Contents

Planning Your Menu

*Eat breakfast like a king, lunch like a prince,
and dinner like a pauper.*

– ADELLE DAVIS

To: Park Hotel Sonnenhof
         Liechtenstein

Date: 21 August

Dear Sir/Madam,

I'm writing to ask for your help with an unusual request!

I'm an author from Melbourne – Australia, soon to travel around the world to visit twenty-six countries from A to Z, where I plan to sample all the 'national dishes', and also to have a dinner 'date' with one or two local men. And why? To get to know them and see if they fit the 'romantic' stereotype of their nationality, then to match them up with the food that best fits their personalities (e.g. Are Brazilians 'fiery' like the local *malagueta* peppers? Are Englishmen stodgy like their egg and bacon pies?)

My aim? To write a kind of global reference book which creatively combines humankind's greatest passions - food, travel and the opposite sex.

I'm visiting Liechtenstein for just twenty-four hours, accompanied by a girlfriend, and I hope you can put me in contact with someone who'd be happy to meet me - preferably a single man aged 35-55, who speaks reasonable English, and has a sense of adventure!
Warm regards,
Bambi Smyth

To: Park Hotel Sonnenhof
       Liechtenstein
Date: 22 August

Dear Sir/Madam,
Thank you for suggesting a local website to help me find a suitable 'date' in Liechtenstein. However, I think you may have misunderstood my intentions.

Firstly, the website features men whom I don't feel have all that much in common with the local stereotypes — romantic or otherwise. Perhaps I had different expectations, but I'm still not sure I'd be doing Liechtenstein justice if it was represented by hairy-bottomed men clad in fishnet stockings, or black-and-red rubber body-suits with panels cut out to reveal rather personal body parts.

Secondly, I am a Ms, not a Mr. I may have confused you by saying I was travelling with a girlfriend. However, either way, we are NOT looking for a threesome, especially with any of the candidates featured above.

Can you please suggest an alternative option?

Bambi Smyth

To: Park Hotel Sonnenhof
      Liechtenstein
Date: 23 August

Dear Sir/Madam,

Thank you for your suggestion to contact the Liechtenstein Tourist Office. Hopefully they will have some good ideas for a 'date' that do not involve me having to expand my wardrobe to suit any fetishist dress codes. I am travelling for three months and need to pack lightly.

Warm regards,
Bambi Smyth

To: Liechtenstein Tourismus
      Liechtenstein

Date: 24 August

Dear Martina,

Thank you SO much for finding me a man in Liechtenstein who is willing to meet me for dinner.

He sounds perfect! I will contact him

immediately to arrange the finer details
of our 'date'.
Bambi Smyth

So that's one country organised. Twenty-five to go.

It has been a particularly bleak Melbourne winter, and the pea-soup fog is so thick that you could stand a spoon up in it. The damp sticks to everything it touches – from the garden statues shivering in its embrace, to the rows of Victorian terraces opposite my home that half disappear into the bilious gloom. The fog even leaves wet little fingerprints on my bedroom window, like a ghoul has been trying to find its way in.

Which is why I don't want to get out of bed the morning after I send the final email to Liechtenstein, even though I'm keen to see if I've received an overnight response from one very brave Dr Ernst Walch from the other side of the world. It's much safer lying under the doona in my flannelette pyjamas than it is to see if my rather madcap mission has legs. Indeed, as the fat winter sleet slaps against my window like tiny lemonade jellies – and my cold bottom unkindly reminds me that the other half of the bed has been empty for far longer than is recommended before One is convinced that One will stay single and tragic for the rest of One's sorry life – I rather wonder what I've started.

It had seemed like such a great idea two months ago. After a sleepless weekend sick of being a boyfriendless, aimless, soulless woman wondering how to inject some meaning into my life, I'd finally had that eureka moment. I would blend my greatest passions – travel, food and men – into one extraordinary experience and write a book about it. Like gathering three basic ingredients from the larder – each palatable enough when served alone, but when all whipped together, create a totally new flavour. Indeed, I was hoping that the everyday staples of my life would become a feast for the senses. A delicious experience to feed my starved soul.

My mouth had watered at the adventurousness of such a quest. The quirkiness of it. The very audacity of it. Dating twenty-six men in as many countries, then trying to match their personalities with their national dishes – just for the fun of it – was undoubtedly not a project for the faint-hearted. But I'd always been curious about different cultures, and was particularly interested in finding out whether the men I met would fit the 'romantic' stereotypes of their countries, or prove them wrong. Would the Italians really be as hot as their reputation suggests? The Dutch as open-minded?

The Brazilians as obsessed with sex? The French truly masters of seduction? I'd begun imagining myself as some kind of cultural detective, dating men in the hopes I could 'taste' who they were – to extract their true flavour, their very essence.

And each date was bound to be different. After all, if a food can be spicy or sweet, sour or salty, delicious or unsavoury, fresh or a little bit off, then surely a man can be too?

I'd name my quest 'Men on the Menu' – how delicious! And right up to this wintry Friday night, I couldn't wait to begin the journey.

But now, all tucked up in a half-cold bed, and as the sleet turns to hail and clatters loudly on the slate roof, it suddenly strikes me: What on earth am I doing? Or more importantly – why?

I am beginning to doubt myself. I'm not a journalist – just a woman who loves to write. And I'm not a psychologist – just a woman who likes to see what makes people tick. And I'm not even a real foodie – just a woman who loves to challenge her tastebuds every now and again.

My life has previously been devoted to more mainstream but still creative ventures – designing puzzles, writing children's books, illustrating wildlife – endeavours that for years have kept me amused and out of the mundane sameness of an office job. Including my current role as the creative manager for a large plush-toy company, in which I spend eight hours a day playing with fabric swatches and colour-wheels, and contemplating whether the new range of dress-up dogs I'm designing should include a Pooch Punk range featuring little metal-studded jackets and safety-pin earrings. The best job in the world really, although I am prepared to give it all up to pursue this latest endeavour.

So what on earth am I doing then? I mean – really?

Fact is, as much as I've been telling friends and family that I am going to travel the world for research purposes, I have begun to suspect that it could be far more personal than that. That it might be less about my thirst for adventure, and more about my hunger for romance. Because with every passing day I've been feeling increasingly empty, much like the imposing but dilapidated terrace house I am renting. It is so large I don't even have enough furniture to make it feel like a real home. And with only one person now rattling around in its maze of rooms with soaring five-metre-high ceilings, it sounds as hollow as my heart.

I finally drag myself out of bed, and decide to stay in my pyjamas for the rest of the day. There's something about flannelette that feels safe and non-judgemental – especially flannelette printed with fuzzy polar bears – like it doesn't care that I'm going to be spending the weekend alone and most likely propped up in front of television watching re-runs of *Boston Legal*.

But first I need to check my emails, and as the computer is warming up, I lean back in my chair and stare out the studio window. The clouds are parting and I can see enough blue sky to make a pair of sailor's pants. Typical Melbourne weather – all the seasons in a day. It seems to perfectly mirror my love-affair of the last eight years that has just recently ended, with its spring of budding love, the summer where it was all hot and dreamy, the autumn shedding, then the turbulent winter filled with storm clouds and violent outpourings.

I shut my eyes against the sudden brightness outside, and think of Mark. It's only been five months since he piled up his ute with all his worldly possession, and moved back to Sydney, and it still hurts.

Because the truth is, I still loved him.

Even if it was me who did the breaking up.

Mark was a rare specimen I found on the beach in Indonesia, a precious Nautilus shell that had found its way to shore reasonably unscathed by the buffeting of wind and waves. He was a full-blooded Italian, but a full-bred Australian, holidaying on the tiny island of Lombok to lick his wounds after recently coming out of a troubled marriage. He was handsome and tanned, and his deep-brown eyes spoke of warmth and kindness. I was struck by his self-confidence, his sense of humour, and his love of nature as we meandered through the rock pools collecting pink and purple sea-urchin shells. I met him when I was thirty-nine and unhappily single, and I thought how lucky I was that I hadn't left my run too late to find a decent guy with whom to settle down.

Mark was an artisan – he designed beautiful bespoke furniture and filled people's homes with colour and texture. As he did with my life too, introducing me to classical music, literature, and ABC and SBS documentaries. He was warm and thoughtful, organising the most beautiful weekends away in romantic country getaways where he'd bring the champagne and I'd cook him delicious three-course dinners that more often than not never got finished because we'd end up in bed. Although we occasionally put the chocolate sauce to good use. The first six years we spent together were very happy. I felt adored, nourished and reassuringly complete. I believed that I'd finally found my soulmate, and that we'd grow old and fashionably ash-grey together.

But then something had started to change, and I spent the next two years of our relationship feeling like a quietly deflating soufflé. Sinking not because of the sudden wrenching opening of the oven door through infidelity or bitter disagreement, but because the heat was slowly escaping. Very slowly. My very being had started to protectively shrink into itself over years of feeling I'd been let down. I began to think that there must have been something wrong with me, as Mark simply couldn't commit to me in the way that I wanted. No ring, no wedding, no babies, no tangible future. We lived together for six years, during which time it began to slowly dawn on me that to Mark the concept of marriage was about as attractive as sticking barbecue skewers in his eyes. So we never talked about it, and would awkwardly attend friends' weddings or stand dumbstruck as new engagement rings were flashed about, and when I once asked Mark whether we'd be together forever, he uncomfortably answered, 'Forever is a very long time.'

So I left him, because there's only so long you can wait on the warming plate in the oven, gradually diminishing, rather than rising up to your full glory.

A sunken soufflé never rises again.

Not without the heat.

Besides, if I was ever going to get around to having a baby – which due to being so busy travelling, happily immersing myself in my career like a worm in mescal, and generally having fun, had only occurred to me in my late thirties – then time was running out fast, and I couldn't afford to hang around whilst the last of my eggs were hitting the skids.

So if I am to be truthful with myself – if not entirely so with my friends and family who think this whole trip is a bit of a laugh – I need it to give me hope. Hope there might be someone out there in the wide, wide world to love me as much as I need to be loved. Someone to give me that future of which I feel I've been cheated.

Hope that I might find The One. Just in time.

Indeed, what has started off as a bit of a cultural exposé has quietly morphed into an opportunity to see who else is out there for me. And yes, I need to travel abroad to find him. Aussie males have never really appealed that much to me. In my personal experience they are pretty true to their 'ocker' national stereotype – drink like fish, swear like troopers, smell like wombats.

I've always preferred the home-grown Europeans, who seem so much more sophisticated and interesting, with their exotic looks – either very, very pale or very, very dark, whereas most Australians are, well, beige. I love Europeans' delicious foreign accents, their passion and virility. And perhaps more importantly, the way they think that it is *I* – being a girl from Down Under – who is the interesting one, even though I am hardly a blonde, blue-eyed, cute little surfie chick. In fact, I am more Olive Oyl meets Cruella de Vil – tall, skinny, angular, brunette, and a bit of a dag.

But still, European men make me feel special. During my twenties and thirties I had romantic dalliances with quite a few of them, and felt decidedly adventurous having an address book that was like a roll call to the United Nations – Klaus from Germany, Thierry from France, Carl from Austria, Sten from Sweden, Edward, Richard and Duncan from England – though not simultaneously – and Terry from Ireland. I learned to say 'kiss me' in many different languages, and found the idea of possibly pulling up stumps and moving overseas to make very, very pale or very, very dark babies oddly exhilarating.

Not that I married any of those European lovers. I think once the novelty wore off for them dating a woman who was more comfortable trekking through Africa than through the frozen-food section of Costco, they decided I was too much of a handful to have as a wife. Men like wives to toe the line, rather than kick up their heels, the latter of which I am much better at. And by not marrying me either, Mark had compounded my belief that I wasn't worthy to be a permanent fixture, but a plaything to be toyed with until Miss Right with her sensible shoes and pale pink lipstick and Margaret Fulton cookbook under her arm came along.

Those repeated rejections hurt. A lot. I'd always just expected to get married one day, and saw my future quite clearly with some slightly eccentric architect or artist who didn't take themselves too seriously, who fancied the idea of snuggling up to my cold bottom at night, and with whom I'd happily ride off into the sunset. Coming as I did from a family with two terrific parents who even after half a century of marriage still celebrated every wedding anniversary with heartfelt gifts and champagne, and four siblings who I didn't want to push under the lawnmower, made me assume that I'd have my own happy home-life too one day.

But here I am, at forty-seven, still unmarried, unbabied and now unloved. I feel like the last chocolate in the box – the one with a colourful foil wrapper that makes it hard to determine what flavour it is, so is left to one side in favour of something more predictable and safe. And it's true that my flavour may not suit every-one – being more of a zesty mint liqueur rather than a bland hazelnut praline or a goody-two-shoes raspberry cream. Which means that I am still waiting for a Man with Adventurous Taste to find me. But I suspect such men aren't thick on the ground in my antipodean neck of the woods, and are unlikely to be hanging about as I am taking out the rubbish on a Monday night.

So I am just going to have to go out and find *them*.

I have a much-adored brother – Os – short for Osmond, a family name dating back to 1884 – which is probably the only reason he puts up with it. Then again, with a name like Bambi, my parents clearly thought unusual names would be character-building. Os is eleven years younger than me, though I think in many ways he's far wiser. When I confided to him that I was worried I was getting past my 'use-by date', he said, 'There's no such thing as a use-by date, just a 'best before'.'

And he was right. After all, I might not be thirty-something any more, but I still feel young and hungry enough to take control of my life. So I decide that I am going to undertake this journey no matter what. Whether during my quest to discover the inter-national flavours of men, I will also find the love I am yearning for is a total unknown.

But what the heck, I'll give it a go.

Choosing Your Theme

To eat is a necessity, but to eat intelligently is an art.

– FRANÇOIS DE LA ROCHEFOUCAULD

Although the trip is turning into a more personal quest than I'd originally intended, I still want to follow through with the exploration of different cultures. So even if I don't find The One this time around, I'll at least have had the chance to nibble at enough men from enough countries to see what tickled my tastebuds, then perhaps go back for seconds.

Besides, I come from a long line of adventurers – travel is in my very DNA. My great-great-uncle was Sir H Rider Haggard, an Englishman who wrote dozens of swashbuckling adventure novels set in exotic – predominantly African – locations. I'm not sure if he actually dated any of the women he came across in his travels though, as doing so would have been precarious in countries where you could be eaten if you so much as looked at the chieftain's daughter. Another ancestor of mine was Lord Baden-Powell, the founder of the scouting movement, who in his early days worked as an intelligence officer for the British Army, frequently travelling disguised as an insect collector, incorporating plans of military installations into his drawings of butterfly wings. Which is handy to know if I ever need to clandestinely take notes on a Russian mobster, or

Japanese yakuza.

With travel clearly in my genes – combined with a personal quest to find The One – it is a logical step to cast my net as far as possible, and see what I can drag in. And having not had any luck with Europeans, why not cast as far as Cuba? Or Japan? I am open to suggestion, and happy to push myself to the limits. For as another ancestor of mine taught me – the astronomer Professor Piazzi Smyth who had a crater named after him on the moon – if you reach for the stars and fall a little short, then no matter, at least you've got the moon. Which will do me just fine. As long as I don't fall really short and end up in a swamp in Tajikistan.

Before I start organising any more dates beyond my lucky break with Ernst in Liechtenstein, I attempt to compile a list of all the other places I'll be visiting. I am hoping to stick with my plan of covering twenty-six countries from A to Z, and spread across every continent, so that I'll give myself the very best chance of finding The One. Besides, travelling literally right around the world rather takes my fancy. But I soon ditch the Antarctic when I discover that it doesn't have – and never did – its own indigenous population, but just a few thousand transient scientific personnel working tours of duty. And I really don't want to date a researcher who keeps the same socks on for three months straight. So that leaves me with just six continents.

Easy.

Well, easy when you're looking at an A4 page in your old school atlas, where everything is only centimetres apart. It's not until I get a poster-sized map to show my proposed route and start sticking dozens of pins into it, connected with endless lengths of red string, that the enormity of my task dawns upon me once again.

I end up rewriting the list at least five times, as some countries are simply too expensive to consider. I've been putting my savings into an 'escape fund' for several years, but it is reasonably modest given the vagaries of my work. Designing stuffed toys might be fun, but it doesn't exactly stuff the wallet. So as much as I'd love to be in far away Greenland for my 'G' country, eating reindeer with a sealskin-wearing Inuit, the truth is that eating pork schnitzels in Germany is far more feasible. And I'd love to cover a couple more Asian countries – especially India, which would be a bollyblast – but I soon discover that a Round the World ticket actually only gets me seven international stopovers, which I have pretty much used up by 'H', so I feel like I've been dudded.

Still, after countless hours of getting tangled in red string, I finally have my A–Z list, and a map of the world that, despite my attempts at simplification, still looks like a psychotic spider's web. So I just need to get Justin – my travel agent – to make it all work.

Three days later and after an impressive exercise in dexterity and creativity, Justin has done it. For the sake of convenience I've swapped Djibouti for Denmark, and Nepal for the Netherlands, which is making my trip a little more Eurocentric than I would have liked, but I have to accept my limitations. And even though there are several African and Middle Eastern countries on my A–Z list – Kenya, Qatar, Tanzania, Yemen and Zambia – they'll have to wait for a second trip after I've returned home, to give me time to top up the war chest, not to mention catching my breath. Which, by the look of Justin's five-page itinerary, I'm going to need, with twenty-two countries across five continents, accessed by nineteen flights, eight different airlines, and ninety-eight hours flying time. Plus twelve train trips across Europe, and one hire car, to make up another fifty-six hours of land travel. Which is a bottom-numbing, leg-cramping 52,794 kilometres I'll be travelling. All in three months.

Phew – it's going to be *Race Around the World* meets *Blind Date*.

But who knows, maybe by the time I get to 'J' I'll have fallen in love and can forget the whole damn book anyway.

Selecting Your Ingredients

Tell me what you eat and I will tell you what you are.

– JEAN ANTHELME BRILLAT-SAVARIN

It's one thing to map out a global coverage of dates, and quite another to actually find them. The Liechtenstein bondage-site fiasco was a great lesson in how *not* to meet men.

I know that if I go down the more journalistic route, and get dates purely for the sake of research, then the men should be easy enough to find. After all, I could just go on a reputable international dating site and take whoever is available. But I am new to this concept of meeting online, and worry that the type of men inhabiting cyberspace chat rooms and dating sites might be single for good reason – like they still live with their mums, keep fleas as pets or collect used toothpicks. I am after a man who I might actually half fancy, and will hopefully fancy me back, which means he is going to have to be more adventurous than the norm. And collect tribal art, not toothpicks. Which is why I'd rather more of a romantic stereotype than just Joe Average, as Joe Average is still boring old Joe, whether he is Jose, Joseph, Giuseppe or Jorgen.

Still, the internet does seem like a convenient option for starters, so I try an international dating site promising 'stylish and exclusive dating for like-minded professionals'. Not that I am exactly up there myself in owning my own tech company or something equally as glamorous, and flying in to meet potential suitors on a Learjet. But what if there is the odd Richard Branson or Owen Wilson intrigued by the prospect of a date with a daring Aussie on a madcap mission? Perhaps it is worth a go. Or not … Although these sites are supposed to be a cut above the ones designed for casual sex, bulk-discount introductions ('Buy 7, get 1 free!') or, good grief, even one for matching up people with the same STDs, the 'exclusive' sites are still brimming over with men sporting pseudonyms such as 'classyrichguy' or 'yrdreamcumtrue', which doesn't exactly whet my appetite. So it is back to the mainstream dating sites, where I realise I can simply filter out the potentially boring men by reading their profiles. Hobbies such as yodelling, mini golf or polishing hubcaps should be a dead giveaway.

But the responses are still decidedly weird.

In Japan, I try a website politely entitled 'Japanese Lifestyle Friends Alert'. I apply to join, requesting to meet 'a Japanese male aged from 35 to 55', but receive this message in response:

```
Dear BambiSmyth
We cannot accept your profile because it
contains insulting or offensive language
including comments about body type, race,
religion or country of origin etc. Please
note that all profiles are reviewed by
human profile editors who notice this
information easily. We appreciate your
```

```
cooperation
Best regards.
```

On a Cuban online dating site I give up after the very first profile:

```
skeetbang, 25 year old man. 'Thizz baby'
chill kick back type nigga black n' puerto
rican by thr way
```

Right.

After several more false starts that include – out of sheer curiosity – a visit to a Brazilian adult dating website where I am asked whether I'd prefer 'spanking/whipping, water sports or hair pulling', I am starting to doubt that I'll find my man in cyberspace.

But where else then? What if my mission doesn't even get off the ground? A date with Ernst from Liechtenstein does not an odyssey make. But then my friend Jan saves the day.

'Here's an idea,' she offers enthusiastically. 'You've got heaps of friends who have connections overseas. Just ask them to set you up. And for starters, I work with a Brazilian guy who might know someone back home who'd take you on.'

And in a split second, it all becomes clear.

All I need to do is dig out my little black address book, which fortunately is pretty much up-to-date, as even if I've not seen people for decades, I still like to keep their contact details current just in case ... well ... just in case I ever need them to find me a date with a chap in Uzbekistan. Which, if the United Arab Emirates doesn't work out, could be handy.

Within half an hour I've written my draft cover letter. I'm not telling the full story though – about looking for The One and all that – because I don't want to scare anyone off. And I've become a bit cheekier with the age range, because, heck, why not a 25-year-old? If Demi Moore can do it, then so can I.

Hi . . . . ,
I hope you can help me out with a rather odd request!

I'm writing a book about food and men from around the world, for which I need 'dates' with men from the following countries: Australia, Brazil, Cuba, Denmark, England, France, Germany, Hungary, Italy and Ireland, Japan, Liechtenstein, Monaco, Netherlands, Oman, Portugal, Russia, Scotland, UAE, Vatican City and Wales.

So if you know an interesting, preferably single, 25 to 55-year-old man who speaks passable English, and who'd be brave enough to meet me for a 'date', please let me know.

He can be an old school friend, work colleague, drinking buddy, ex-boyfriend, whatever. As long as he's a local, and better still, a 'romantic stereotype' of his country - think Italian Stallion, Frisky Frenchman or Dreamy Dane!
Bambi xx

On the stroke of midnight, as the spring rain lashes violently at my windows as if to herald an impending storm of overwhelming magnitude – surely an allegory of my life – I send out into cyberspace, emails to every single person I know on the planet.

And then I sit back and wait.

Cooking up a Storm

Variety's the very spice of life, that gives it all its flavour.

– WILLIAM COWPER

Within two weeks I receive emails back from dozens of contacts right around the world, who offer up their friends and business associates to me like sacrificial lambs.

```
Bambi,
I got a mail from a man whose name is
Vori. He's a cheerful graduate student
who is capable to talk in English. He
is typical Japanese man, but maybe not
so 'romantic' as you asked for. Would he
still be suit for you?
Take care,
Rie
```

Not romantic? Ah well.

But it soon gets better …

```
Bambi,
Got you one! Lucienne — the Brazilian guy
I work with has an uncle called Paulo,
who lives in Rio de Janeiro. He is a
professor at the local uni. He would be
```

very happy to meet you. But be careful, I
hear he is a bit of a handful!
Jan

Dear cousin,
Yes, I have a date for you in London. He
is actually an old boyfriend — dashing
and dangerous, very good-looking, and if
you sleep with him I will never talk to
you again!
Eva

Hi Bambi,
I have lined you up a great dinner date.
Stefano Corona. He is Italian ... what
more can I say? Actually, I can say lots:
Stefano is a naval architect. He is highly
educated, well-travelled, attractive and
charming, charming, charming.
Ciao ciao,
Karen

And perhaps the most exciting one of all – given his
celebrity status – and me not being averse to a bit of
schmoozing with the rich and famous. Or even just
famous will do.

Hi Bambi,
I have arranged for you to meet my
colleague, and Madonna's piper, Mr Lorne
Cousin. He is single and was recently
named the sixth most eligible bachelor

in Scotland.
All the best,
Hamish x

The response has been so good that rather than limiting myself to just one date per country, I decide to take as many as I can get. Besides, isn't variety the spice of life? And as well as giving me a broader knowledge of the locals – which is great for my research – it will increase my chances of finding The One.

But there are still a few countries where no-one seems to know anyone, so with just over two weeks before I am due to depart Australia, I make a decision that will undoubtedly test the very foundations of my self-esteem – putting myself out there like a platter of diced cheese at a food-tasting, at the risk of being humiliatingly snubbed. Or – even worse – spat out mid-mouthful. In those countries where I have no pre-arranged dates, I'll simply go it alone. I'll chat up men in bars and cafés, railway stations and airports. I'll ask waiters whom I half fancy if they care to join me after work for a drink. I could even make eyes at the security guard at the local bank to see if he is up for a bit of foreign exchange.

Risky – maybe. Cheeky – for sure. But I'll do whatever it takes. Although I draw the line at a suggestion made by one online dating site: 'Hit a sports bar and wear the local football team's jumper, and chat up a cute guy wearing the same.'

Because, apart from not even knowing the difference between a fullback and a halfback, I'm not *that* much of a dag.

Appetiser

appetiser / ˈæpətaɪzə(r) / noun a small savoury or drink taken before the main meal to stimulate the appetite, and to alert the tastebuds of the pleasures to come.

I should have known better than to cook Moroccan lamb tagine for my farewell dinner with a group of close friends. It has a gazillion spices that have to be freshly ground with a mortar and pestle, and then has to be left to marinate, so by the time I get it into the oven it is already nine o'clock, and my guests are getting twitchy. And to make matters worse, I've read the handwritten recipe incorrectly. The '1/2 hour' of cooking time for which I've allowed half an hour, is actually meant to be one to two hours. I really should have figured this out first-up, but I guess when you've got other things on your mind – like how on earth to get a date in Oman – it's easy to miss the small stuff.

So I make sure everyone's wine glasses are filled, and hope that the entree of artichoke soup will keep them quiet while I crank up the heat in the oven for the tagine. And as the eight of us sit here surrounded by the bric-a-brac of my previous travels – a Maasai honey pot, a Balinese footstool, a Venetian Carnivale mask, a Tunisian camel-hide lampshade – I once again outline my journey to them, skirting the issue of hunting down The One so they don't think I am romantically deranged.

But talking up the fact I am hoping to meet with well over thirty men, just for the heck of it. Surely a perfectly reasonable objective for a woman in her mid-forties whose love life is as exciting as watching jelly set. Still, my plan has my friends somewhat bemused, because most of them can't even contemplate going on a blind date in Australia, let alone Liechtenstein.

'But what exactly do you *mean* you'll be comparing the men you date with the food you eat?' Edwina asks. She's an old school friend whose favourite food is rather bland meat pies, so she clearly can't see the intellectual wit of my mission. 'Sounds a bit weird to me.'

'Yes, give us an example,' pipes up Fiona, despite being more of a laksa girl so someone who should really be more imaginative. 'It does sound like you're stretching similes a bit.'

'Do you mean,' asks Simon, before I can even get a word in, 'that the lawyer you were dating who dumped you right before Christmas would be, say, a turkey?'

'No,' Fiona interjects, 'he was more a stuffed pork roast, wasn't he? Rather full of himself if I remember correctly.'

'Ah, I get it,' Edwina hoots gleefully. 'Well, what about that two-timing George you dated? He'd have to be some sort of tripe, or sheep's testicles, wouldn't he?'

And so it continues, as my closest friends pick through the remnants of my love life like vultures scavenging on a zebra carcass – although I don't think vultures would be quite so brutal. Not that my friends are deliberately trying to be cruel; half the men I dated years ago *do* deserve a fair degree of savaging, as back then I was more interested in style than substance.

I mistakenly thought that if a man could afford to buy me a glass of Bollinger then he was a worthy catch, even though he more often than not turned out to be of the scum-sucking bottom-feeding variety. There were many with whom I got it equally as wrong, and they were all destined to break my heart. Time and time again. But I really only had myself to blame – if it looks like a player, talks like a player and behaves like a player, it usually *is* a player.

And as for the Nice Guys – well – I think I just scared them off. I was fiercely independent and wanted to make my own way in life. I've decided of late that most 'nice' men want to settle down into a life of suburban bliss. Whereas, what I wanted – well, once I'd got over the Bollinger phase – was someone with whom I could dance barefoot in the moonlight, go skinny-dipping in the ocean, trek through deepest darkest Africa, and heck – why not – build a his-n-hers treehouse in the jungle in which we could live happily ever after. Back then responsibility and raising families were for Boring People, and I didn't want to join that camp. I figured there was plenty of time to settle down later, and in the meantime I just wanted to have fun.

So after a perfectly cordial date with Mr Nice, where I may have been a teensy bit guilty of talking all night about my latest camel-back Tunisian adventure, we'd part ways, and he'd find someone who was far easier to handle. And before I knew it there'd be wedding bells and a Labrador puppy followed by a designer baby, all neatly tucked away behind a white picket fence, through which I could only peer, wondering what I'd done wrong. Because deep down some domesticity was actually what I really wanted too. But I simply didn't realise it at the time, and I'd just carry on partying, hoping to attract someone's attention any way I could. But what guy really wanted to marry a girl who wore a transparent cling-wrap skirt to cocktail parties? Or who danced on tables when she'd had a few too many drinks? Although, if he'd just looked a little deeper – and I'd given him the chance – he would have found a woman who was actually so socially awkward that she compensated by being outrageous, and hoped that no-one would notice the insecure Ugly Duckling within.

And if I'm to dig even *deeper*, there has actually been something else going on all through my dating years that has prevented any meaningful relationships.

I'd wanted to marry my father.

For the whole of my life I've regarded my father with awe and admiration. He was a senior officer in the Royal Australian Navy, and my first defining memory of him was as he inspected his cadets at the naval training college of which he was in command. The sight of two hundred young men in their 'whites' standing to attention like phalanxes of chalk, as my father sternly looked them up and down to ensure everything was ship-shape, is a sight I'll never forget. To a five-year-old it seemed that he was a cross between Captain Marvel and God. And not much has changed – he's still just as large in my world, and I'm still living in his shadow, never quite feeling I can measure up to his expectations – nor indeed can the men whom I have dated.

I have a photo of my father beside my bed – tall and reed-slim and dashingly handsome in much the same mould as Gregory Peck, although my father was far more impressive in his naval uniform with four double rows of gold coat buttons flashing in the light. On formal occasions he'd also wear a row of service medals, so broad and heavy on his chest that he was in danger of tipping over sideways. His latest medal is the French Legion of Honour – a magnificent gilt five-armed Maltese 'asterisk', which was pinned to his chest personally by Jacques Chirac. It's France's highest honour, presented to my father in 2004 on the sixtieth anniversary of the D-day landing in Normandy, where with thousands of other brave men he helped turn the war around.

My father's not all pomp and ceremony though. After twenty-five years of retirement – and now aged eighty-three – he smells of Winsor & Newton oil paints rather than Nugget boot polish, wears only slightly less than loud Hawaiian shirts, and drives a clunky old Rambler instead of a 26,000-tonne naval tanker. But even now he still stands tall and strong and proud, with a mind as sharp as mustard, and a heart as soft as butter. Well, perhaps slightly firmer gouda cheese, given his habit of looking at me with steely eyes if he thinks I am up to no good, which in my early twenties was quite often.

But either way, he was – and still is – my consummate hero. A man of integrity, valour, honour and enterprise. A leader of men and a follower of principle. Captain Marvel with gold epaulets. However, he is still human enough to donate generously to the Lost Dog's

Home and the Salvos, and cheerfully sing so out of key in church that people turn around and stare.

So how could any man, let alone boy, ever compete with him?

They never stood a chance.

'Are you still with us Bambi?' I hear Eddie saying, and am brought back to earth as my friends continue to debate what foodstuffs my other boyfriends were. 'What about the actor?' Eddie continues. 'Wasn't he a bit … um … stupid? What would he be?' Eddie never was one to mince words.

'Hmm, I wouldn't say stupid,' I counter defensively, 'just inarticulate. He was Irish after all, and you really don't know what they're on about half the time. So maybe he was alphabet soup. With a few letters missing.'

'But David was nice,' Anita kindly offers. 'He was like a fine old port, although being twenty-two years older than you, we were all worried he might be slightly corked.'

'Rather than comparing the men with food, why not compare them with cars?' Simon grumbles – clearly impatient that there's still no food on the table. 'Like an Italian would be a Maserati, and a Swede a Volvo? Much more masculine, I reckon.'

'Or furniture?' suggests Jan, who works in interior design. 'A lovely laid-back Frenchman could be a chaise lounge.'

'Well,' I reply, having already thought this through

in great depth. 'The problem is I don't know anything about cars or furniture. Besides, I don't want to miss the opportunity to try as many local dishes as I can whilst I'm over there, so I may as well base it on food. And you can learn a lot about a culture through its cuisine – the way it's acquired, the way in which it's cooked, the way it's consumed at the table.'

'If it ever gets to the table,' whines Eddie, upon which I quickly top up her glass again.

'So if I can understand the food, then perhaps I'll have a better understanding of the local men too,' I continue with renewed enthusiasm. 'Because don't you think that national dishes can also say something about the national psyche? France's joie de vivre, for example, is reflected in the rich complexity of its national dishes. Think pot-au-feu, or coq au vin.'

'And champagne,' says Anita, taking a slug of her own, and pointedly looking at her watch.

'Exactly!' I hoot, and get up to serve the tagine before my guests start chewing on their rice-paper table napkins.

Grace

For what we are about to receive, may the
Lord make us truly thankful. Ah – men.

And so – after ten weeks of planning, and wondering
whether I'm certifiably mad – it finally begins. And
with thirty-plus complete strangers lined up across
twenty-two countries, let's just hope that I don't end up
with a terrible case of indigestion.

Entree

The entree sets the tone for the whole meal.
It should be light and delicate, and served in
quantities that just satisfy, but do not sate.

– RENÉ GORDON, *THE COMPLETE AUSTRALIAN COOKBOOK*

I'd love to write about each and every date – and meal – that I'll have on this odyssey, but I'd risk ending up with a tome longer than *War and Peace*. And although mine would potentially have equally as colourful characters and dramatic twists and turns, for the sake of brevity I'll pick and choose which experiences most tantalise my tastebuds.

Because my primary mission in my journey is to find The One, unless a married date has so much flavour that I simply have to share him around for all to enjoy, or alternatively, the date is single but has about as much fizz as a flat lemonade the morning after a Salvation Army Christmas party, I'll spare all the gritty details.

Australia

Beef 'n' reef never tasted so good

Given I've never had much luck dating Australian men, I am excited by the challenge of casting my net a little further than the Aussie lawyers and stockbrokers and advertising sorts, who collectively contributed to the precarious state of my self-esteem. Usually by dumping me well before I was ready, even though I should have known it was doomed at their very first 'Hi, I'm George, and I'm a total tosser.'

Or words to that effect.

It's clear to me now that I simply chose badly, and even though I tried to avoid the less desirable 'ocker' stereotypes – lazy, laconic, beer-guzzling, sports-mad larrikins who put mateship ahead of their girlfriends – I still ended up with lazy, laconic, chablis-sipping, golf-mad lads who put their careers ahead of their girlfriends. But I still believe that somewhere out there another type of Aussie male exists – easygoing, uncomplicated, devoted and fun-loving. It is just a matter of finding him.

But where? I don't have a clue where to start, given I've been out of the dating scene for over eight years.

Then one morning as I am sitting at my desk contemplating whether my friends know any nice Australian men who haven't recently gone through a hideous divorce, filed for bankruptcy, or had a botched hair-transplant that has ended up looking like the scalp on a cheap plastic doll – I am startled by the wail of an ambulance speeding past, followed closely by two fire trucks, their red lights flashing frantically and horns blaring. And as I peer through my ghoul-smudged window, only to see that thanks to a million too many cars on the road the air has gone from pea-soup to Scotch broth, it suddenly occurs to me that perhaps a Boy from the Bush might be the perfect antidote to city living. I've spent most of my life in concrete jungles, so perhaps a change might do me good. If not for my heart, then at least for my lungs. And besides, a jackaroo, farmer or shearer are quintessential Australian icons, so I'll be killing two birds with one stone – a romantic stereotype for my book, and a country hunk for me. Perfect.

My friend Tim spends the occasional weekend 'up bush' on a large family property, and he offers to introduce me to his next-door neighbour, Matt, a 34-year-old cattle farmer. Tim describes him as 'a bit of a stud', and before I've even met him I am contemplating whether I could swap my civilised 8 a.m. wake-me-up cappuccino in a city café, for the jarring 3 a.m. call-to-arms of a rural rooster. I know which one I'd enjoy more, but I would be happy to give the pre-sunrise option a shot if it means bucolic bliss. And I'm not bothered by the age gap, because although having anything in common with a 25-year-old man – as my cover letter dared suggest – might be pushing it a bit, I reckon 35 is doable. At least he'll know that Icehouse was an '80s rock band, and not a place he might get his hands on some party drugs.

And besides, if I am going to end up with a farmer, then I may as well go for a strapping young bullock rather than a grumpy old bull.

It's a four-hour trip to Matt's property, and before we're even halfway there I feel I'm on another planet – the landscape sparsely spotted with straggly yellow box and river-red gums, and the earth beneath a vast slice of overcooked toast – dry and brittle from the worst drought in one hundred years. Dust devils dance angrily through the parched fields, and the dams are empty and cracked. A forlorn sense of desolation hangs in the shimmering air – brooding and heavy. Despite my earlier excitement, I feel an increasing sense of emptiness, as if I'm being sucked into a vacuum.

Another hundred or so kilometres on and deep into cattle country, Tim and I unload our bags outside his little weatherboard cottage. But before we can enter, we have to chase off a bedraggled mob of sheep that have taken a fancy to reclining on his veranda, and are using its balustrades as scratching posts. Then, after delicately removing an enormous huntsman spider from my bedroom, we straddle Tim's quad bike to find my date on 'Kalamunda' – Matt's property next door. I soon realise, however, that in this part of the world, 'next door' takes on an entirely different meaning than in the suburbs, as at 5,000 acres it's ten times larger than Monaco – one of my future date destinations.

Failing to find Matt at home, Tim uses a walkie-talkie to tell him we've arrived, and soon a column of rust-red dust billowing down the road heralds his imminent arrival. Matt pulls up in a four-wheel-drive with massive bullbars and a sky-high radio antenna, and a back tray loaded with hay-bales bigger than your average Fiat. He jumps out of the cabin and I swear I go a bit weak at the knees. Matt's very handsome, with a strong jaw, perfect white teeth, deeply tanned skin, a strong muscular body and a broad easy smile. He's wearing a huge Akubra 'ten-gallon' hat – with what I'd swear are a couple of bullet holes through its crown – dark sunglasses, a faded-red polo shirt with a frayed upturned collar, and cow-wrangled jeans.

Within minutes Matt's offered to show me around his property as he checks on the stock before nightfall, so I clamber up into the cabin of his truck, only to find myself practically sitting on his gleaming Remington rifle. As we bounce jarringly up the heavily rutted dirt track, I nervously wonder if it's loaded.

In the first paddock Matt proudly shows me his stud bulls who he declares 'have the best job on the planet', and which I can't help noticing have the most enormous and pendulous scrotums I've ever seen, almost dragging along beneath them on the dusty earth.

'It's not polite to stare,' laughs Tim, at which I blush – deeply.

Matt refers to his cattle not as living animals, but as 'T-bone steaks', and as we pass a mob of sheep in another paddock, he cheerfully announces, 'We'll be eating one of them tonight. I'll slit its throat and bleed it, and they'll be the freshest lamb chops you've ever eaten.'

Suddenly I'm not looking forward to tonight's barbecue quite so much.

We meet Matt's three old working dogs that can't wait to be let off their leashes and sent off to do some rounding-up. But it's late in the day, and all that's around to muster is a flock of pink-and-grey galahs wheeling chaotically overhead. So Matt roughs their coats up with broad tanned hands – powdered soil rising from their fur like flour being smacked onto a kitchen bench

– then off we go again. And although there are fences to be mended and holes to be dug, and there's dust and rust and cow pats and flies everywhere, Matt looks as happy as a pig in mud.

As dusk settles, we do one last circuit of a paddock that's heavily patchworked with clumps of trees, and all of a sudden the scrub around me seems to be surging forward. Alive.

'Roos,' Matt says matter-of-factly. And sure enough, we're surrounded by scores of leaping kangaroos, grey fur morphing into the grey scrub, like semi-invisible figures in a *Predator* movie. Some pass just metres from me, springing gracefully on powerful back legs, keeping effortless pace with the truck before bounding ahead and melting into the bush once more. I'm speechless, feeling quite overwhelmed – and humbled – by how close I've just been to Australia's most iconic creature in its own backyard.

Now tonight's barbecue has become even less appetising. I have kangaroo steaks marinating back at the cottage, which I chose because they're top of the list for Australian 'bush tucker'. But after coming face-to-face with the main meal – their gentle black eyes and pretty little faces close enough to touch – I'm not so keen to misplace their trust. When I explain my dilemma, Matt laughs. 'Don't worry, roos are just giant rabbits. They're vermin, they eat all my feed, and they're most likely worm-infested. Nothing to cry over.'

But still – vermin or not – it *is* Australia's beloved national emblem, and now I feel like I'm about to commit high treason.

For our date I've invited Matt over to Tim's cottage

for a home-cooked meal. Having a threesome – as such – isn't quite the romantic scenario I'd been hoping for, but Matt hasn't offered his own place, and I can hardly ask Tim to go away and leave us alone. But perhaps it will work out for the best, as with a friend around, Matt might let his guard down and I can find out more about him – beneath the stockman's swagger and the flashing white teeth. He's even given to the occasional flexing of biceps if he knows I'm watching him. Indeed – he comes across as about as macho as they breed them in the country. But I have a feeling there's more to Matt – something sweetly sensitive hidden beneath his manly flexing. I caught a glimpse of it earlier when we came to a paddock gate and he wouldn't let me open it for him. And I want to see more.

We go our separate ways to tidy up before dinner, and when Matt's truck rolls up an hour or so later, I can't quite believe my eyes as he strides in with a Little Red Riding Hood basket loaded with food. There's a homemade garden salad, fresh lamb chops – a little too fresh for my liking – a choice of mustards and dressings, and even a parsley garnish handpicked from his veggie patch. Offerings I'd never have expected of – dare I say it – a country bumpkin, let alone a male one. He's even changed his clothes and brushed his hair, and I'm slightly suspicious that there's a hint of Hugo Boss wafting around after him. So much for country blokes being thin on style and thick on bulldust.

As I knead the dough for the beer damper, feeling pleasantly like an Early Settler – I've even got the eighty-year-old frilly apron happening – the boys set up a campfire in a six-foot-wide pit outside, using enormous logs from a felled Murray pine. Before long they have an inferno raging, and we're sitting on sling-back camp chairs in our own little amphitheatre restaurant, created by leafy drapes of eucalyptus and yellow box trees on either side of us. Our tables are small up-ended logs, our flooring a dirt carpet littered with rabbit poo and spent bullet-casings, and our light the campfire before us and the blazing universe above. We sit silently sipping on stubbies of XXXX and Fosters beer, and stare into the flames as they shoot up tiny red sparks into the chilly night, with the rich, sweet smell of burning pine hanging in the air. I couldn't ask for a more idyllic setting, and for the first time in ages I feel at peace. Even the urgency I've been feeling of late to find The One and finally 'get on with my life', seems to simply melt away into the night sky, leaving me with a deeply serene feeling that if the universe can take its time to get things done – after all, it's been thirteen billion years and it's still expanding – then so can I.

As the fierce embers do their work on the foil-wrapped potatoes and damper, Matt necks his stubby and good-naturedly answers my questionnaire. I've compiled a list of twenty questions that I'm intending to ask each date, having determined it to be the easiest way to extricate information from nervous participants. Or if indeed *I* too ever get lost for words – given that I'm way out of practice chatting up men. The questions mostly relate to relationships or food, and – perhaps more importantly – how each date sees himself in the world. Apart from opening up a fascinating range of cultural idiosyncrasies that I can compare from country to country, this will also help me gauge whether they're worth pursuing on a romantic level. I hate to be so brutal, but if one of my date's definitions of foreplay is 'you awake?', then I'm sorry, but it's never going to work.

Matt is much more relaxed now, and maybe the beer is helping too, for he's quite happy to tell me what life is like for a bachelor living 'out bush'. And it's clearly not all that easy, which is perhaps why he's still single at an age that most city blokes have a couple of kids. Or at least have to share their wardrobe with forty-six pairs of designer shoes. Indeed, if Matt wants to meet girls, he has extremely limited options, either heading to the nearest pub – forty kilometres away – or waiting for a big occasion.

'Weddings are good, always meet girls at weddings,' he smiles broadly. 'Oh, and B&S balls. Huge fun.'

I can't help but laugh. I remember those country Bachelor and Spinster Balls, where two hundred women in formal party dresses, and four hundred men in various interpretations of black-tie, congregate from dawn to dusk in wool sheds, drink far too much, and see how long it takes to either rip, lose, exchange or vomit on said clothes before passing out. From what I recall of B&S balls – and having once had a dead rabbit put in my sleeping bag – they certainly aren't the venue to find a prospective lifelong mate.

The 'date' with Matt is running as smoothly as a shearer's blade, and although it's becoming clearer to me that perhaps he's too young to be The One – or in all fairness I'm too old to be His One – there's still plenty to talk about, and I'm loving getting a fresh perspective on his view of the world, and how he ultimately sees a woman fitting into it. He'd love to get married and have kids – one day – although it will need to be with a woman who pulls her weight. 'Bloody oath she will. No barefoot and pregnant in the kitchen for me.' Although that said, my guess is he'll still be wearing the pants, as when I ask him how he'd impress a girl on a first date, he does the bicep-flexing thing again.

'Bring her along to watch me ride in a rodeo,' he says proudly, and I have to admit the sight of Matt lunging around on the back of an enraged 900-kilogram bull would do it for me. Especially if he can last longer than three seconds.

Matt is certainly turning out to be the ultimate example of a vital, robust and red-blooded male – give or take a parsley garnish or two. And testosterone? I'm betting he's got buckets of it. So I'm not surprised when he suddenly reveals that he's got a girl back at his house who's staying over for the weekend.

But Tim is. 'A girl?!' he exclaims. 'And when were you going to tell me about her? Or is this the same one you've been dating for a year, and who you've never bothered to introduce me to?'

Matt stirs the fire vigorously. 'Same one,' he replies elusively, and that's that. So I'm very glad that I didn't fall for him, as if she's a bit of a country lass then she's bound to be handy with a shotgun, and I'd be in trouble.

I've discovered a sneaky way to try and get my 'dates' to divulge their deeper personalities without quite realising it. It's a tried and true tactic for businesses to build a psychological profile on prospective employees, by helping identify who they really are, not who they would like to be, or how they would like to be seen. It's a simple question to which there are a thousand answers: If your personality was an animal, what would you be?

This way, rather than an unlikely confession of, 'Hi, I'm Wayne and I'm emotionally insecure, a bed-wetter and terrified of anything larger than a housefly,' the person-in-question may feel comfortable enough to say, 'I'm a mouse.'

Which pretty much means the same thing.

And I'm certainly not wanting to confuse the issue of what animal my date sees himself as, compared with what food I think he best matches – the latter being half the point of my mission. But if I'm trying to find out who he really is, within the challenging limitation of just a few hours spent with him, then how *he* sees himself can give me a great leg up.

So I ask Matt this question, and wonder what other surprises on top of the Mystery Girlfriend he has up his chambray sleeve. He laughs as he tosses six lamb chops onto the hotplate, oil spitting furiously on its surface like tiny firecrackers.

'Stud bull,' he answers, and I swear there's that flexing of biceps once again.

'And why?' I ask – a little hoarsely.

'Because of my attributes,' Matt replies, his face deadpan.

Tim cracks up, and I suddenly find myself quite unable to look Matt in the eye. Or anywhere else for that matter.

'Buying a bull, you look for structure and sound-ness,' Matt says, and I honestly can't tell if he's pulling my leg or not. 'And it has to be appealing to the eye,' he continues, at which Tim hoots with laughter.

'And a bull needs stamina,' Matt goes on, studiously ignoring Tim's ongoing chuckling. 'It needs to service a cow three, four, five times in her cycle. And remember, there are another hundred he has to look after too.'

'Dream job,' sighs Tim.

'Too right,' says Matt, and throws the roo steaks on.

When the meat is cooked, Matt uses a shovel to dig the potatoes and damper out of the embers, and we lay the meal out on wooden breadboards on the bare earth. At first I hesitate in helping myself to the kanga-roo steaks – with visions of little black noses twitching at me – but then I reason that I'm here to do a job, and can't be too sentimental about it. I'm surprised when Matt says he's never eaten kangaroo before; even as a city girl I regularly eat it, given it's 98 per cent fat-free, and most supermarkets stock it as the result of carefully monitored culling programmes. I suppose familiar-ity breeds contempt, although by the look on his face Matt may well now be a convert, for it's hard to resist the meat's rich and interestingly gamey flavour, and extraordinarily tender flesh. The fresh-as-fresh lamb chops are incredibly sweet and finely textured, with an earthy, chargrilled finish, and a wonderful smoky flavour from the Murray pine logs. Matt is tucking into them with relish, and I'm guessing that he's most likely a 'meat and three meat' kind of guy. In fact, if I were one of his sheep, I wouldn't be venturing too close to the homestead.

Whilst I eat, I'm a little distracted as the lads talk graphically of boning rooms and slaughterhouses. Sensing my discomfort, they gently chide me.

'If you eat it, you should meet it,' Tim says.

'But it's best not to name it,' adds Matt, explaining that he has a pet cow called Chooky, whom he could never eat, because it would be 'far too personal'. Such an admission rather surprises me, because farmers aren't known for being all that sentimental about their stock. Particularly when they have over two thousand head of sheep or cattle to run around after. Although perhaps after Chooky, and Daisy, and Buttercup, and Dixie, they've simply run out of names and it's not so personal any more.

For dessert I serve up lamingtons, another great Aussie national dish. They're named after Lord Lamington, who was the governor of Queensland from 1896 to 1901. Apparently his cook was called upon at short notice to feed unexpected guests, so he cut up some leftover vanilla sponge cake, dipped the slices in chocolate icing, and rolled them in desiccated coconut. Unpretentious beginnings to be sure, but right now they taste better than most fancy desserts that take hours to make.

As I clean up after dinner, dropping the empty stubbies into one of two bins fashioned from rusty 44-gallon oil drums and set beneath a flowering yellow box gum, something small, warm, furry – and very much alive – suddenly drops onto my head from the branch above, leaps onto my shoulder, scampers along the full length of my arm, balances a moment on my outstretched hand, and then hurls itself into the darkness.

As I jump in alarm, steadying myself against a pile of empty Quarter Pounder cartons, another small furry thing leaps from the mound, runs *up* my arm, cartwheels across my chest, runs down my other arm, and disappears off my wrist into the night.

I confess to squealing, at which Matt and Tim dutifully trot over to see what all the fuss is about, although I'm sure both are thinking I'm just an idiot city slicker who's been spooked by a harmless little bat, or a perfectly friendly and only slightly rabid dingo. But upon hearing scuffling behind me, Matt flicks on his torch, and soon we're all peering down into the second oil drum. It's empty, save for a spent stubby of beer, and the sweetest wide-eyed baby sugar glider I've ever seen. In fact, I've never seen one before full stop, let alone just worn it on my head. It must have a nest in the tree above and been out foraging, and mistaken me for a ladder.

'Ah-hah,' says Tim, matter-of-factly, 'so that's what's been eating my roses,' at which both boys head back to the campfire to finish off their beers, leaving me to figure out how to safely extricate the tiny creature from its metal prison.

Mission accomplished, I join Matt and Tim beside the fire, where we toast our faces and toes, as our backs grow chilly and damp with the cold night air. Matt takes a long swig from his stubby, his face glowing ruggedly handsome in the firelight, and although I haven't figured out what his secret is, I feel that perhaps it's simply more to do with him wanting to keep something private from the outside world. I'm thinking that he's really quite gentle and sensitive – although I'd never tell him that, for fear of being crammed into a cattle press and branded with a hot iron. Men need to be men, after all. Especially when they're a thousand miles from anywhere. He sits wordlessly by the fire, and is eventually lost in the flickering shadows as the fire dies right down, and the embers start to go black at the edges.

'Now *this* is a turn on,' Matt finally murmurs, 'you asked me before what an Australian aphrodisiac was, and this can be my answer. Food cooked on an open fire under the stars. Nothing but nature all around. You feel like you want to explode. To howl into the night.'

And in that very moment, I finally see a more complex picture of Matt. A man of the dirt and of the dust. Of the eucalypts and of the Murray pines. Driven by instinct and some ancient primal need to connect with the land. At one with Mother Earth.

And all of a sudden I have a perfect food match for him, for even though I'm not expecting all my dates to fit the dishes we share during our actual time together, I simply can't go past matching Matt up with the big juicy kangaroo steak we had tonight. He's sweet, slightly gamey, and not too heavy or rich to digest. He's best cooked medium rare, and lightly smoked – preferably on an open fire under the stars – and marinating him will bring out the fullness of his flavours. He's free-range, pretty much organic, and – sorry Matt – very cute indeed.

Matt needs to be up at dawn to truck cattle so we call it a night, and as I kiss him goodbye on a cheek still flushed brick red from the fire, I couldn't have asked for a better evening. Even though Matt's not a match for me, he's given me faith that there will be other decent men like him out there. Somewhere. Somehow. Someday. And I'm going to find me one.

Well, if I ever get outta here that is. I suspect that pissed-off huntsman spider has been plotting his revenge all evening.

I have time for one more date before I leave Australia, and I'm keen to have a shot at winning over the affections of another quintessential local icon – a surfer. I used to have a thing for them in my teens, when I'd sit on the beach pretending to read surfing magazines, hoping that an Aussie Adonis in salt-bleached board shorts would strike up a conversation with me, fall madly in love, and we'd live happily ever after. I spent three entire summers doing this, and not once was I approached. Not even by a weedy kid in Speedos. It may have had something to do with my knobbly knees, or my orthodontic braces that used to catch the sunlight like reflector lamps, but either way, the closest I ever got to a 'surfie' was being hit on the head by a boogie board on Portsea back beach. But now that I'm forty-seven and the braces are long gone, I wouldn't mind another chance. But how to find one? When I ask my friends to help, the nearest offer I get to meet someone who regularly surfs is a date with an internet junkie.

So I take matters into my own hands.

I know a beach abutting some of the wildest seas in the Southern Ocean. The surfers love it. They're out there nearly every day of the week, bobbing about on the green waves like pie-floaters, waiting to catch a thundering breaker back to shore. They're young, tanned, fit and well-built – exactly what I want.

At the beginning of the track leading down to the beach is a turning circle where surfers park to change into their wetsuits, providing great bare-bottom-watching opportunities. From there they head off to get tossed about in the surf like rag dolls in a washing machine. So one wintry but sunny Sunday morning – after making sure that no-one is around to catch me in the act – I tuck flyers under all the windscreen wipers.

> WANTED: one surfer!
> Female author would like to meet a surfer to take out for lunch or dinner. I'm writing a book on male stereotypes from around the world, and want to know what makes an Aussie surfer tick.
> If you're bronzed, buffed and brave enough, I'd love to meet you! Please call Bambi on the following number.

Now some people might think this approach a tad forward. Brazen even. Possibly mentally unbalanced. But to me it seems like a perfectly reasonable solution. I need a surfer, and maybe there's one out there who'd like a free feed. The only reason that I dive behind the Kombi van when I hear some surfers returning to their cars is because I've been caught off-guard. I would much prefer someone to have read the flyer before I actually meet him. But I have to quickly change tactics when the voices start heading right for the Kombi. And I have to move even faster so they know I'm here, before they start stripping down to their … well … nothings. So I pop up cheerfully from my hiding place, pretending I've been tying my shoelaces.

There are three of them, with wild sea-spiky hair, and faded black wetsuits like battle-worn seal skins, which are peeled down to well below their fuzzy bellybuttons.

Bingo.

They haven't noticed my flyer yet, so I decide to wing it.

'Hi,' I say a little breathlessly, 'I wonder if you can help me. I need a … um. Would any of you be interested in … um … a date? Not necessarily a real one, but … um. Oh dear.'

The trio look at me like I'm a previously unidentified and potentially toxic sea slug, and don't say a word, so I find myself gabbling on slightly hysterically about dates and fish 'n' chips and comparing Hungarian men with spicy sausages. Not that this helps, and now they must think I'm looking to score some drugs – or indeed am already on them – because they start to quietly back away, muttering something about being too busy or having to be out of town for the next month. So I thrust flyers into their hands and scoot away as fast as I can, feeling utterly humiliated and not expecting to hear from them ever again.

I shouldn't have worried, as within the week I receive two phone calls regarding my 'WANTED' notice. The first is from an old work friend, whose grown-up children I also know.

'Bambi,' Jocelyn says sweetly, 'My son Richard is

wondering why you're trolling for dates with surfers? He got the flyer, and although he'd love to help you out, he thinks it would be too weird.'

I nearly die of embarrassment. I'm mortified to think that Richard may have regarded my actions as no more than the desperate pick-up ploy of a sad and lonely middle-aged woman. Even though there's perhaps an element of truth to it. My mission is surely doomed if everyone else is going to think the same way.

But the very next day I receive the second phone call.

'Hi, it's Bear.'

The gruff voice sounds a little awkward.

'One of the guys you met down at the beach. I'm happy to meet you this weekend for lunch.'

Game on.

The next Saturday I make my way to Snatches Oceanside Takeaway. It's the local fast-food joint, and the perfect place to meet Bear, with its garish neon sign of a surfboard flashing above the front door. Inside, the pale blue walls are bleached by harsh fluorescent strip lighting, with a floor-to-ceiling mural of a beach scene studded randomly with kitsch ceramic whales and pastel-coloured starfish. Clear plastic strips cover the open doorway to keep out the flies, and are flicking violently – like impaled eels – as the wind picks up ahead of a forecasted storm.

I'm feeling as unsettled as the weather, as although I've already briefly met Bear, it's quite another thing to actually sit down and try to carry on a conversation with a near-stranger. I'm still a bit starstruck from my gawky teenage days when I thought surfers were the ant's pants, but at least Bear has already told me he has a long-time girlfriend, Chris. Although putting paid to my fleeting romantic notions of us ever skinny-dipping in the ocean together, this information takes the pressure off me. This way I don't have to worry about him meeting me with a grubby ulterior motive. Well, I hope not anyway. Although that's still certainly something I'm going to have to watch as I 'date' my way around the world, as no doubt I'll be regarded as fair game. I don't mind being seen as a cougar on the prowl – because that's kind of cool these days – but the last thing I want is to be viewed as a sad old flea-bitten moggy looking for someone to scratch my itch.

Bear arrives and pads inside with bare, broad, Hobbit feet. I can get a good look at him now without the distraction of a car park full of naked torsos. He's solidly built, medium height, and wears a faded t-shirt and shorts that appear to have been taken directly out of the tumble dryer. His hair is well past shoulder-length, bleached to a warm straw colour and crinkle-cut like potato chips, and pulled back untidily with an elastic band and don't-care-attitude into a ponytail. I'm guessing he's in his mid-forties, although he has surprisingly good skin for a guy who's probably spent more time in the sun than most solar panels. And he's so quintessentially Aussie that the cultural detective in me nearly faints with delight.

'Hey,' he says cheerfully, throwing himself into the seat opposite me, showering sand everywhere, 'I'm here, what do you wanna know?'

To help break the ice, I slide six stubbies of beer across to him. They're popular local brands, including one called Piss Weak, which I have just tossed in for effect. Bear reaches across to expertly snap the cap off a Vic Bitter, whilst I go for a Fosters.

'Cheers,' he says, his eyes twinkling mischievously, and looking like he's already thoroughly enjoying himself.

After checking out the menu which could well be a Suicide by Cholesterol Manual, with everything on it either deep-fried or ... well ... deep-fried, I order fish 'n' chips. It's one of Australia's most loved national dishes, and I'm guessing it might be a good match with Bear, given his affinity with the sea. Then I get out my questionnaire and try to look as nonchalant as I can, although I'm slightly amazed that we're both even here. I mean, I picked him up in a car park just a week ago, and now we're sitting down to a cold beer. And even though I already know he's not The One – as I'm no home-wrecker, and besides, I'm not sure I could put up with zinc-cream smears on the couch – the whole experience will undoubtedly be good practice for the thirty-plus men still to come. So, mixed in with the fear of failure, embarrassment and rejection, there's also the excitement of what might ultimately be. If not Matt, or Bear, then perhaps Paulo or Stefano. If not today, then perhaps tomorrow. If not for ever, then perhaps just long enough to fill my life with meaning again. To replenish the empty larder.

'So why are you called Bear?' I ask to get things started.

Bear smiles broadly. 'Well, mostly because of my

hair, as in grizzly bear, but if I'm having a bit of fun, I say it's B.A.R.E. as in butt.'

'Bare? Oh cute,' I reply, getting a flashback to the cheeky line-ups at the beach car park.

I blush knowingly, and Bear laughs, enjoying my mild discomfort. Indeed, I get the impression that he's a bit of a loveable larrikin, and before long I'm chuckling over his tales of 'trying to pick up' during his youth. The first gaffe occurred when Bear originally invited Chris out, and he turned up with no shoes on, whereupon she flatly refused to go out with him until he bought a pair. Then on the next date he wore shoes, but had to ask for her help to push-start his car in the pouring rain. It seems that being a smooth operator wasn't a high priority for Bear, but I'm guessing he got away with it because he has such a gentle, and delightfully uncomplicated, confidence about him.

'So how would you impress a girl on your first date?' I ask, at which Bear looks nonplussed, and studiously scratches his armpit as if to make sense of my question.

'Chocolates? Flowers?' I prompt. 'What would you do to show you were interested in her?'

There's more silence, and I hold my breath.

'Shoes,' he finally offers.

'Shoes?' I ask, confused.

'Yeah. I'd wear shoes,' Bear sounds sincere. 'I've learned my lesson. And then I'd take her to a barbie, or to see a band. Nothing flash. I wouldn't try to buy her, you know, with posh dinners and stuff. Nah ... you can't buy love.'

We crack open another beer, and Bear talks about how he sees himself in the world. It soon becomes apparent that he's not all that fussed what other people think of him. The fact that he drives a battered old station wagon with more dents in it than an orange on steroids, has a head of hair that may well be home to several species of endangered Australian wildlife, and would only get married 'to have a get-together and a bit of a laugh with friends', suggests he's a down-to-earth, no-nonsense, no-frills kind of guy. And although I wouldn't say he comes across as particularly deep, but more of a splash-in-the-shallows character, I still find him very likeable, and his attitude to life refreshingly honest. Especially with me coming from the city where image, money, career, and whether or not you're prepared to flash your butt in public, is all important. Indeed, all Bear really seems to care about are his kids, and surfing. But I suspect not necessarily in that order.

'Surfing rules your life,' he says passionately. 'It's only now and again that the waves are going to be huge, so you just gotta be ready. You have to drop everything or you'll miss it.'

'And what about sharks?' I ask.

'Less dangerous than girlfriends,' he replies cheerfully, I suspect alluding to his choice of surfing over babysitting duties. 'One time a fin came up fifteen metres from me, and I pulled my feet up and hoped it wasn't hungry. That was cool. And another time a killer whale came up to check me out. It just barrelled up out of the water like a 44-gallon drum.'

'What did you do?' I almost squeal.

'I turned to my mate,' Bear replies with a deadpan face, 'and I said, "Do they eat people?" And he said, "I dunno, let's wait and see," so we just bobbed about for a bit until it went away.'

'Really?'

'Fair dinkum.'

Our fish 'n' chips arrive, and are great. The fish has a subtle, smoky flavour, and is surprisingly sweet. The chips are perfect – golden-brown and crispy on the outside, and white and mooshy in the centre. Bear and I are momentarily silent as we focus on the meal, the only other sounds in the café being the occasional, slightly disturbing 'zzzt' of a fly getting roasted in the electric insect zapper. Outside it's raining. Hard. The wind is whipping up more ferociously by the minute, and the plastic strips over the door are convulsing frantically, sounding like sweaty thighs slapping together in a fat-camp marathon. I'm thinking we should both get going before the storm breaks. But I'm not quite finished yet.

'So if you were an animal, what would you be?' I ask Bear, upon which he looks uncertain, as if he's more used to looking without than within.

'Nothing harmful,' he finally replies, 'and something a bit cheeky. Perhaps a dolphin. They're smart and happy and free. They're very sociable and they try to get along with everyone else. And they're in the water 24/7 doing what they love best.'

It's with this comment that I believe I glimpse the essential nature of Bear. He's a creature of the sea for sure, which gives him a certain innocence and softness that's much harder to find in us concrete-hardened city folk.

Which gets me to thinking about Bear's food match, and I can't go past the fish in the fish 'n' chips. He's fresh, natural, honest, uncomplicated, and doesn't need to be eaten with silver cutlery. He's either grilled or deep-fried, is salted just right, and surprisingly sweet. Perfect.

As lightning starts to pierce the fizzing air outside, Bear suddenly jumps to his feet.

'Now I've really gotta go or my missus will kill me,' he says with a blazing smile. 'I told her I was meeting the boys for a quick beer, and you don't look much like Snake or Oopsie to me.'

And with a toss of his unruly hair, he's gone, leaving behind a scattering of sand and a warm stubby of Piss Weak beer.

And as I contemplate the fact that neither of my two Australian dates turned out to be The One, I'm not all that put out. I really wasn't expecting to find love in Australia anyway. I've been looking for it here for over thirty years, and it's pretty much evaded me – apart from Mark – so it's time to set my sights further afield. And I resolve to find it somewhere out there, even if I have to travel to the four corners of the earth. It's just a matter of keeping Hope alive, because as a very wise young man once told me, there's no such thing as a use-by date.

So watch out world – here I come.

Main Course

A main course is usually the heaviest, heartiest,
and most complex or substantive dish on a menu.

My tastebuds suitably piqued by my two Australian
'entrees', I'm practically salivating with the thought
of what's to come. Wining, dining and dating my way
across twenty-two countries for heaven's sake! If I
sometimes lacked good taste in the past with such activities, this is a sure-fire way to test my appetite anew …

Brazil
Sweet Jesus!

I arrive in Rio de Janeiro just as evening is settling like
a warm blanket over the grimy hillside favelas and the
luxury waterside apartments – cocooning rich and poor
alike in an eerie purple haze. Jesus watches me curiously from atop his pedestal on Corcovado Mountain,
and I feel a little self-conscious that I'm here on such an
indulgent mission. Then again, he did say to 'love one
another', didn't he?

I'm here with David, a friend who's accompany-
ing me on this first leg of my journey before he heads
for Jamaica. I'm grateful for his company, as I know
nothing at all about Brazil, apart from the facts that it

hosts the world's biggest Mardi Gras, it produces nuts and talented soccer players, and its official language is Portuguese.

Which I don't speak.

But I'm more clued up on the men, who, I've heard, are passionate, hot-blooded, jealous, vain, tactile, fun-loving and chauvinistic. I'm both nervous and intrigued by such a combination, particularly as I'm about to date one. My friend Jan made good on her word to organise an introduction via her Brazilian work colleague Lucienne, who came up with his Uncle Paulo.

Hi Paulo,
Thank you for agreeing to be my Brazilian date! I'll be arriving in Rio on 2 October, and am travelling with a male companion. May I suggest we meet at our hotel for a drink first, and then head out for dinner somewhere cheap and cheerful?
Bambi

Hi Bambi,
Why don't you bring a female friend? How can we have that atmosphere you want with a men waiting for you?

Why don't you send me a foto? Do you'll pay for the dinner?

You want a typical 'Restaurant Brasileiro'? Okay, I'm not gona charge you for that, only a dinner, talk and may be.
Hugs&Kisses,

Paulo

Hmm. I wonder what he means by 'and may be'.

Our luggage has gone missing and nobody at the air-port has a clue when it might turn up – if at all. When we get to our hotel, David and I head straight to the bar, for I'm in need of a stiff drink as I contemplate how to cope with one pair of undies for the next eighty days. Conveniently, the hotel is offering a compli-mentary *caipirinha* – the national cocktail of Brazil. It's made from muddled lime, sugar and special rum called *cachaça* extracted from sugarcane. And it's dangerous. Very dangerous. Especially when you knock back two in quick succession. Which is most probably why I start chatting up Chico – a famous Brazilian TV anchorman I meet at the bar. He's in his early fifties, handsome, with slightly overgrown silver hair, deeply tanned skin, dark eyes and full, pale lips. Indeed, I can't help noticing the lips, deciding I'd watch the news every night too, if those lips were presenting it.

'Chico,' I say, smiling stupidly, emboldened by a dangerous mix of sugar and rum. 'I'm writing about Brazilian cuisine, as well as men, so maybe you can help me?'

Chico doesn't miss a beat. 'Have a drink with me,' he says authoritatively. 'Now.'

David considerately heads for bed, whereupon Chico orders me another *caipirinha*. Which makes it three I've had in less than an hour, and probably isn't such a great idea on top of jetlag. Indeed, I'm soon more muddled than the limes, so I'm only too happy to let Chico do all the talking. Not that I'm really taking in much of what he's saying, so mesmerised am I by Those Lips, and his habit when making a point of softly touching my wrist, my arms, my knees and my thigh. Though not for a moment does he make me feel I need to toss a drink in his face to protect my honour. His tactility is simply very expressive and natural – as if it's his second language – and I find myself drawn to him like a moth to a warm, gentle light. But my time with him is short, and he soon bids me farewell, taking my face tenderly in both hands and kissing me four times on both cheeks.

'How many kisses are normal in Brazil?' I ask breathlessly.

'Ten times if you want. This is Brazil. We live for today.'

Another two tender kisses follow – this time on my lips – and then Chico is gone. And although I'm a little disappointed that it's over before it's even begun, at least it's given me a taste of him. And that is a *caipirinha* – a silky mix of sweet and sour that is vibrant, refreshing and most certainly a little intoxicating. And as I wearily head to bed, I hope that my 'real' date tomorrow will be even half as delicious.

Despite my hangover the next morning being akin to a tribe of Amazon Indians playing wooden drums in my skull, I still head out to sample the local cuisine. David and I wander along the main drag with people of every imaginable shape, size and colour cramming the foot-paths – cartwheeling buskers, toothless street-vendors selling fried pineapple, big-breasted Spanish-looking girls unashamedly flaunting all under barely there tank-tops and brightly coloured bras, and big black mamas with bottoms like huge over-ripe peaches. It's a true cel-ebration of cultural diversity, and as we're swept along by the energetic samba music flooding the streets, I feel like I'm diving through an exotic fruit-punch.

A corner café gives us a chance to come up for air, as well as try out the local coffee, whereupon I have an epiphany. It seems to me that the various styles of coffee being served in the café are pretty much a mirror image of all the people in the street outside. They're the full colour spectrum – from the creamy white macchiatos to the cinnamon-sprinkled café lattes, to the darker café au laits and jet-black espressos. It's as if God has been trying his hand at being a barista here for the last few hundred years, blending new combinations of people to result in this extraordinary brew bubbling away across the country. Magic.

As the street lights start to flicker on across the smog-shrouded city like luminous jellyfish, I head back to the hotel bar with David, and soon have another *caipirinha* at my lips to soothe my increasingly jumpy nerves before I'm on my own with Paulo. I want David to check him out for me first, just in case it's perfectly clear to everyone but me that Paulo's a serial killer. Or just a regular murderer, given that Rio has one of the highest

homicide rates in the world. I chat with David distractedly, occasionally laughing at nothing in particular and
tossing my hair from side to side in order to appear
relaxed. But the truth is, I'm deeply anxious about how
the night will go. Even though I've been planning it for
months, nothing has quite prepared me for the moment
of truth. Surfers and farmers on home turf are one thing,
but a total stranger in a foreign country? I'm starting to
feel I've made a dreadful mistake and this whole trip
will leave me utterly humiliated, because – quite apart
from possibly never finding The One – what happens
if the men I'm meeting don't even like me? Even the
serial killers? I've been on enough blind dates in my
life to know that if men don't fancy you in the first sixty
seconds, then the next sixty minutes are usually as comfortable as sitting on a nest of army ants. I wonder for
a moment if I can wriggle out of the whole thing, but
then as a figure cuts across the room toward me, I know
there's no turning back, so I turn to flash a cheery smile
– come what may.

Paulo is handsome. Ruggedly so, with a healthy
Caucasian tan, dark brown eyes and silver-grey hair
with strikingly contrasting black eyebrows – a Brazilian
version of Steve Martin. He's showing off an impressively fit body in a figure-hugging black t-shirt, and
looks younger than his fifty-seven years, which is a
relief because having described himself in his email as
a 'Professor PhD at Rio University', I was half expecting
an Albert Einstein lookalike. But no, he's cute.

So far, so good.

Paulo greets me somewhat guardedly, so I buy
him a drink to get things going, and we make light

conversation as the bartender looks on with a bemused smile. He's probably wondering how I could have talked three different men into having drinks with me in less than twenty-four hours.

Maybe I shouldn't be so hard on myself after all.

Paulo doesn't appear to be all that relaxed, sitting up straight as a ramrod and frequently flexing his considerable biceps and pecs. I'm not sure if this is for David's benefit or mine, but I'm reminded of pigeons puffing up their chests to impress the ladies and intimidate the opposition, upon which I carefully avoid catching David's eye in case I get the giggles.

After drinks we part ways with David, and Paulo walks me through the dimly lit back streets like he doesn't have a care in the world. The guidebooks say, 'when in Rio walk quickly and with purpose', but Paulo positively saunters, as if daring thugs to take him on. Not that they would I guess, as Paulo radiates an aura of being able to deal with anything. And perhaps justifiably so – he tells me he has a black belt in karate, and also in judo, which is very impressive, especially compared to my white belt in ju-jitsu at the age of eight.

We eventually end up in Copacabana at a huge open-air restaurant right across from the beach – one of the most famous in the world. Outside, the open-sided marquees are filled with young *cariocas* tucking into a multitude of small dishes, similar to tapas. It's all very animated and cheerful, but Paulo seems disdainful of such frivolity, and leads me inside to the practically empty restaurant, which has an atmosphere of an old people's home, with its plastic carnations and wall-mounted TV blaring out a B-grade soap opera. It's not at all what I was after, so I encourage Paulo to sit beside an open window from where I can at least get a sense of the pulsating ambience outside. And even though I'm beginning to suspect that Paulo and I don't have much in common – me being a tapas-tasting, toe-tapping sort of girl – I'm happy to go with the flow. After all, I can't possibly expect to get along famously with all my dates, so I may as well just enjoy the experience. If he's not The One, then I hope he can show me a culture I know little about. I'm frustrated, however, to learn that the restaurant doesn't offer any of Brazil's famous dishes such as *feijoada* (a stew of black beans with beef and pork) or *churrasco* (barbecued meat), which had been half the point of the date.

'But the *moqueca* is very popular with locals,' Paulo assures me. 'In fact, it's one of my favourites.'

I don't have a clue what *moqueca* is, but tell Paulo I'm happy to give it a go, crossing my fingers it's not guinea pig stew. I used to have a pet guinea pig as a kid, and I'm not so sure I could go there. Then again, as a cultural detective I can't be squeamish, so if Mr Willy-Wiggles is on the menu, then so be it.

It soon becomes clear that Paulo has neither a great sense of humour, nor a fondness for small talk, and indeed, when I resort in desperation to my question-naire for inspiration – upon which he flicks it back to me across the table, and flares his nostrils in obvious displeasure – I get the slightly unsettling impression that he thinks I smell like a four-day-old empanada. But I've dated plenty of difficult men in my time, so when I persist with a mix of witty asides and more buttering up than a footlong hotdog, he eventually starts to open up, and little bursts of light occasionally reveal themselves from behind the gloom. It's hard work, and Paulo doesn't smile much, but when he does his whole face glows. I discover that he's an oceanic structural engineer, designing 'ecologically sensitive artificial reefs' around the world. He also has two marriages under his belt with Japanese and Brazilian women, which have resulted in four kids, who Paulo proudly informs me 'all look quite exotic'. He rockclimbs, he goes trekking, he cooks, and when I ask him what his favourite childhood meal is, his eyes sparkle.

'Sweet apple pie that my grandmother used to make,' he sighs happily. Which has me thinking he has a gentle side after all.

But then I make the mistake of asking him if there's a particular Brazilian dish that's used as an aphrodisiac. Paulo must think I'm suggesting that he needs help in that department, for he slowly raises one Steve Martin eyebrow and glowers at me. But I gamely press on.

'You know, something that's used to ... um ... increase sexual pleasure. It's here, written in my questionnaire,' I say lamely, as if that gives it intellectual credibility.

'Black mussel, and oyster,' he finally answers, his voice somewhat strangled.

'And do they work?' I blunder on like a swimmer heading into the open jaws of a four-metre crocodile.

Paulo sits back in his chair and grimaces. He doesn't answer. He doesn't even at look me. There's a good thirty seconds' silence as he rearranges the napkin on his lap, and I'm pretty sure I've just overstepped the boundaries of international goodwill.

I'm saved when the meal arrives, and I can focus solely on the *moqueca baiana,* which is handsomely presented in a large earthenware pot. Paulo stops grimacing, waits for the waiter to top up our beers, and appeasingly nods, *'Saúde.'* Then he graciously explains the dish, which is a seafood stew of prawns and grouper, with tomato, coriander and red chilli, all swimming in coconut milk and a thick yellow palm oil called *azeite de dendê.* No guinea pigs, thank goodness. It's served with *farofa,* which is a toasted manioc flour mixture, and good for soaking up the oil. I start to work my way through it, savouring each mouthful as if I'm a judge on *Master Chef,* and inhaling the sweet, fish-scented steam as it spirals upwards.

I initially wonder whether this dish is a good match for Paulo because it's very rich and full-bodied, but then decide he's nowhere near as flavoursome or colourful. The *farofa* comes close, as it's slightly dry and hard to swallow. Or perhaps he's the coconut from which the milk is extracted – being such a tough nut to crack. But even though I've not yet found a dish to sum up Paulo's complex character, it doesn't matter. I'm starting to enjoy this date, as challenging as it is. Getting to know Paulo is like dancing the samba – constantly shifting my weight to get the right balance, and trying to get the steps right without falling flat on my face. I hated dancing class when I was at school – being the tallest person there so none of the boys wanted to partner me – but I grimly stuck it out and the skills of 'two steps forward, one step back', also taught me some life skills. So even if there's not a whole lot of rhythm happening between Paulo and me, I'm still enjoying the exercise.

Paulo's well-toned physique combined with that somewhat unnerving flexing of his muscles, along with a slightly arrogant air, makes me suspect he could be a tad shallow. I certainly don't want to judge him unfairly just because he takes pride in his appearance, but I've met plenty of men at the gym with bodies of cast iron, and the depth of a stainless-steel sink-strainer. To see if I'm right, I ask Paulo if he only dates beautiful women. I await his answer with some trepidation, as given I'm no beauty myself I take such slights personally, as if I too am being judged.

'Beautiful. Of course,' he answers, puffing out his chest proudly. 'But beautiful is different with every woman. And I would not go with a beautiful woman if that woman is not also intelligent.'

His response redeems him somewhat in my eyes, as it suggests he also values what's happening behind the scenes – like a Mardi Gras float that's all about theatre and glamour on the outside, but has been put together with thoughtfulness and creativity.

'Right,' I say, rather dreading my next question, as I'm expecting Paulo to think it beneath him. 'If your personality was an animal, what would you be?'

But Paulo smiles, as if pleased at the opportunity to get away from talking about what he thinks, to what he *is*. Because despite some gravitas, I still get the impression he's more used to holding up the mirror to see how good he looks, rather than for more soulful reflection.

'Orca,' he replies after a few moments.

'Orca?'

'Yes, a whale.'

'And why?'

'A whale is king of all the sea,' Paulo replies. 'No-one can beat him. But a whale doesn't have to fight anyone like a lion who's king of the jungle. A whale can just be left in peace.'

And there it is. The hint of vulnerability – even a certain world-weariness – that once again suggests he has a rather sweet side.

That is, until the bill arrives.

Now that I'm far from home, wining and dining my way around the world and imposing myself upon total strangers, I can't ignore the elephant in the room. And it's a big elephant too. With whiskers.

Who pays for dinner? Not just this one, but also all of them to come?

It may seem screamingly obvious that as I have invited the man out, then I should cover it. But in my mind it's actually not that black and white, because I'm concerned that if I insist on paying – or even if we split the bill – then it could spoil the traditional male/female, hunter/gatherer dynamics, and risk deflating the sense of romance and intrigue that invariably comes with them. I don't want these dates to turn into calculated business transactions, but rather be possible launching pads for something special. Besides, being a ballsy women's libber is hardly very attractive. Not to most sensitive guys anyway. Of course I'm happy to pay my own way. Of course I don't expect a stranger to pay for my meal. But paying for his too? Now that's a curly one.

Or have I got it all wrong?

'Of course *he* should pay,' Lou, my not-working, married, no-nonsense friend, said when I asked her advice at my farewell dinner party.

'Of course *you* should pay,' Jan, my working, single-mother, and equally no-nonsense friend, snorted.

'Why don't you just go Dutch?' Fiona suggested. 'Then you can't be accused of freeloading.'

'But if he insists on paying for you,' Simon – who likes to be The Man – said, 'you should graciously accept.'

'Just pay the tip,' Anita said, 'so he feels like you've made a contribution.'

'I'm confused,' my dear elderly mother said when I rang her the next day, asking her advice. She'd been raised in the '30s and '40s when there simply weren't so many options, when men took women out to dinner as a matter of course, and women would reciprocate by baking cheese-and-pumpkin scones, and it all seemed to work quite nicely. 'I'm really quite confused,' Mum repeated. 'Who is taking who to dinner exactly?'

Good point. And that's exactly why I had simply decided to see what would happen when the issue raised its whiskery head.

Which it just has.

In Paulo's case he'd expressly asked me in his email who was going to pay for dinner, to which I'd responded that I would as otherwise it may have been a deal-breaker. But as it happens, the bill is twice my daily food budget. It seems the *moqueca* is the most expensive item on the menu, which multiplied by two has hardly made it a cheap and cheerful outing – as I in turn had expressly requested from *him*. But as much as I'm horrified at the blowout, and wondering if my bank balance will last the distance, I'll just have to suck it up. So I pay cash for the two of us, and leave a small tip, then watch in morbid fascination as Paulo slowly leans across the table towards me, pulls out another – not insignificant – note from my purse, and slaps it on the table. Clearly my tip wasn't generous enough.

Still, I'm totally gobsmacked.

And Paulo doesn't even thank me for dinner. In fact, he's busy pouring salt into the wound.

'I am surprised by how expensive that meal was,' he says cheerfully. 'I thought the waiter must have made a mistake.'

I'm even more gobsmacked.

But Paulo is now the most upbeat he's been all evening – as if a weight has been lifted from his shoulders. He even suggests that we have coffee in a local bar, and although I wonder if I'm being masochistic, I accept. It might be a more pleasant way to finish off an evening where half the time I'd felt about as welcome as a dose of malaria. But I'm not sure of Paulo's motives for extending our date. Over dinner he'd shown absolutely no intention in pursuing any level of meaningful – or even meaningless – association with me. In fact, he hadn't asked me one single question about myself. And although during these dates I'm trying to put the focus on the men rather than me, so I can get inside their heads – and maybe their hearts – it would have been nice if Paulo had shown just a smidgeon of interest.

Because heck, what girl doesn't enjoy a bit of attention from a handsome man? Especially when she's travelled halfway around the world to meet him? Still, given his indifference, I feel confident that accepting a late-night cuppa won't give him the wrong message, like that perhaps I'm up for a bit of horizontal samba dancing.

Which I'm most certainly not. Or at least, not with him.

We find an appropriately dingy little bar where Paulo orders two espressos, and the moment the cups hit the laminex, he leans his head against the wall and smiles oddly at me. He reminds me of the Cheshire Cat.

'So where are we sleeping tonight?' he asks.

'Where?' I ask limply. I hadn't seen it coming.

'Yes, where? You have a man back in your room,' Paulo replies. 'Why bring him to Brazil? It would have been easy to go back to your hotel, but now we will need to find somewhere else.'

I stir my espresso nervously, wondering how to respond. I've put myself smack bang in the middle of this situation, and I need to deal with it with diplomacy. Besides, who knows, maybe it's just the polite thing to do in his social circles. And perhaps I should have taken his original 'may be' more seriously, so that I'd have been better prepared with an answer, rather than sitting here looking like a stunned mullet.

'How can you understand me if we don't really get to know each other?' Paulo goes on. 'The only way to truly learn about someone is to be with them.'

And suddenly Paulo holds up his broad well-manicured hands, and splays his fingers out like a piano player. 'I am very good with my hands,' he says proudly. 'All ten fingers. With massage like shiatsu, and touching, and making love. I know what to do to make a good experience.'

Oh. My. God.

I can feel myself blushing hotly. I'm used to a slightly more subtle approach – usually after a whole evening of whispering romantic sweet-nothings across the dining table, and a nice foot-tickle to get me in the mood. But this is so out of the blue that I don't know whether to be insulted or flattered. Sure, I've been thinking about sex since I broke up with Mark, and I haven't embarked on this trip to suddenly turn all prim and proper the minute I get a proposition, but this is decidedly wham, bam, thank you ma'am, which just isn't the way I operate.

I still don't know how to respond, so I just keep stirring my coffee, wondering how I'm going to get myself out of this one. Eventually I take a deep breath, and use a soothing tone I once used quite successfully in coaxing an over-amorous boy at a school social to put it back in his pants.

'You're very charming, Paulo,' I say, 'but I need a lot more time before I sleep with a man. I'm sorry.'

And it's true – only once in my entire life have I had a one-night stand, and that was after eleven strawberry daiquiris at my thirtieth birthday party. But every other act of … um … whatever … has taken me at least half a dozen dates, over several weeks, to warm up to.

Paulo leans back and does the muscle-flexing thing again. 'I know when I walk down the street that people look at me,' he says earnestly. 'They look at me, and they talk about me.'

I nod solemnly in agreement as if I quite understand

his dilemma – the burdensome responsibility of being far too handsome for his own good. And then I slowly become aware – as if waking from a dream – that Paulo is crooning a romantic Brazilian ballad at me, which I can only guess is another angle to get me into the cot. Although, I suspect he's only doing it out of fear that he wouldn't be much of a man if he didn't give seducing me his best shot. He persists, which is a smart move on his part, because before long I'm wondering what it *would* be like to have a quick fling with him. To live for today. Just like Chico had said last night. Why not?

After all, if I truly want to find out about Brazilian men, within a culture where overt sexuality – and arguably promiscuity – is a driving force, then perhaps no-one would judge me harshly for it. So nor should I.

But no. I simply don't fancy Paulo. Yes, he's handsome and cares about homeless fish, but he's far too confident for me, which I find more of a turn-off than a turn-on. Besides, he's just told me about the 26-year-old girlfriend who's waiting for him at home.

'But what would she think?' I respond, slightly offended to think he's been keeping his options open.

'She has other boyfriends,' he shrugs nonchalantly.

'Do you love her?' I ask.

'Yes, I love her, but life is complicated.'

It's all getting a bit complicated for me too, so I toss down the last of my espresso, and suggest it's time to go.

Paulo shrugs, but I can't tell if it's resignation, or his way of saying, 'Well, you don't know what you're missing out on *mocinha*.' We leave the bar and head towards my hotel, with Paulo strolling slowly beside me, as if to play for time. He looks glum.

'The change of season makes my skin very dry,' he suddenly says. 'I notice my body is flaking. I think I am turning into a snake.'

'You told me you were a whale,' I respond lamely.

'Well, we are all animals in some way. We are driven by instinct,' he says mournfully, and I can't help but feel sorry for him. Maybe the shrug had been one of surrender after all. Perhaps I've just caught a glimpse of the true Paulo behind all the bravado and posturing – something a little bit sad and lonely. We stop outside the hotel and stand there awkwardly. I firmly shake his hand just in case he's thinking of making a last-minute lunge at me.

'Thank you, Paulo, it's been a great night, and thank you for showing me the whale.'

'Perhaps just an old tiger,' he says, and looks me in the eye with a slightly haunted expression, then turns on his neat designer heels and is gone.

In the morning I play David a recording of my date with Paulo. After my rather clumsy Australian dates where I was constantly scribbling notes, I'd hoped a digital recorder would make things easier. But all we can hear is some shuffling, the scrape of a chair, footsteps, the squeak of a door opening, the squeak of a door closing, the sound of a latch being drawn, and then for the next thirty seconds the unmistakable sound of ... well ... splashing. I'm absolutely mortified as I realise that I must have accidentally turned the recorder on when

I intended to turn it off, which means that apart from not recording any of my date with Paulo, I now have a full unedited recording of Me Having A Wee. At least David thinks it's hilarious.

My date with Paulo over, I'm now able to relax and look forward to a few days simply absorbing the whole Rio experience. And even though Paulo didn't turn out to be The One, I'm not disheartened, as with twenty countries still to go, there are bound to be plenty more opportunities. And hopefully more palatable ones at that. Which reminds me that I still need to find a food match for my tricky professor, so David and I spend the next two days trying out as many *tradicional* restaurants as we can, including one in which a serving of chicken and *tutu* nearly brings me undone.

Tutu is one of Brazil's national dishes, but it fails to excite me. The name might sound cute, but it's simply mashed black beans with a decidedly bland flavour and an odd, floury texture. Hoping to liven things up a little, I reach for some red peppers, which look identical to the delicious sweet *pimentos* I ate in a previous local meal. However, as peppers in general are not to be trusted – much like an arsonist who says he doesn't play with matches – I squash just half a pod into the *tutu*, and take a bite.

Before the fork has left my mouth I suddenly recall reading about the different types of peppers used in Brazilian cooking. There are *pimento biquinho*, which are sweet and tasty, *aji pineapple*, which are citrusy and moderately hot, and *pimenta malagueta*, which are only slightly less fiery than Vulcão do Paredão's eruption several thousand years ago – the latter specimen of which I've just consumed, causing my mouth to catch alight and my eyeballs to weep sulfuric acid. Or so it feels.

'Hot are they?' David cheerfully asks once I've finished frantically spitting the half-chewed mess out into my napkin, and sticking my tongue as far into the beer as it can stretch, quite convinced I can hear it sizzling.

I don't bother replying.

But being a doggedly glass-half-full kind of girl I decide that this is an experience not to be wasted. Perhaps *this* is Paulo – all hot and red and showy, on first bite at least, until your tongue goes numb. And certainly something you want to spit out sooner rather than later to prevent permanent damage.

There's another national dish I want to try – *feijoada*. So the next day we track down a restaurant that promises to serve up 'a tasteful Brasileiro experience of the pigs'. Despite such an eloquent introduction, I'm still not looking forward to it very much.

'You must eat *feijoada* only at lunchtime,' Paulo had told me.

'Why?' I'd asked.

'Because you will be so full that unless you walk around a lot after eating it, your stomach will split open like a watermelon.'

And he's quite right, for after an eight-course

banquet that includes an enormous cast-iron pot full to the brim with a thick purplish-black broth of beans and rather confronting pig bits – including a whole pig's ear, a little pig's trotter, and what I strongly suspect to be thinly sliced pig's penis – I'm about to burst. Indeed, when we finally get back to the hotel and the concierge says he's booked a table for us tonight at a *churrasco* barbecue house, I wonder how on earth I'm going to fit it in, let alone cart around a belly the size and weight of a bowling ball.

At the up-market Porcão, David and I are ushered into a cavernous room where the heady smell of barbecued meat has me salivating before I even sit down. Clearly accustomed to this effect on diners, there's a waiter at our elbows in seconds, offering us metal skewers of little sausages, which he disimpales with a dramatic flourish so that they tumble onto our plates like acrobats. The restaurant floor is constantly in motion, with waiters gliding between tables as if on roller skates, clearing wobbly towers of dirty plates, or bringing out meat fresh from the kitchen. The skewers are enormous – the length of swords – and the waiters pause momentarily for our nod of approval before pushing lamb chops, spare-ribs, chicken livers, and chicken hearts the size of twenty-cent pieces, onto our plates. There's a choice of twenty-three different cuts of barbecued meat from just about every farmed beast imaginable, and although I didn't think I'd be able to stuff another thing in after today's *feijoada*, I sample most dishes, and as I lick my lips with the sort of delight a piranha feeding on a boatload of tourists would appreciate, it suddenly hits me. Of course.

Paulo is the eye-fillet steak in a *churrasco* barbecue. He's as red-blooded as they come. Well-seasoned, prime cut, lean and served rare. And although with careful cooking he might tenderise quite nicely, he's still too rich and gamey for my liking.

I leave Brazil the following day, happy that our luggage has finally been returned, which means for the first time in four days I don't have to wash my undies last thing at night, and spread them over the warmth of my computer screen to dry. But I'm a little disappointed that I didn't find The One here. Not that I actually expected that to happen quite so soon – like winning the lottery on your first-ever quick-pick – but I'm the impatient type, and am beginning to wonder how long it's going to take to find the soulmate who's going to fill my heart. On the next date? The one after? As the plane arcs high over a landscape deeply scarred by deforestation, and pocked with mining shanty-towns like huge festering sores, it's slowly dawning upon me that I may end up in much the same state.

Cuba
Bean there – done that

I've not come to Cuba necessarily expecting to find some romantic Che Guevara love child with whom to fall madly in love – although heck, if I find one I'm happy to give him a go. I'm here because Cuba exists in an extraordinary time warp. America's embargo has essentially frozen it in the '60s, and I'm wondering how that affects the local men. What I've read about them might reflect their frustrations – 'loud, hot-headed, lazy, controlling, misogynistic and promiscuous', although on the upside they're also known to be generous, warm and friendly, with strong family values. But just who I end up with for my Cuban date is anyone's guess, because I was unable to initiate any personal contacts from home, or even – as a last resort – to access an online dating site. Being a communist country, Cuba has such repressive laws that even connecting to the internet 'illegally' can lead to a five-year prison sentence. And that would be a really bad start to a date.

David and I are met at the airport by the lovely Marta – with a personality as bubbly as a Cuba *libre* cocktail – who'll be our tour guide tomorrow. If we survive that is. An enormous lightning bolt has just split the sky almost horizontally, followed immediately by an Armageddon-worthy crack of thunder, and the rain is absolutely bucketing down as we make a dash for the taxi to take us into the centre of Havana. It's hot and unbearably humid, and I'm crossing my fingers that even though I've arrived smack bang in the middle of the hurricane season, we might be spared. I've got far better things to do than strap myself to the nearest palm tree for three days.

Within minutes I feel like we've stepped back in place and time, as every car we pass is a classic American relic from the '50s – Buicks, Dodges, DeSotos, Pontiacs and Chevrolets, most on the verge of collapse and stuck together with brown packaging tape or frayed canvas strapping. But it's not just the cars that are relics – the houses and apartment blocks are old and dilapidated too, with broken windows, peeling paint and buckled corrugated-iron roofing. And as I pass by droves of scruffy people on the outskirts of town, waiting for buses, or just lethargically standing about on cracked footpaths and seemingly oblivious to the downpour, I already sense that not only is Cuba a place lost in time, but perhaps also in spirit.

However, it seems I was mistaken, as when David and I open the green-and-white shutters in our hotel room, we're instantly drenched in a rich broth of salsa and rumba and reggae music, bubbling up from the myriad of laneways below, and suggesting that the Cuban *alegria de vivir* is alive and well. It's absolutely intoxicating as it pulls us inexorably downstairs like the Pied Piper of Hamelin, luring us to a place where it seems that music can transport one's lives of privation to a far happier place.

The main thoroughfare of Calle Obispo is seething with a colourful mix of ethnicities, mostly from Spanish, French, African and Portuguese roots. The women are incredibly sexy, with their flat tummies and belly rings, firm breasts, tiny hips, slim waists and smooth caramel skin. And they're dripping with attitude, the sort that says, 'I'm hot and I know it, so what are you going to do about it *cariño*?' The younger men are impressively muscly, and walk with a certain macho swagger, but seem a bit rough around the edges, like they've not shaved for a week, and have worn their clothes to bed. Which would be quite understandable given that most Cubans live in relative poverty. However, they all smile back at me if I smile first, showing they're neither impoverished of warmth, nor skint on manners.

In the morning Marta takes us on a walking tour of Havana's Old Quarter and its crumbling facades flecked with peeling paint in turquoise and lemon-yellows and mint-greens – exotic gelati colours good enough to eat. Delicate wrought-iron balustrades and elaborately carved doors line the cobblestoned streets, telling of a city once prosperous and proud, although the faded grandeur is repeatedly interrupted with electricity lines strung chaotically overhead like tree snakes in a mating frenzy. A withered old woman hangs her washing over a balcony railing, but the air is so humid that I don't hold out much hope that even her neatly darned stockings will be dry within the week. And where the music doesn't quite reach – down the crooked side streets and dead-end alleys – the positive energy noticeably decreases, and even colours seem to fade like they're flowers that need the hydrating qualities of music to keep them alive.

One can't live on music alone though, as I learn when Marta takes us to a Food Distribution Centre, with raw wooden shelves displaying a selection of items – a six-pound bag of rice, a three-pound packet of sugar, twenty ounces of beans, twelve eggs, powdered milk, two cups of cooking oil, a bunch of bananas, a mound of spotty potatoes. Marta tells me that every Cuban gets these rations at heavily subsidised prices to get them through the first ten days of each month. But I note that there's no meat here. No green vegetables. No choice of fruit. No chocolate bars.

No joy.

I'm shocked, but when pressed, Marta concedes that some meat can be purchased with coupons at the local *carnicería*, or meat store. But Cubans are on their own with fresh fruit and veggies, where a large guava can cost an entire day's wages.

'So what happens for the next twenty days?' I asked Marta, choosing not to tell her that in Australia I regularly throw out spoiled food from my fridge that I haven't got around to eating.

Marta smiles sadly, as if she's seen a great many injustices in her life. 'They suffer.'

When I feel I've won Marta's trust that I'm not some creepy tourist preying on other people's misery – like the busloads gawking at Rio's slums as if they were exotic scenery – I describe my mission and ask her if she can help me meet a Cuban man.

'What about my husband?' she suggests. 'Would you like to meet weeth 'im?'

'Your husband?'

'Yes. He speaks very good English.'

'Are you sure that's okay?' I ask, embarrassed.

'Yes, no problem,' she replies cheerfully. 'I trust you weeth 'im. I will tell 'im to meet you tomorrow in your hotel.'

'How should I recognise him?'

'Easy,' Marta replies, 'he ees very handsome. His

name ees Alberto. And he ees in a wheelchair.'

I'm delighted that Alberto is locked in as a date, as it means I won't have to resort to more sneaky methods, such as taking salsa lessons in order to chat up the teacher. Some women might find dancing with a hot Latino with a butt of steel exciting, but not me. I'm about as coordinated as a daddy-long-legs on smack, and it would end in total humiliation. And although of course I'm disappointed not to be meeting a single man in Cuba for the sake of my heart, at least I'll have met a local for my research.

However, Marta has more trouble with my next request – finding a restaurant that will cook *ajiaco*, one of Cuba's national dishes. It seems that it's a 'peasant dish', and usually only cooked in the home. But after several cajoling phone calls to her friends, she has David and I heading off for a specially prepared lunch at Hostal San Miguel. I'm expecting a dinky little restaurant with dried gourds hanging from the rafters and Mama Concepcion in a floral apron doling out fried beans, but I couldn't have been more wrong. The restaurant is located in a magnificent three-storey hotel, where we're whisked upstairs to a wide marble terrace dotted with small potted palms, overlooking the entrance to Havana's harbour. It's an extraordinary setting, and even better, no-one else is here.

The *ajiaco* arrives almost right away, beautifully presented in two fine white porcelain soup bowls on matching plates, with a small dish of lime wedges on the side, and a breadstick still steaming from the oven. I feel a little guilty because I'm guessing this restaurant is totally out of reach to most Cubans, unless of course they're wearing green army fatigues and their last name is Castro. Plus, the soup looks much more palatable than some of the other food I've seen around, with lots of tasty things floating around in a rich orange broth – corn, fried banana, onion, pumpkin, red pepper, green pepper, taro, sweet potato and neat cubes of pork. I soon discover a thick flap of pork skin sporting an impressive patch of bristles though.

'Our soup's got hairy bits,' I say to David, who luckily is slurping his soup so loudly that he doesn't hear me. Or at least he pretends not to, having already dealt with what may have been sliced pig penis in the Brazilian *feijoada*.

Despite the stubble, the *ajiaco* is absolutely delicious – rich yet mellow, and with a luscious velvety texture, with the added lime juice making it really zingy. Indeed, it's so good that I'm growing increasingly nervous as I wipe the bowl clean with bread as light as fairy floss, then ask for *'la cuenta, por favor'*, bracing myself for a peasant's soup worth a king's ransom. The waiter smiles ominously as he gives me the bill.

It reads '12 pesos', which I assume is a mistake, as that's not much more than the price of two coffees back home. But it's correct, and the waiter's eyes light up like the Catherine wheels at Fidel Castro's eightieth-birthday celebrations, as I leave a tip equivalent to a month's wages for both he and the chef to share. Well, fifteen dollars won't ruin me, but it might mean they can buy their kids chocolate for a year. If they can find any.

That evening David and I have dinner in one of the world's most famous restaurants – La Bodequita del Medio. It was writer Ernest Hemingway's favourite hangout in the '40s and '50s, and lays claim to popularising the mojito, a more basic version of which was drunk by thirsty African slaves as they laboured in the Cuban canefields. La Bodequita's front bar is already stacked with ready-to-mix mojitos, which I waste no time sampling, and am instantly sold. A mojito is made from fresh mint muddled with lime juice, sugar, white rum and soda water. It's much like Brazil's *caipirinha*, but packed with minty freshness, and just a little punch from the rum. However, I suspect that more than one may well turn into a knockout.

The menu here has been exactly the same for fifty years, but it's not all that inspiring – much like a decades-old marriage that started off exciting, fresh and delicious, but over time has settled back into a comfort zone best described as ... well ... mildly palatable, simply because no-one really cares any more. There are somewhat ho-hum black beans and white rice, fried pork chunks, black bean soup, and fried green banana. Not to mention an incongruous side plate of limp french fries – adding weight to my marriage metaphor. It's all a bit bland, and I'm getting heartily sick of beans, but to be fair, the history of the restaurant and the animated atmosphere more than make up for the food.

After dinner David and I head for El Floridita, Hemingway's other favourite hangout, and the place he'd go for his daiquiris, a Cuban invention of the Spanish–American War. I order a grapefruit-juice daiquiri, and munch on deep-fried banana chips as I happily settle back to listen to a musical quartet playing a romantic mix of accordion, maracas, violin and cello. The maracas player doubles as the singer, her black hair exactly the same colour as her eyes and her skin, so that in the flickering shadows her bright lime-green sequinned blouse seems to take on a demented life of its own. She's belting out songs with that typically infectious Cuban beat that I'm beginning to love – the one that lifts your soul and makes you feel incredibly alive. So alive that when David and I eventually head back to the hotel, we practically dance, our toes tapping one-two-three, one-two-three, one-two-three as we go. And as the palpable energy throbs down the narrow streets, and the humid air cocoons me in its sticky embrace, I feel like I'm in quite another world – somewhere between starring in an old-time movie and infused in a warm bottle of rum.

The following afternoon I wait for Alberto in the hotel lobby. I feel bad for putting him to so much trouble – as making his way to the hotel over the bumpy cobblestones of Calle Obispo would test the resilience of a moon buggy, let alone a wheelchair. But when he arrives, he doesn't seem unduly concerned, and introduces himself warmly and sincerely. He's in his early thirties, and is indeed very handsome as Marta had said, with pale skin, a neat Steven Spielberg beard, silvering hair, a trim body in a figure-hugging red t-shirt, a drop-dead-gorgeous smile, and the most amazing blue eyes sparkling with good humour. And yes, he's in a wheel-chair – his legs quite lifeless before him – although within seconds I don't even notice them, so struck am I by a personality that's easily standing ten-feet-tall. We tuck ourselves away into the coolness of the hotel's bar, and away from any prying eyes that may want to make a big deal of our meeting, as it's frowned upon – if not illegal – for Cubans to fraternise with tourists. I'm so conscious of not getting either of us into trouble that I start writing my notes in schoolgirl code, so I can get on that plane to Europe tomorrow, rather than the secret police charging me with crimes against the state.

At first I'm a little tongue-tied with Alberto; as he's married, I don't want to misplace Marta's trust in me. But when I defer to my questionnaire to get me started, and ask Alberto who wears the pants in his family, he laughs heartily.

'I am the man,' he replies confidently, 'I prefer to 'ave the power. It makes me feel good to look after my woman. Besides,' he adds with an electrifying smile that matches his high-voltage personality, 'Cuban women love men to be een control.'

I'm not sure how true this is. I got the impression from Marta that she felt Cuban women could do with a bit more equality. So I try to trip Alberto up by telling him that Marta claimed Cuban men are 'always unfaith-ful to their women', whereupon he laughs again, his blue eyes twinkling mischievously.

'Oh yes, eet's true,' he replies without hesitation. 'Weeth one, two, three women. It ees normal. But we can't 'elp it – the women make us do it. They are erotic. What they wear een the street. When it ees hot and the women are almost naked een your face, it ees very difficult for us.'

'Even with a lovely wife like Marta?' I playfully chide, not really expecting him to answer.

'Oh yes,' he replies easily. 'It ees important for me to have women. They make me feel good. Een Cuba it ees normal.'

Alberto continues being remarkably open with me, with stories of picnics in the park, his love of music, his almost obsessive passion for baseball, and of a very happy marriage with Marta – notwithstanding the odd affair. Although as I pick my way through the pretty shells on the beach that are his life, I'm also gleaning there's a lot of rubbish mixed in with it. He has a salary – but it's too low. His basic needs are met – but he's not comfortable. He's connected to the internet – but 'the government is always watching'. He has a wheelchair – but it has a flat tyre and there's nowhere to get it fixed. He hates Fidel Castro – 'e 8's F Castrol Oil' I write in code, hoping I'll be able to decipher everything when I get out of the country – and he's totally against communism. But as hard as his life is, Alberto still rises high above the quagmire. He smiles often and easily with that amazing, dazzling flash of exuberance where his whole face lights up. Indeed, I don't think I've met such a genuinely positive and likeable man in a very long time. And sexy too.

'Do you see yourself as a typical Cuban?' I press.

'Maybe not,' he replies, 'most Cubans think they are a bull or a tiger and they like to roar, but me, I prefer intelligence first, like a horse.' Alberto hesitates for a moment. 'But in some ways I am typical because I like the women too much,' he says, smiling broadly, then gestures a shape in the air with his hands – a very curvy rounded shape.

'And bottoms?' I ask, laughing.

'And bottoms, yes,' he replies, those blue eyes blazing again. 'Big bottoms. Eet's nice.'

A grim-faced man with a suspiciously new polo shirt enters the bar and settles down at the next table, intently scanning the drinks menu, although he doesn't order. I don't like the look of him, and neither does Alberto, so we finish our date, and I bid Alberto a warm farewell at the hotel entrance, keeping watch as he manoeuvres his wheelchair with its wobbly wheel up Calle Obispo. And I can't help but think what a darling he is, a little ray of sunshine peeking through the dark clouds of a Havanan spring, where brooding storm clouds – low standards of living, food shortages, poor infrastructure – are ever present on the horizon.

As Alberto disappears around the corner, it occurs to me what food he is, and I almost high-five the man in the polo shirt as he comes barrelling out of the hotel. He glares at me, but I don't care, because Alberto – who's safely away – is definitely *ajiaco*. He's exceptionally smooth, tasty and nourishing, yet humble and not bothered with pretentious airs. A little bit zingy, a little bit spicy, a little bit sweet. He has lots of other flavours too, and it takes time to discover them all as you dig through the bowl. Delicious.

Alberto has set me up on a date with his friend Christian, so on my last day in Cuba I wait in the hotel lobby looking forward to a coffee and a chance to compare notes. If all Cuban men are as delightful as Alberto, it might be worth coming back one day. Christian is running ten minutes late, then twenty, then sixty, and in the end never turns up at all, without so much as an apology or explanation. Although perhaps I shouldn't be surprised.

'There are two types of okay in Cuba,' Marta had warned me. 'The first means, "Okay yes, I will do it, it's great." But the second is, "Okay. Maybe."'

Right. No wonder nothing much seems to get done around here.

Still, I got to meet Alberto, and I got to feel the very heartbeat of Cuba, so when later that afternoon I fly out, after a warm farewell to David, my toes are still tapping one-two-three, one-two-three, and I make a wish that next stop it will be my heart that skips with excitement, and leads me on a merry little dance into the future. Because I'm ready now – ready to face my next batch of dates with renewed confidence that I can do it.

As long as those beans I've been eating all week don't bring me horribly undone.

NETHERLANDS
Cockles, and mussels, alive, alive, oh!

I have great hopes for who I might meet in the Netherlands. I've spent my entire dating life in Australia wearing flat shoes and sitting down a great deal, so that no-one notices that I am close to six feet tall. But with Dutch men on average the tallest in the world, and invariably described as 'open-minded, honest, reliable, faithful, domesticated and good-humoured', it looks like this could be my utopia. And with three dates already lined up – thanks to my frightfully efficient friend Catherine with whom I'm staying – I'm off to a great start.

Despite just having flown for thirteen hours in cattle class with my long legs wrapped around my ears like a cheese roll-up, I don't waste any time getting out and about to sample what Amsterdam has to offer in the way of national cuisine. With three dates to match I'll have my work cut out for me, and it won't be made any easier if an article I've read is true, describing Dutch food as 'one of the five most horrible cuisines in Europe, along with Icelandic, Lithuanian, British and Czech'.

Great.

Wandering through Amsterdam is like stepping back in time. The canals are lined with narrow four-storey seventeenth and eighteenth-century buildings of doll's-house perfection, although it's alarming many are leaning forward like stiffly collared maiden aunts at a wedding reception after one too many *brandewijns*, and seem about to topple off their perches. The tilt has something to do with hoisting furniture up and down via pulleys on the gables, because the internal staircases are too narrow, but I half suspect they've also lowered the odd occupant down after a lifetime of too many smoked sausages, or *rookworst*. Which I'm already concerned might not be a good mix with my beans, my gut full of gas having nearly exploded at 10,000 metres.

There are people on bicycles everywhere, cruising the streets as if their wheels are a second pair of legs. There are men in business suits, grannies in long skirts, fresh-faced teenagers dinking their friends, and kids in *bakfiets* – big wooden boxes fixed to bikes to carry around ... well ... kids.

And. Oh. My. God. I simply can't believe how many handsome men and beautiful women there are – tall and slim with gently sun-tanned skin, and perfect white teeth. They have delicate features, and invariably blond hair that catches the sunlight to shine like silken threads. The men here are definitely the most handsome en masse I've seen so far in any country on any of my travels – anywhere – and I'm finding it hard not to stare.

Which gets me to wondering what my dates will think of me, given that they're surrounded by such gobsmacking perfection day after day. It's a hard act to follow, and right now I'm feeling more like Thumper than Bambi. Still, I hope they give me a go, and that 'open-minded' covers open-hearted too.

After eating a *broodje haring,* which in Dutch sounds much more tasty than what it actually is – a sandwich stuffed with raw herring and raw onion, and which tastes ... well ... raw – and then *patat frites* served with *knoflook* garlic sauce, I'm beginning to appreciate that earlier description of Dutch food. So I head for a coffee shop to try something less mainstream. Not the sort of coffee shop where you can relax with a nice latte and a blueberry muffin, but where you sit at nasty laminex tables and try to look cool as you order a hash cookie. Or a joint. Recreational use of cannabis in the Netherlands is legal in certain licensed establishments, and indeed is an integral part of the whole Amsterdam scene. So I feel obliged – for research purposes only of course – to at least nibble on a cookie. Just in case it matches the personalities of any of my dates – think a dreamy Paul Newman, or hyperactive Jim Carrey.

But there's a slight problem: I don't take drugs. I don't smoke them, or inject them, or snort them, or – good grief – stick them up my bottom like some people apparently do. And until today I didn't eat them. But I like to live a little on the edge, so I take a deep breath as I sidle up to the counter in the Andalucia Lounge, my hands sweaty and my heart pounding. There's a sweet smell permeating the thick blue haze floating across the room, and a few vacant-eyed customers are puffing on bongs. The bartender looks at me suspiciously – no doubt because I've got my camera out and tape-recorder on, its little red light blinking anxiously. Which lacks discretion, but I'm playing it safe because I'm worried that if I eat a cookie, I may forget everything that happens between taking the first bite, and waking up three days later in a downtown window-front clad only in suspenders and fishnet stockings. I nervously buy the smallest slice of space-cake available, which frankly looks more like Mum's homemade carrot cake than something that in most countries could land me in jail. But then as one of the bong-puffers starts staring at me like I have snakes crawling out of my nostrils, I lose my nerve, and thrust the cake deep into my handbag, planning on eating it in a day or two back at Catherine's, where at least I'll be in a safe place if I pass out.

Next morning Catherine and I head off to buy cheese, which is as much part of the Netherlands' national identity as windmills, tulips and clogs – although I've not seen a single person wearing the latter. Not that I'm particularly surprised, given the nickname for clogs is *klompen*, which suggests they're hardly very conducive to tiptoeing through the tulips. We soon end up in a cheese shop unlike anything I've ever seen – or smelt – before. Stacked right up to the ceiling are every type of cheese imaginable – from huge wheels one metre in diameter, to neat little billiard balls. They're covered in red wax, yellow wax, brown wax, and some are so mouldy and wrinkled you'd only want to go near them wearing full HAZCOM breathing apparatus. I buy thin wedges of the most popular for afternoon tea – gouda, edam, truffle brie and Dutch blue, hoping they don't make my breath smell of stinky feet, as I'm meeting Harry tonight, and that's one way to stop a date dead in its tracks.

Harry calls late in the afternoon to arrange the finer details of our date. He has a deep, resonant voice, and his English is nearly perfect, with a slight Dutch accent – much like German but without the scouring-pad abrasiveness.

'Catherine tells me you are a princess,' he chuckles.

'Well, if I'm a princess, will you be my prince?' I sweetly ask, barely believing I can be so cheeky. But what the heck, it's time I did some flirting.

And Harry embraces it. 'For tonight, I will be your prince,' he laughs richly. 'See you at seven.'

As I'm getting dressed I find myself with an unfamiliar dilemma. Harry sounds great. Strong and masculine, and seemingly very confident. And sexy. And he's single. And I can't help but wonder if he might end up being The One. And although that may seem a little presumptuous before I've even met him – much like seeing what my new signature would look like using the surname of boys to whom I'd taken a fancy in dancing class – finding The One *is* after all why I'm here. And even if Harry doesn't end up being a permanent fixture, I can't help remembering what half my friends had said about just letting 'whatever happens happen'. The intimation being that I should sleep with the occasional date if it felt right. After all, they'd reasoned, if I was going all this way, then I may as well get 'value for money'. And besides, isn't Amsterdam the city of sex, drugs and rock'n'roll?

But no – I'm not that sort of girl. I might be physically ready for some hot romance after nearly six months of feeling like a microwave permanently set to 'high' and with no-one around to push the start button, but I'm simply not sure that I could go there right now, even if Harry turns out to be cute as pie. I need time to get to know a man before becoming intimate, and time is something I don't have. Not this trip anyhow. My schedule is as tight as a thumb in a dyke – one date per man, and then I'm outta there. Besides, meeting total strangers in completely artificial circumstances is unlikely to morph into something more meaningful. Sexual – yes. No problem. Microwave on – easy. But emotionally – which is what I'm really craving – now that's a harder ask. And to be honest, after all the heartache over Mark, I'm terrified of ever getting close to another man.

But as my date with Harry looms closer, I give myself a good talking to. I can't live in limbo forever. I need to be brave. So I take off a layer of clothing, put on a layer of Chanel No. 5, and decide to be as dramatic and sexy and princessy as I possibly can, and just see what happens.

The doorbell rings and Harry's bounding up the stairs, all smiles and handshakes and bonhomie. He's handsome in a strongly masculine, rugged sort of way, with deep brown eyes and dark, slightly receding hair. Not a hint of blond locks or blue eyes, but that's okay, as he's actually much less intimidating than all the golden Adonises I'd spotted in the street, whom I'm scared would judge me harshly, given what else is on offer. I can tell that Harry is indeed very confident, expressive and open, and lots of fun, which bodes well for the evening, one way or another. Indeed, after a couple of glasses of wine in the apartment for Dutch courage, and the teeniest tiniest bit of space-cake nibbled at surreptitiously between sips, I can almost feel the microwave being set to 'full steam ahead'.

It's a twenty-minute drive to the restaurant just outside Amsterdam, during which Harry presses me to recount some of my dating disasters in Brazil and Cuba, which he takes in with awfully good humour, clearly enjoying my gumption. But then he slows the car down, and looks at me earnestly.

'So Bambi,' he booms, 'I understand you are 'aving dates in many countries. But tell me, are you prepared to fall in love?'

'Of course,' I say, caught off-guard and feeling myself blush.

'I'm glad to hear it,' Harry says. And I sense that he means it.

'But I'm not in a hurry to get involved,' I half lie, squashing to the floor a tiny overnight bag I'd packed at the last minute of Hot Date Essentials – fresh undies, elbow moisturiser, baggy-eye concealer, make-up, deodorant, toothbrush and perfume. 'It takes me time to get to know someone first,' I add, realising that I've quite forgotten to pack condoms. Which surely betrays that I'm far more Minnie Mouse than Jessica Rabbit, and perhaps not quite cut out for this seduction business after all.

'How long are you in Holland?' Harry persists.

'Only four days,' I reply. 'But I'm in Europe for much longer, so anything's possible.' I smile encouragingly at him, wondering if I'm batting my eyelashes winsomely, or whether he'll just think I've got something in my eye.

It must be the former, as Harry smiles. 'Well, I'll 'ave to show you a good time den.'

We drive on through the exceptionally pretty countryside, with a thin mist hanging over tiny villages snuggled into embankments on the left of the road, and the sea at slightly unnerving eye-level on the right, its ribbon of beach lined with old wooden fishing boats, and still-wet nets strung out like dew-hung spider's webs. As Harry carefully manoeuvres past a flock of white geese waddling with great self-importance down the main road, he speaks passionately of his love for the sea, and his need to be 'very still, and quiet, and gentle with it', which makes me wonder if I'm beginning to see the real Harry. The relaxed one who's not just all bluster and jokes, but something far more soulful. Which I'm finding very attractive.

We pull up in front of De Oude Taveerne, a 300-year-old converted fisherman's cottage. Inside, it's dark and cosy and chock-a-block with all things nautical – harpoons and sea chests and flags and knotted ropes, and dramatic paintings of storm-tossed ships, which make me feel a little seasick just looking at them.

Harry orders the saffron mussel bisque to share, and I'm already salivating at how fresh the mussels will be – visualising them straight off the boat, being skipped across the cobblestoned yard like river rocks to land directly in the cooking pot. We settle into the comfortable leather wingback chairs and start chatting like we've known each other for years. My head is clearing now from the wine and space-cake, and I'm keen to find out more about Harry, sensing there's some real depth below the waves. Indeed, Harry turns out to be a bit of a philosopher – searching to make sense of the world, and his place in it.

'I am already thirty-nine years olt,' he says, a little anxiously. 'So I need to find someone I can settle down wid, and 'ave children together.'

He says this with such a clear ache in his heart that I suddenly feel guilty that I'm flirting – as inept as it is, and as harmless as my intentions are. Because at forty-seven I reckon my eggs are more scrambled than sunny-side-up, and although I haven't totally given up hope of cooking up a kid or two, I don't want to toy with a man who should be looking for a woman more his own age, so they can have loads of kids who'll spend their winters ice-skating to school and eating pea-and-ham soup, and their springtimes *klompen* through the tulips.

'Maybe you should find yourself a nice preschool teacher. Or a midwife,' I say lightly, hoping to get myself off the hook.

'Well, children are important but de relationship is first,' Harry says, searching my face for some kind of response. 'If I meet someone who doesn't want children, den dat's fine.'

I'm not sure what to say – being torn as I am between already genuine affection for Harry, and a sense of responsibility not to lead him on. Thankfully our meal arrives in the nick of time, so I can stop fretting and concentrate on eating. The mussels are spectacularly served in a big black enamel pot, and when the lid is removed, fragrant steam billows up and fills my nostrils. It speaks of leaden seascapes and salty brine, and weathered fishermen in yellow oilskins heading out to sea. And although I don't see any fresh scuff marks on the smooth black shells from being skipped across those cobblestones, I'm sure they're only hours out of the water. The waiter also brings out a large plate of *patat frites*, and little pots of gherkins and sweet onions, all of which appear to require eating by hand. In anticipation of a sloppy repast, I follow Harry's lead and tuck my napkin into my collar. The princess in me can wait until dessert.

'*Eet smakelijk,*' Harry says cheerfully. 'Eat deliciously.'

We work our way through the mussels, and between slurping up the broth I discover that Harry goes on many internet dates.

He just can't find the right woman though, as they all seem to be afflicted with weird 'psychological issues' – arachnophobia, agoraphobia, a girl who couldn't bear to be touched, and another with such a 'filthy temper' that he ended the relationship before she ended up killing him.

'But they were all very pretty,' he laughs good-naturedly.

And I laugh too, as he really has a heart of gold. Indeed, I'm being drawn to Harry once again. I like him. A lot. So I can't help but think that I should stop worrying about leaving him for someone younger to snap up. Surely all's fair in love and war? And baby – it's a battlefield out there.

Harry must be reading my thoughts. 'So Bambi, are you here for a long time, or a good time?' he asks. A loaded question for sure.

I dunk my sourdough bread into the last of the mussel broth, and wonder how I should answer. Right now I want to keep my options with Harry wide open. Right now I just want to enjoy the moment and not have to think two years, five years, twenty years ahead when he'll leave me for a woman who still has firm breasts, and can go ice-skating without subsequently needing a hip replacement. Right now I just want to have fun, so I take the easy way out and I ask him what animal he is, feeling rather appalled at what a coward I am.

But Harry doesn't seem to be offended at my obvious deflection, and ruminates awhile.

'A young lion,' he replies carefully. 'Just olt enough to roar. A young lion is nearly a leader but is still learning. But he's unstoppable when he's needed.'

It's a good answer, although it makes me even more conscious to do the right thing by him. Harry's simply too nice to mess with. Besides, I've got another date tomorrow, and I'm not sure it would go down too well with Harry if I threw myself at him and then the very next day went gallivanting off with someone else. Thick skins are worn by old rhinos, not young lions.

After we finish our meal and head back to the car, Harry turns to me with a twinkle in his eye.

'I would like to suggest something else we do now,' he says, and my heart gives a little leap. And then a little lurch as I wonder if … well … if we're going beyond harmless flirting, am I really ready for it? It was exciting thinking I could step over that moral line that has for so many years defined my life and labelled me as a 'nice girl', and instead be a gloriously fabulously wildly wanton woman who eats men for breakfast. But when it comes down to actually doing it … well … maybe not.

But I shouldn't be getting my knickers in a knot. Not only because they're my best just-in-case French lace ones, but because Harry has other ideas anyway, suggesting we head back into town for a nightcap. Which suits me just fine. It gives me some breathing space, because either way we go, I don't want the night to end just yet.

We walk along the Keizersgracht – Emperor's Canal – and past all the beautiful houses shrouded in a honey-yellow light cast by a nearly full moon. The maiden aunts are at rest now, and seem to soften in their slumber. We find a bar so tiny and narrow that it's standing room only at the mahogany counter, smoothly polished from decades of cable-knitted elbows. Harry and I stand in the corner, with him pressed up tightly against the wooden panelling with barely any room to fit his heavy frame. Our faces are dangerously close in the scrum, as we talk earnestly and for many hours, mostly about finding love, and what we want from a partner. It seems we have much in common – love of travel, cooking, dogs, French films and jazz music, and even skinny-dipping in the ocean, as long as it's 'not in winter', he stipulates, 'as it gets so cold here that ducks have been found with their bottoms stuck fast in the frozen lakes'.

But as lovely as Harry is, and as potentially compatible, I still don't think that it could work between us. Simply because my gut instinct – that annoying one that seems to pipe up even when the heart and head have reached a perfectly amicable agreement – is that ultimately it might be too great a compromise for him.

Forgoing kids isn't quite the same as forgoing chocolate at Easter. Once the opportunity is gone you can't just pop into a 7-Eleven to stock up on a few boxes.

So why prolong the inevitable? It's time to go.

Harry drives me home even though it's miles from his apartment in The Hague. When we get lost momentarily, I'm pretty sure it's not only me who thinks it's a sign we should just head for a hotel and let whatever happens happen.

But we don't.

Eventually Harry finds his way to Catherine's place, and leaves the car running as he hops out to kiss me lightly on both cheeks. And once again. We hug each other warmly, then I plant a delicate kiss on his lips, trying to make up for all that's been left unspoken between us, and what Could Have Been if only I wasn't so scared to take a risk. Or I had more time up my sleeve and I could really get to know him. After all, you can't cook a slow lamb roast as if it's two-minute noodles.

As I wave Harry off, I think of the meal I had last night. It was venison and angel hair pasta with apple sauce, and it's the perfect match for him. My initial impression of the dish – and Harry – was that they were mild and sweet, thus perhaps a little insubstantial, but with each bite I took, the flavours deepened and the textures intensified, and I could more fully appreciate their rich, nourishing and delightfully heartwarming natures. And as Harry's car disappears into the early morning gloom of Amsterdam, and mist rises off the canals like steam off a wet barge dog, and once again I'm left all alone, I feel very, very sad.

Next evening, when I open the door to my next Dutch date, I'm delighted. It's not that I'm fickle, but neither is this the time to wallow in regret over Harry. Eduard is very tall, with a slim build that fits ever so neatly into his elegant blue shirt with fine red pinchecking, and a matching red tie. A navy-blue jacket is tossed casually over his arm, like he's posing for a Ralph Lauren fashion shoot, and he's wearing fine-rimmed black glasses that make him look intelligent, as if he's just been reading the *New York Times*. He's handsome too, with chiselled features, ash-blond hair, and eyes the colour of aquamarines. As I leave the apartment, Catherine winks and gives me the thumbs-up sign.

Eduard is chatty and friendly, laughing easily at my tales of adventure thus far, and as the husky-voiced Grietje on his car's GPS guides him to a restaurant to which he's never been, I suspect he's gone to quite a bit of effort to make this a unique experience for me.

And I was right. On the outskirts of the city we pull up outside an enormous old windmill, its torso fat and round like a huge black mama, sails fluttering above like she's hanging out freshly washed table runners. It's something right out of a child's picture book. Although it's not just a windmill, it's also a restaurant – De Jonge Dikkert, which means 'the young fatty'.

Eduard and I have a pre-dinner drink at the downstairs bar, and I'm loving talking to a man standing a full head and shoulders taller than me. It makes me feel feminine and not quite in control, which is oddly intoxicating. Eduard's conversation is sharp and witty, and surprisingly personal – he wants to know all about me, and that's surely a good sign. Indeed, I'm already feeling like there might be a real connection between us – a clog that fits the minute you slip it on.

We're eventually seated on the second level, surrounded by tall white lilies and flickering tea lights to create a mood of hushed opulence. Eduard orders a four-course banquet, starting with *bouillon van lagostina* served in a shot-glass – an outrageously decadent single gulp of rich shrimp *bouillon* (broth) topped with velvety cream. Eduard cheerfully admits that this isn't traditional Dutch fare, even though I'd already guessed, as it's about as opposite to the stodgy national dish of *erwtesoep* (split pea soup) as a swan is to a common shelduck. But I don't care. I'm in heaven. I could definitely get used to this sort of food. And Eduard too.

As we eat our way through the second course, I neatly turn the focus back onto Eduard, as a clog can't only fit, it has to be comfortable. Fortunately Eduard is very happy to talk about himself, although I'm not imposing my questionnaire upon him as I'm guessing he's not the type to want his life reduced to a mere formula. But I still find out plenty about him. He travels a lot through Europe for work, but would much rather it was Africa, on holiday, at which my ears prick up because I'd love to ramble around there too, but with a partner rather than a jeepload of loud American tourists. Indeed, being the hopelessly romantic type, I already have visions of us in matching safari suits paddling down the Zambezi. However, I'm not sure I'd get him skinny-dipping in it, as I suspect he's a bit … well … proper. And possibly a tiny bit lazy, as although Eduard likes entertaining, he doesn't like cooking, which conjures up more images, this time of a table full of guests politely nibbling on gherkins and smoked mackerel dip. And he really, 'really' hates cheese, which apart from seeming somewhat un-Dutch, must limit his entertaining options even further. Still, he has lots of good qualities too, which I find engaging, such as having three older sisters he just loves to death, and a home in Apeldoorn that he fills with fresh flowers and the strains of Vivaldi. He briefly mentions something about a German girl who broke his heart eight years ago, but then quickly changes the subject.

The third course arrives – *bresse duif met opgerolde eendenleverpannenkoekjes en saus van mais en aceto balsamico,* which is the longest food description I've ever come across. However, it turns out to be less of a mouthful to eat, with a delicate plate of pigeon breast served with a tiny duck liver pancake. As I watch Eduard savour it like a pedigree cat enjoying a snack of endangered wildlife, I'm prompted to ask my favourite question. I'll get back to the German girl when I can catch him off-guard.

'If your personality was an animal, what would you be?' I ask.

'I'd like to be a lion, because they are strong,' Eduard replies. 'But I think I am actually an elephant, because they are trustworthy and family oriented, and look after each other to the very end.'

I'm intrigued. Such an answer suggests that although he's confident, he's not necessarily a predator, and in fact, has a certain sensitivity and generosity of spirit – all of which I find attractive qualities in a man. My father has them too, and perhaps that's why I'm liking Eduard quite so much.

But then he's suddenly back to asking *me* the questions.

'And what do you want from your life Bambi, in the next five years?'

I can't help but wonder if he's fishing. To see if I'm available. So I take the bait.

'To be happy,' I reply with a smile to soften the sudden twinge of pain behind it. 'To be with a man I love.

That's all.'

'And to write your book back in Australia?' he adds.

'I can write my book anywhere,' I say, swallowing the hook shamelessly. 'Australia, Europe, Amsterdam.'

I know I'm being forward, but why not? It's about time I put myself fair and square on the line, as that's the only way I'm going to get anywhere in my quest for love. I want a relationship where I don't have to hold back for fear of rejection, like I've done for most of my life. Time to get naked. But before I can expose my own underbelly, Eduard's mood dramatically shifts. It changes in a split second from a warm demeanour of 'yes I might be interested in you', to him sullenly slouching back into his seat with a definite air of 'I've lost interest now, and may even be a little bored'.

I'm confused, and embarrassed, and don't know what to say, so we wait for our dessert separated by a half empty wine bottle and an uncomfortable silence. I've obviously said something wrong, but what? Was I too pushy? Too wish-washy? Or both? I get the feeling that Eduard knows exactly what he wants from life, and I'm guessing it's not an Ugly Duckling that never quite made the grade to Elegant Swan.

'Well, you're lucky to live in Holland and have the choice of so many beautiful women,' I eventually say, trying not to sound too hurt. Which I am.

'Yes, but I am very picky,' he replies – haughtily now. 'None of them have exactly what I am looking for.'

'And what's that?' I mumble, my hurt quickly turning into indignation, like curdling bearnaise sauce.

'Something my German girlfriend had, and no-one else can match,' he says, carefully folding up his napkin and placing it on the table, as if the conversation is Now Over.

I'm starting to lose my patience. I mean, really, Eduard's relationship with German wunderfrau ended eight years ago, so I feel like I've been summarily passed over for a ghost. I reckon he should just get over it. Indeed, I'm rather thinking he deserves a clog where the sun doesn't shine. But then he sighs heavily and looks a little lost, and I start to wonder if he's simply a wounded beast in the woods licking his wounds, and growling at anyone who tries to get close.

But my sympathy doesn't last long, as when I ask him if I can take a photo of him for my records, Eduard shakes his head firmly. 'No, take a photo of someone else,' he says impatiently, 'and just pretend it's me.'

'Fine,' I reply, trying not to sound like I'm deeply offended. Although actually, I'm uncertain whether I'm offended, pissed off or heartbroken. Eduard's clearly not interested in me, but he needn't be so rude.

We finish our meal and walk to the car without saying a word. As Eduard warms the engine, he plugs Grietje in again to get us home. I don't think it's a coincidence she has a German accent.

'You need to move on and find someone new, Eduard,' I say, as kindly as I can, as he grimly grips the steering wheel. 'You have to let go of the past so you can have a future.'

And I should know.

There's silence in the car all the way home. And there's sadness brooding behind it like an unwanted back-seat passenger. Then the night ends abruptly as Eduard pulls up outside my apartment block. He remains seated, keeping the engine running.

'Thank you, Bambi,' he says, as if closing off a business transaction. 'It has been nice to meet you. I wish you well in the rest of your adventure.'

There's no opening of car doors, no kiss on the cheeks, no rendezvous in Africa, no possibility of little blue-eyed white-haired kids running around in clogs. Whatever connection we'd had earlier in the restaurant has totally dissolved, like Dutch cinnamon stirred into milk. Then he half smiles, and is gone.

I don't know what to think as I sadly trudge up the four flights of stairs to Catherine's apartment. The night started off so deliciously, but ended like a bad case of indigestion.

Which makes me wonder what Dutch food Eduard is?

Certainly not the delicious truffle brie – too moreish. Nor the comforting national dish of *stamppot* (potatoes mashed with kale or endives, and topped with a whopping great sausage) – too common. And definitely not the Wieckse Witte beer I enjoyed on one of my other dates – too sweet and refreshing. Then I recall a snack I ate yesterday. It was an *appeldrie-hoek,* a triangular pastry filled with baked apple. At first it had looked very appetising, and being sprinkled with icing sugar, the first lick was tantalisingly sweet. But it turned out to be a bit of a struggle getting past the brittle crust, and then a slightly stodgy filling, so I finished up feeling hungry and oddly dissatisfied. Just like with Eduard.

The next morning I receive an email from Harry, and once again I'm reminded that Substance wins out over Style any day of the week.

```
Dear Bambi,
Thank you for a great evening. You are
really a wonderful girl and fun to spend
time with! Last night I had a drink
with another internet date. It was an
interesting evening but I had a much
better time with you. I hope you find
what you are looking for. Same as me.
Whatever that is.
Harry xx
```

Whatever that is. Indeed.

GERMANY
No sauerkraut here!

I like Germans. When I was twenty-five and backpacking around Europe, I fell in love with Klaus from Munich, and I still have fond memories of our brief time together. He was sweet, and kind, and compellingly burdened by the weight of the world. It broke my heart to leave him when I returned home, and I thought I'd never love again. But I soon found out that he was just the first in a long line of relationships that would leave my heart looking like a badly mended china vase. And each time it broke, another piece would go missing. But I still like Germans, and I'm hopeful that my limited vocabulary of Germanic sweet-nothings – courtesy of Klaus – may even get an airing after idling for so long on the shelf.

As I wait in the Frankfurt train station for my New Zealand friend Aron to collect me, I notice there are lots of Klaus's milling around. Klaus wasn't the hand-some-but-ruthless Aryan hunk portrayed in most James Bond films – all angled cheekbones, blue eyes and blond hair – but was a darker, softer, brown-eyed version that seems to be more the norm these days. Which gets me to wondering if the traditional German stereotype still exists for their personalities – serious, polite, frank, disciplined, tolerant and friendly enough, although somewhat unsentimental and humourless. The latter perhaps because of the war.

Which I'm not going to mention.

Aron arrives, and we head off on foot to the old part of town, where I'm keen to sample the local cuisine in readiness for my date tomorrow with Jens – a friend of Aron's. Our destination is the massive cobblestoned Römerberg town square ringed by towering Tudor-style buildings, their facades crisscrossed with thick wooden beams so elaborate they look like the heavy brown lace on a German peasant's Sunday dress. Lined up shoul-der to shoulder they remind me of Amsterdam's rows of stiff-necked maiden aunts, although these German Fraus are decidedly broader in the hips. There's a vibrant cluster of open-air cafés at their feet, with long trestle tables set beneath sun-bleached red market umbrellas.

The whole place is abuzz with locals enjoying the last of the warm weather before winter, when no doubt they'll hibernate indoors like dormice. Indeed, by the ample girths of some, they too must be attempting to double their weight in preparation for the long fast ahead.

I order an *apfelwein*, which looks like heavy warm-yellow cider, but without the bubbles. It tastes sweet at first, then sour. In fact, decidedly sour, but nicely so. And as Aron and I prop ourselves on bottom-worn stools and catch up on the last few years since we've seen each other, I suddenly feel deliciously lazy. And a bit light-headed. It's a sunny day here in Frankfurt, the town-hall bells are ringing, and I have a date with a gorgeous young man tomorrow. What more could a girl want?

Well, she would have liked some forewarning, as Aron suddenly waves at someone walking across the square towards us, before cheerfully informing me that he's organised a second date, 'as a bit of a surprise'. It certainly is a surprise, as I'm dressed for a five-hour train trip and not a date. Besides, I've just downed half a litre of fermented apple juice, and have no idea what might come out of my mouth. But it's too late to worry, as Christian, my date, wants to introduce me to some of the highlights of German cuisine. 'Now,' he demands warmly. So after a quick visit to the basement *toiletten* and some confusion as to whether I'm a Damen or a Herren, we're off.

Christian is a typically untypical-looking German – average height, average build, homely face with rounded features, nice smile, brown eyes and brunette hair with an unruly fringe that keeps flicking into his eyes. Even his accent isn't what I'd expect of a German; instead of harsh *ach*'s and *ich*'s, his accent is soft and almost sing-songy. He owns the advertising agency where Aron rents office space, and they've become good friends. I immediately like him, as he's engaging and sweet, and very keen to take me on 'not just a date, but a discovery of the senses'. We head for the famous Kleinmarkthalle, a two-storey indoor market stocking produce from all over the world. This is where the discovery of the senses kicks in, the very moment I pass through the unprepossessing olive-green front door, like a gateway to a whole other world – the cupboard into Narnia. There are fragrant flowers and colourful fruit and vegetables, pungent cheeses and eye-watering spices, salt-tanged fish and velvety Belgian chocolates begging to be eaten. But it's not all so pleasant. The sight of lifeless rabbits with their skinned, naked little bodies stretched out as if still running, their lidless eyes frozen in shocked eternity, and limp quail with tiny blue feet that will never scratch about in the dirt again, upsets me so much that I have to turn away.

But there's no avoiding the wursts – they're everywhere I look, stacked on glass shelves, stuffed into baskets, and hanging from hooks. Smooth ones and wrinkled ones, long ones and short ones, straight ones and looped ones. And they're all different thicknesses too, from weensy weiners just a few centimetres in diameter, to chunky stallions as wide as your fist. Which, being a girl with a vivid imagination, is causing me some consternation. But as tempting as it is to make cheeky comparisons with all those sausage-shaped wursts and ... well ... the males of our species, in all probability I won't be getting that close to either Christian or Jens to check for any similarities. Which is just as well, as some of them are downright scary.

Christian picks up on my fascination for these ugly beasts, and takes me across to a stallholder who's happy to let me sample the most popular varieties. Otherwise, with over fifteen hundred types of wurst available in Germany, I could be here until Christmas. Not to mention requiring a shoehorn to get me into my slimline travel pants.

I'm apprehensive as I take a bite of a blood-red slice. 'What's this one?' I ask, not really wanting an answer.

'*Blutwurst*. With fresh pig's blood.'

I knew this wasn't going to be easy.

'And this?' I ask, nibbling on something grey with an oddly smooth texture.

'*Leberwurst*. Pig liver.'

I smile somewhat stupidly at the vendor and manage to swallow without gagging.

'And dare I ask?' I query, throwing all caution to the wind and popping into my mouth a whole slice of a pretty yellow-skinned sausage with bright-white insides. It can't be as bad as the *leberwurst*. Surely.

'*Gelbwurst*. Pig brain,' Christian replies cheerfully.

Charming.

Christian heads off to the greener fringes of the market to find some bok choy for his dinner tonight. He's never heard of it before, but he's found a Jamie Oliver recipe that uses it, and is keen to experiment. It strikes me that he's a bit of a New-Age German, and I'm impressed, given that Germans are more renowned for their efficiency rather than their creativity.

As I wait for him to return, I notice all the bread. Well, I smell it before I see it, yeasty and warm and sweet, filling my nostrils with a heady purity that could only be matched by the scent of a newborn baby. There are knotted rolls and rounded kaiser rolls, chunky pretzels and twisted breadsticks, plaited loaves and dome-shaped buns, each studded generously with a richly textural mix of poppy seeds, sunflower seeds and pumpkin seeds. There's even one loaf covered so thickly with oats that it looks like a dachshund has been rolling in glue and white confetti.

'Now for lunch,' Christian says when he returns, bok choy under his arm and looking rather pleased with himself.

'I thought the wurst was lunch?' I reply, conscious of the heavy lump of animal bits in my stomach that I think at this very moment are planning an uprising.

'That was just a snack,' he replies, shepherding me down a tree-lined street. 'Now for something really special.'

It's clear that Christian is enjoying himself, and I'm relieved, given some of my recent experiences with dates where I felt like I was a mild dose of food poisoning. But Christian is treating me with the utmost respect and warmth, and I'm rather disappointed to have just found out that the bok choy is to impress his girlfriend over dinner tonight. Pity – he really is a darling.

We soon come to a restaurant tucked in behind a high courtyard wall, where a large hairy man wearing a singlet and black rubber apron – making me wonder if he's related to anyone in Liechtenstein – is pouring shrivelled little apples into a wooden slatted press, and then squeezing the bejeezus out of them. The juice cascades out a surprisingly burnt-orange colour, then it's into a sieve and into a jug and into our glasses. It's known as *süsser*, or 'sweet', and it's fresh, mellow and deeply delicious, like I'm drinking from an alpine wellspring laced with honey.

Christian smiles wickedly. 'I have something else for you,' he says, 'and even if you don't like it, you have to taste it. It's cheese,' he continues, without giving me the chance to protest. 'It's called *handkäse*. Nicknamed "the Musician".'

'Musician? Why?'

'It's cheese – with music,' he replies, and gives no further explanation, which makes me suspect that he isn't quite as innocent as first appearances would suggest.

When the cheese arrives I nervously poke at it, half expecting it to let out a possessed soprano screech. It's pale yellow and semi-translucent, and heavily slathered with finely chopped onion, brown vinegar and a sprinkling of cumin seeds. It looks harmless enough, but I soon realise what Christian is up to.

It absolutely stinks. It's like a mixture of rancid parmesan cheese and something scraped from the back of the fridge. A German soccer player's jockstrap after two back-to-back matches would be a treat in comparison.

'You've got to be joking,' I smile through gritted teeth.

He smiles back. 'Try it.'

It's not going to be pleasant. Not with the odour reaching up into my nostrils like sticky fingers searching for even deeper crevices to pick. But Christian's watching me like a hawk, so I nibble at it cautiously, trying to ignore its texture of overdone gelatine, which is almost grossing me out more than the smell. Still, I persist, and am surprised that it actually tastes nice enough – tart, sour and mildly spicy – not bad at all.

'So why is it called the Musician?' I ask, taking another bite after realising that if I hold my breath as I take a mouthful, it tastes even better.

'Well,' Christian says, grinning like a naughty schoolboy, 'after you eat it, you make music.'

I look at the plate, trying to make sense of his comment. Cheese, cumin, vinegar and loads of onion. Oh, I get it.

'Music? You mean, music like it makes you … fart?' I stammer.

'Yes,' he smiles broadly. 'Maybe for a few days.'

Delightful.

The more I chat with Christian, the more my suspicions are confirmed that he's not a particularly German German. Not the traditional model I grew up with anyway. Not with his bok choy, and his willingness to please, and his ever-smiling face. Plus he doesn't eat frankfurters or drink Jägermeister – activities that Germans are supposed to enthusiastically embrace, along with wearing tight leather shorts and drinking huge steins of lukewarm beer. And he's adventurous – having driven from Berlin all the way to China in a remodelled jeep Cherokee – whereas Germans are more known for lolling about in beach resorts, and bagging their sunbeds beside the pool well before dawn so no-one else can get them. And while I thought Germans were supposed to be cool and unemotional, Christian is really starting to open up to me, even admitting that he's still getting over a broken heart from his last girlfriend. All up, he's a real surprise package – a little Chris Kringle bottle swap at the office Christmas party that turns out to be not the headache-inducing *liebfraumilch* in the blue bottle, but a far more refined riesling. Yes, that's what Christian could be, a nice riesling *kabinett* – sweet, light, refreshing and not too acidic.

We finish our meal, and are walking back into town when Christian suddenly pulls me into a *bäckerei* smelling deliciously of fresh bread. 'Okay, last stop,' he announces excitedly. 'This place sells the best *käsekuchen* in the world.'

'What's that?' I ask, but what I really want to say is, 'More food? No way.' Because if I keep on stuffing my face I'll be the size of the Hindenburg.

'Cheesecake,' Christian replies, beaming as he buys a whole *kuchen,* which we take back to the office to share amongst his staff. And as I try to find a few spare square centimetres of gut in which to fit it, it suddenly occurs to me that I'm eating Christian.

Yes, Christian's a cheesecake, not a riesling lacking in complexity and substance. Sure, at first nibble a cheesecake is light and sweet, but the more you eat the deeper the flavour becomes, and the more interesting the textures. It's firm at the edges, but soft in the middle. It's safe, dependable and homely. And you'd be hard-pressed to stop at just one slice. Damn that girlfriend.

I spend most of the next day being followed around by

a really annoying little kid with a trumpet. At least – that's what I thought it was until I realised that it was the *handkäse* doing its thing. In fact, by the end of the day I've just about got 'Oom-Pah-Pah' down pat. Poor Jens, I wonder if he knows what he's letting himself in for tonight.

I'm meeting Jens at the restaurant because he's working late. Coincidentally he works for Christian, so I'm going to have to keep myself nice or they'll be comparing notes. However, when he finally arrives – half an hour late – he's clearly stressed, and decidedly grumpy, which is a real letdown after a couple of earlier emails in which he'd come across as lots of fun. But at least he's still as cute as the photo he'd sent – very tall and slim, with bright blond hair spiked up with gel so he looks like an albino hedgehog. He has matching blond eyebrows, delicate Aryan features, and amazing blue eyes that bore right into me. Indeed, apart from his accent – which is deliciously light and lilting with nary a trace of *Hogan's Hero's* glottal stops – he perfectly fits my original image of the stereotypical German. In fact, as a kid he could easily have been the unassuming pin-up boy for Hitler's Youth Camps.

Not that I'm going to mention the war.

Dauth-Schneider is one of the best-known taverns in Frankfurt. It's a barn of a place, with heavy wood panelling and whole tree-trunks piercing the canvas ceiling, and with a cheery ambience so thick that you could cut it into neat slices like pumpernickel bread. Jens looks like he needs a drink, so I join him in a Jägermeister. I'm excited to try it, as it's a herbal digestive – made from fifty-six herbs and spices no less – so I figure it will help with my tooting problem. But even though it's bright green and looks innocuous enough, it tastes like it's mixed with scorpion venom and fire-lighters, and threatens to ignite my insides and turn my relatively harmless trumpeting into a World War II flamethrower.

Okay – did it that time.

As I choke on the Jägermeister as politely as I can, Jens tells me it's seventy-proof – 35 per cent alcohol – which means that I better take it easy or he might have a little too much information to share with Christian tomorrow. Like how ridiculous a middle-aged woman looks doing the German Chicken Dance along the full length of a communal trestle table. Jens also informs me that it contains tiny quantities of deer's blood, which rather stops me in my tracks. I mean, even though I've happily eaten venison this trip, there's something slightly more unsavoury about drinking the actual blood of my namesake. I'm relieved when Jens admits that it's just an urban legend, although I suspect the locals quite like to perpetuate the myth to freak tourists out.

By the time we're staring at the bottom of our second glass, Jens has cheered up no end. Indeed, he's now delightfully easy to talk to, which means that the evening won't be spent dealing with a sauerkraut after all. Feeling more relaxed myself, I tell him that Aron had warned me that 'Jens loves dating', at which he laughs good-humouredly.

'Yes, I am recently going out with four girls at the

same time,' he cheerfully confesses, 'but it's just sex. Although this can still get me into trouble.'

The trouble turns out not to be so much the fact that the girls are jealous of each other – because they don't actually know that Jens is seeing anyone else – but because they are 'liars'.

'Liars?' I ask, confused. 'How?'

'At the beginning I told them that I just wanted sex, and they all say, "*Ja*, okay, fine." But then after three or four times sleeping with them, they want more. They want a relationship. Commitment. And that wasn't the deal.'

I laugh at such sweet naivety. At twenty-seven Jens still has a whole lot to learn about the vagaries of the female race. I mean, we initially say we're happy to keep things simple, and that we don't mind playing second fiddle to his mates, or his football, or his career. And that we don't need to live together, or have a ring on our finger, as proof of his love. But what we *really* mean is that we'll give him exactly one year of free rein, then expect him to pretty much devote himself to us. Shopping together at Ikea, going to Broadway-style musicals, watching David Attenborough wildlife shows on TV. Oh, and giving us a ring as proof of his love.

Or at least that's what I'd expected when I was younger. Which, come to think of it, may be why I never got married.

'So, are you a typical German then?' I ask Jens.

'No, I'm not normal,' he says, those bright blue eyes boring into me until I feel quite giddy. 'Most Germans are shy, and don't have much self-confidence. But my grandmother taught me to be charming, open-hearted and chivalrous. So I like girls very much, and have no problem being close with them. In every way.'

I think I might be in trouble. Jens certainly *is* charming – dangerously so. And I'm finding myself thinking thoughts I really shouldn't – at least, not for a man twenty years younger than me. In fact, he's practically still a boy, and I'm sure in Germany there's some kind of law against that – like the *Keep Your Mitts Offen Young Boys Act 1943*.

Fortunately the spell is broken when the waitress takes our order, and I can switch my focus to trying to correctly pronounce *gebratene schweinshaxe mit sauerkraut und brot.*

'Ut's very big,' huffs the waitress in a broad Scottish accent, making eyes at Jens and clearly wondering why he's with me. 'Very big. I hope yoo're hungry.'

I'm not. After yesterday's orgy of eating, my stomach is as solid as a medicine ball. But still, roast pork-knuckle is my all-time favourite, and I simply can't resist. Besides, it will help take my mind off Jens's extraordinary blue eyes, which are big enough to fall into like bottomless sinkholes, to be lost within forever. And although floating about in there may be nice – a bit of emotional weightlessness wouldn't do me any harm right now – ultimately it would most likely be a waste of time. Men Jens's age want hot little chicky babes, not clucky old hens.

Still, he seems happy enough chatting with me, and even keener to keep on talking about his love life. And I keep on listening as, who knows, I might even learn something.

'Having sex is the best,' he tells me, grinning broadly.

'But there's Fun Sex, and there's Love Sex, and for the moment I am happy just with Fun Sex.'

Jens's eyes drill into me again, and I can totally understand the dilemma of his poor girlfriends. Apart from being very good-looking, he's sincere in his own way, and delightfully unassuming. But perhaps his greatest asset is that he appears to be so sexually confident. We don't get that so much back in Australia, where younger men – the handful I knew at least – tended to see sex as something a little bit shameful, and when they'd had their fun would more often than not suddenly remember they had a replay of last year's Grand Final to watch. At three in the morning. But Jens is different – he positively celebrates sex – and although I've only had two drinks, I can easily imagine us both swinging from a pair of wall-mounted deer horns in an alpine lodge somewhere up in the Alps.

God help me.

As the clinking of glasses around me starts sounding almost melodic – like a glockenspiel at a Bavarian wedding – it occurs to me that Jens's food match is something quite festive. Perhaps even a Jägermeister. Yes – that's it. At first he's smooth and mellow, and rich in flavour. But halfway down your gullet his personality suddenly hits, and burns like fire, before eventually settling down, leaving you with a very warm and slightly naughty after-glow. And as much as you want more, you know that you might lose your self-control, so it's best to take it easy.

Or not.

The pork arrives and really *is* huge – the size of a small Mercedes. It's rich, sweet and unbelievably succulent. And although I can't possibly finish it all, I make a good fist of it, just to annoy the Scottish waitress who keeps making eyes at Jens. The sauerkraut tastes – well – sour, and I'm struggling to understand why the Germans have taken such a liking to cabbage fermented in salty vinegar – a process that results in a decidedly mouth-puckering and eye-watering experience. Then again, Australia's got Vegemite, so who am I to talk?

Jens's phone rings. It's work. They want him back by 11 p.m. to meet a deadline, which means that any teeny-weeny itsy-bitsy harmless thoughts I may possibly have been thinking to be another notch in his lederhosen, have just been cruelled.

Damn.

'Okay, just one more question,' I say. 'If your personality was an animal, what would you be?'

'A cat. Definitely,' Jens replies, almost purring himself.

'Why?'

'A cat has its own will. If I don't like you, I will totally ignore you. But if I like you, I will do anything to make you happy.' Jens lowers his voice and grins wickedly, 'And cats are hopelessly enthusiastic about sex. They just can't help themselves.'

It's at this point that I can't help myself either, and I find myself ditching the questionnaire and asking Jens about things you'd be lucky to find in the sealed section of a *Cosmo* magazine. Indeed, at my shameless encouragement he fills me in on what Fun Sex actually entails, including such knuckle-biting topics as favourite sexual techniques, multiple orgasms and swinging from wall-mounted deer horns. Well – just about. And then

Jens leans forward earnestly, his eyes soft little ray guns slicing into mine.

'I know how to please women,' he says. 'There are five types of orgasm a woman can have. With different places on her body to stimulate. Did you know that?'

'Hmm,' I respond, trying not to look surprised, and doing a quick inventory. Let me think. One, two ... um ... three, four. Okay. Four yes, but five?

'Where?' I ask. I'm blushing deeply now, and madly fanning my face with a Heineken drinks coaster.

He reels off the four with which I'm well acquainted – if not personally then courtesy of *Cosmo* – then hesitates as if he's about to reveal some amazing Secret Men's Business handed down through generations of horny Huns.

'And the neck,' he says triumphantly.

Ohhh. Yes, he's right. What a spot. Get that kissed in just the right place and your whole body goes into spasms. Jens sure knows his stuff. But then I remember something.

'And there's another one,' I challenge him.

'Where? I thought I'd found them all,' he says, a little peeved.

'The soul,' I say, feeling sad now, remembering the times with Mark when the energy between us was like the splitting of the atom. 'When you just lie very close together and your whole soul is filled with an intense luminous energy, and it's like you're part of the universe. It's amazing.'

Jens looks thoughtful, and there's silence for a while.

'I think perhaps I'll try that one too,' he says softly.

Jens's phone rings again. 'I really do have to go now,'

he apologises, before walking me through the shadowy streets of the old town, and along the licorice-black river to Aron's apartment. My head is spinning, I suspect not so much from the Jägermeister, as the extraordinary conversation.

'I've had a great night,' he says. Then, in quiet disbelief, 'I've talked about things I never have before with anybody.'

As we stand at the front door, I stand just a teeny bit closer to him than I ordinarily would on a blind date. He kisses me goodnight, one kiss on each cheek, but as he turns to leave I gently grab his arm because – well – I'm not done with him yet.

'Some advice from an older woman to a younger man,' I say, in not much more than a whisper. 'A soul orgasm. You should try it sometime.'

Jens stops and smiles. He looks at his watch then looks me deep in the eyes, and ever so slightly cocks his head. There's a split second where we both might fall into temptation, and twenty years' age difference is as insignificant as finding a cherry in your black forest cake.

Then we both laugh, and he's gone.

And as I crawl into bed just as the church bells of Alte Nikolaikirche in the old town square ring twelve times, like bursts of honey into the blackness of the night, my faith is once again restored that I'm not past my use-by date. If I can get a gorgeous 27-year-old to spend five whole hours with me on a Friday night, then surely I can find someone twice his age to spend the rest of his life with me?

Surely?

As long as I can stop farting.

FRANCE

She sells seashells, by the seashore

As the train approaches Paris I'm both excited and sad. On my second trip to Europe back in '85, I fell hopelessly for a Frenchman named Thierry, an investment banker. He taught me much about art and French music and truffles, and Random Acts of Kindness, such as retrieving an old man's vastly overshot *petanque* ball in a public park. He was quite unique – a man of both style *and* substance. Our love affair spanned two continents over six months, and I was blissfully certain that he was The One, even naming our future children – Clementine, Josephine, Emmanuelle and Devereaux. Not that I ever let Thierry know what I was thinking. Although maybe I should have, because then he mightn't have left me for that pretty little Swedish scientist, who got herself pregnant faster than I could say *allez-oop*. Yes, I discovered even more that year about broken hearts and cracked china vases, and how, even if you could find the pieces, they never fit back quite the same way.

It's misty outside, like one of those magic paintings that starts off black and white, and then as you stroke a wet paintbrush over it, comes alive, the colours emerging surprisingly from the nothingness. A chateau materialises up ahead, poking its elegant spires up out of the woods, and suggesting wealth, romance and foie gras for dinner. Who lives there, I wonder? An ageing marquis? The heir to Cartier? I'll never know. As much as they'll never know this Australian nobody hurtling past on a silver train.

And I suddenly feel very lonely. I should be sharing all this beauty, this magic, with someone special. I'm even beginning to regret breaking up with Mark, and wonder how I'm ever going to replace him.

Which makes me wonder what I'll find in Frenchmen this time around. Popular opinion suggests that on a good day they're romantic, sexy, passionate, chic and sophisticated. And on a bad day – well – arrogant, chauvinistic, rude, lazy and intolerant. So I only hope I'm getting here on the right day.

But perhaps I shouldn't be worrying – I've been set up on a date through my brother-in-law, whose friend Lynda clinched the deal for me to come to Paris. Not that it was ever going to be a difficult choice for my French destination. Not with Paris being widely referred to as the Most Romantic City on Earth. And I'm going to get me some.

Dear Bambi,
Olivier has said yes to a date! You are so lucky, as he is one of the most charming, highly educated men I know. He's even studied at New York University in the same year as Oliver Stone and Martin Scorsese, and he lives on a *pe'niche* (boat) on the Seine just next to the Place de la Concorde. People would die for this.
Happy adventure,
Lynda

My date with Olivier isn't until tomorrow evening, so I'm planning to spend the interim sampling my way through the patisseries and charcuteries of Paris, to ensure I have lots of culinary options with which to match Olivier. Well, that's my excuse anyway. Although when it comes to stuffing my face with *marrons glacés* – chestnuts candied in sugar syrup – I don't even need an excuse. My first stop is a café beneath a giant plane tree cloaked in the fluorescent yellows and greens of early autumn. And as I sit and watch the world go by, I notice that practically everyone is kissing. They just stand in the middle of the footpath and kiss without a care as to who might be watching. A pretty blonde with full red lips tenderly kisses her boyfriend beneath the Art Nouveau metro sign. A beautiful black girl with lots of spangly beads passionately locks purple lips with her dreadlocked boyfriend. Indeed, there's so much smooching going on that I can understand why lipstick sales in France is a multi-billion-dollar industry, if all they ever do is rub it off onto someone else.

I can tell the Frenchmen from the tourists not just because they kiss more, but because their big Gallic noses give them away. And their eyes pop out just a little bit – probably from looking at the girls kissing all the boys. The men are generally quite nice-looking, but I wouldn't say that they're collectively handsome, as the Dutch are. Not that they really need to be – they just have to speak and they're delicious, the words dripping off their tongues like the syrup on a crepe suzette, embodying romance and passion and all that is lyrical and sweet, and completely validating why French has been dubbed the Language of Love. Which makes me even keener to meet Olivier.

By the time my rendezvous with Olivier comes around, I'm beside myself with excitement, and have decided to go all out to impress him. I've already let one Frenchman slip from my grasp, and I'm not about to let it happen again. There's something about Frenchmen – a certain *je ne sais quois* – that makes me go weak at the knees. So to make sure Olivier doesn't overlook me, I'm wearing my killer Black Widow Spider outfit – knee-high boots, shiny black stockings, short black skirt, push-up bra, and lace body-stocking peeking out cheekily from beneath a figure-hugging black jacket. If this doesn't win him over, nothing will.

Olivier greets me warmly in the hotel lobby. In his early sixties, he's quite a bit older than I was expecting, and shorter, but he's also twice as elegant. He has silver hair and matching silver glasses, and a gentle face with a handsome Gallic nose – not so much big as aristocratic. He seems pleased to see me, and is completely charming from the word go. He holds my arm confidently as he walks me to his car, and then as we crawl through the traffic he points out famous landmarks – the Seine, Conciergerie and finally the extraordinary Notre Dame, bathed in a soft yellow light, and so ornate and delicate it looks like it might tear in the breeze.

'Like an embroidery in stone,' Olivier says, upon which I feel my legs starting to wobble. But I suspect this is just the beginning of a night of jelly-legged captivation, for on the side of the road I see a young couple kissing.

'Is that all you French ever do – kiss?' I laugh.

Olivier turns in his seat and looks at me intently, before smiling wisely. 'No, that's not all we do.'

At the Restaurant le Bel Canto, we sit at a tiny table with heavily starched white linen, and enough silver cutlery to build another Eiffel Tower. The room has a Baroque feel to it, with red-ragged walls trimmed in dark green, gently illuminated by flickering tea lights in crimson tumblers. It feels suspiciously Italian – which wasn't what I'd had in mind for the French leg of my research – but I'm only too happy to have a night off worrying about food, and just focus on Olivier. He orders champagne – the real stuff – and then scans the menu, his spectacles cutely perched on the end of his nose.

'What would you like Baum-bee?' he says, in a delicious accent that's a cross between Gérard Depardieu and a vintage cognac.

'I'm in your city Olivier. I'm in your hands,' I tease.

'Then I will 'andle you with care,' he smiles.

When the meal is ordered and the glasses are filled, Olivier makes a toast, looking deep into my eyes.

'*Santé,*' he says, '*à tes amours.* To your many loves.'

I laugh. My French date is already flirting with me, and – unlike with Paulo – I don't mind a bit.

It doesn't take me long to find out why our go-between Lynda had been so enthusiastic about my date with Olivier – he's truly intriguing. He lives in a large Dutch barge moored on the Seine, and spends the weekends either at his family's ancient lighthouse on the wild coast of Brittany, or on his property in the Loire

Valley. His job as a corporate headhunter requires him to travel the world collecting scalps. And a few hearts along the way too I'd guess. But most impressively, as a boy he taught himself to speak Russian, solely because he wanted to read *War and Peace* in the untranslated words of Tolstoy. He is indeed an exceptional man, and although I'm thrilled to be here, I'm also beginning to feel that I may well be out of my league. What happens when he finds out that I'm a mere mortal? That the closest I've ever come to speaking another language was after those eleven strawberry daiquiris at my thirtieth? Swahili I think it was.

But I shouldn't worry, as Olivier genuinely seems to be enjoying my company, so I just let myself be immersed in the experience, barely believing that I'm here – in Paris, in an amazing restaurant, with a fascinating man, drinking real champagne and eating goat's-cheese mousse, which is perhaps the most elegant entree I've ever had. And just as I thought it couldn't get any better, a woman starts playing a grand piano only two tables away, upon which our waitress saunters over to join her, smooths her frilly white apron, takes a deep breath, and starts to sing. But it's not some schmaltzy, bordello-singalong-type singing – it's full-on opera. The real thing. Amazing Italian opera that sends shivers down my spine.

I look at Olivier, dumbfounded.

He smiles. 'These are not waiters who sing,' he explains. 'These are singers who wait. They are the best music students in Paris who sing in this restaurant to earn extra cash.'

Another waitress joins in, and then a waiter, and

soon there's a quartet filling the room with melody – *Rigoletto, Figaro, Violetta* and *Carmen* – and finishing off with a soaring, sweeping, heartbreaking rendition of 'O Sole Mio', which in anybody's language is enough to make you cry. Which I do.

A few hours later and we've somehow arrived at coffee, although I can barely recall eating the meal, so captivated was I by its operatic accompaniment, and indeed, the whole experience that Olivier has so generously bestowed upon me. Rather lost for words, I mention my theory on the different styles of Brazilian coffee reflecting the flavours and colours of the local populace.

Olivier leans forward with a wicked smile. 'Well, in France, there are also as many different types of coffee as there are different types of kisses.'

It's about now that I realise I'm up against a master. Jens was certainly charming too, but Olivier seems to have it down to a fine art only equalled by the paintings of Renoir.

But who is Olivier – really? During dinner I'd gleaned the superficial from him, but now I'm anxious to dig deeper. So it's time for my favourite question – what animal he sees himself as.

'Albatross,' he replies after thinking for a few moments. 'Because it travels the world and is always restless and independent. But sometimes I'm a tiger,' he adds with a smile, but without further explanation, and I get the impression that's as much as I'm going to get from him tonight. Indeed, he now turns the spotlight firmly onto me.

'You have very elegant hands Baum-bee,' he purrs.

'Sexy hands. Why don't you take off your jacket?' he adds, and then spends the next half hour making me feel like I'm the only woman in all of Paris. And I'm loving it to bits.

It's getting late and the waitress is hovering, so we get up to leave, at which point Olivier spots my knee-high black leather boots.

'Oh, I didn't notice the boots. Nice. But where are the spurs?'

'I don't need spurs,' I reply, 'I'm already fast enough.'

'Good answer,' Olivier smiles, and we head out arm in arm into the chilly Parisian night.

But the evening is far from over. Olivier takes me to a basement jazz club where a DJ is spinning out Dizzy Gillespie and Nat King Cole, and we hit the dance floor where Olivier proves he has more energy than someone half his age, even though it has to be forty degrees Celsius and is as hot as Dante's inferno.

'But why don't you take off your jacket?' he tries again, and even though I'm melting, I don't, because the black lace body-stocking beneath is a little too flimsy to completely expose in public. It's designed to titillate, not satiate. Not here anyway.

'You have gone to such an effort to look elegant, and now you don't show it all,' Olivier grumbles good-naturedly. 'You should share.'

'I never show it all,' I reply, trying my best to be coquettish. 'I like to leave something to the imagination.'

Olivier nods approvingly, and spins me around so fast I nearly clear the floor.

At 3 a.m. Olivier drops me back at my hotel, and as I lean forward to kiss him goodnight – one on each cheek which I believe is the accepted ritual in France – he goes straight for the lips and kisses me passionately. Just like that. I wasn't expecting it, and am momentarily taken aback. But then I reason that I'm in Paris, and a kiss is only a kiss, so I let him keep going before I eventually drag myself away and dash inside.

Besides, he's a very good kisser.

In the morning I receive a text from Olivier saying he'd like to see me again if I am ever back in Paris. Which leaves me feeling oddly conflicted. On the one hand he ticks so many boxes, and even adds a few more – effortless sophistication, graciousness, gentility. But on the other hand he doesn't tick the box that asks, 'Does he make my heart do somersaults?' Yes, I love Olivier's company, but could I ever really love Olivier? It is close but not quite close enough. Maybe because of his age. Or maybe because he's so sophisticated and I'm not sure I could keep up. Or maybe – and I think this truth is dawning on me slowly like a sunrise behind Montmartre – maybe it's simply because it's much easier for me to make excuses, than to commit to anyone. Maybe I still have a long way to go before I'm prepared to trust a man not to break my heart, and then spend years trying to glue the pieces back together.

Maybe it's less painful this way.

But thankfully I don't have much time to wallow in regret or self-analysis, as my friend Candace has just flown in from Australia. She's travelling with me for the next week, and as she's gorgeous and blonde and

irresistibly vivacious, I might even have some luck picking up the odd stray and adding him to my menu. Just
for a little nibble before putting him aside and going
onto the next course, like an indulgent degustation.

Maybe it's more fun this way.

After a glorious morning of sitting in cafés, inhaling
the scent of Chanel as it wafts languorously from
parfumeries, and wandering through antique shops pretending we can afford 5,000-euro gilt-framed mirrors,
I get a call from Olivier. He's inviting us to stay the
night on his *péniche*, and we can't resist such an amazing opportunity. Besides, maybe something more will
come of it second time around – especially if I take off
not only my jacket, but also my man-proof Kevlar vest
that I seem to have been wearing of late.

Candace and I make our way across Paris to meet
Olivier, marvelling at the travel-brochure familiarity
of his neighbourhood, with the magnificent Jardin des
Tuileries just across the road, and on the other side,
the Eiffel Tower, so close I can see the yellow elevator trundling up through her bony skeleton. Upon the
Seine, a line of boats – mostly old Dutch canal barges
– are moored bow-to-stern and three-deep, hugging
the murky water. Olivier is waiting for us on the gang-
plank, eyes smiling. He welcomes us onto his beautiful
Feijtje – built in 1908 – and as we plunge into her bowels
I can already feel the history whispering at me from
her dark redwood walls, curving elegantly towards
the floor. And if *Feijtje*'s hull is her bowels, then I'd

say she has a serious case of constipation, as there's stuff everywhere – a beautiful bronze statue of Pan, a huge terracotta relief of two dancing Thai women, leather-bound books spilling out of shelves, and countless paintings and sketches and prints propped against the wall on one side of the boat, and on the other side framed photos of Olivier's family.

'And this is my country 'ouse,' he says, showing me a photo of a beautiful chateau in the Loire Valley. Yes – a chateau, with limestone walls three storeys high, and a grey slate roof studded with spires. It's stunning, and I'm beginning to appreciate the calibre of the man who French-kissed me last night.

But now he's showing me a postcard of one of those gobsmackingly enormous chateaus you see in the movies, with a hundred windows and acres of roof with dozens of turrets, and rambling gardens and topiary hedges, and God knows how many peacocks strolling about. Although I'm not sure what point he's trying to make.

'And 'ere is our old family 'ome,' Olivier says matter-of-factly. 'But it is ours no longer. It was taken in the Revolution.' He goes on to explain that back in the Reign of Terror of 1793–94 when French aristocrats were merrily getting their heads lopped off, a few members of his well-heeled family managed to flee, but most of their wealth was confiscated. Including this chateau. I'm still contemplating this travesty when Olivier shrugs his shoulders resignedly, and turns to me with that by now familiar naughty twinkle in his eye.

'You 'ave the choice of three rooms for sleeping,' he tells us. 'There is my room with a large bed which you both can 'ave, and I will sleep in the sitting room on the couch. Or there is a little *cabine*, which one of you can 'ave. Or we can work it all out later.'

I certainly don't want to toss Olivier out of his own bed, and 'working it out later' may be fraught with risk – much like Paulo's 'may be' – so I opt for the couch, and then we all prepare to head out again. I've offered to cook Olivier dinner, and I'm keen to try his local market for inspiration. As I grab a basket from the galley to carry back any goodies, I notice a trapdoor in the floor.

'Is this where you keep your slaves?' I ask playfully.

Olivier doesn't skip a beat. He smiles, looks me directly in the eye, eyebrow arching, and with a tilt of his head, replies, 'It's for those who say "no".'

The market sprawls beneath an elevated train track, and is bustling with Parisians. Fish stalls heave with huge white octopi, alongside stingrays frozen in flight like miniature stealth fighters. Woven-cane baskets brim over with oysters nestled on cosy beds of black kelp, filling the air with a sharp, salty tang.

'Are these good?' I ask Olivier, pointing to a tub of *bulots* – little pointy-ended shells with fleshy bits sticking out one end.

'Everything in France is good. Everything is very tasty,' he replies, with a suggestive lift of his eyebrow. Which I pretend not to notice.

We soon have armfuls of treats, including a paper bag of the *bulots*, three fillets of wild salmon, and a handful of *girolle* mushrooms with almost luminous golden tulip-shaped caps, looking like the sort of thing the witch in Hansel and Gretel would sauté up with a nice toad or two. Good grief, I hope to God I don't poison us all.

Dinner for three has evolved into *dîner pour huit*, with five neighbours from other boats joining us, bringing extra food to stretch things out. My entree is surprisingly good. The *bulots* may be no more than lumpy little sea-snails steamed in white wine and fresh herbs, but they taste like a cross between calamari and abalone, and have the guests good-naturedly fighting for the last one. Indeed, they seem to be impressed that an Aussie can cook French food.

But then it all comes horribly unstuck.

My *girolles* taste like wet cardboard, and the wild salmon like I've marinated it in sump oil. I'm mortified – I was trying so hard to impress Olivier, hoping that if I threw myself into the fray with unbridled enthusiasm, then my heart might follow, potentially sparking something between us to burn brightly for years to come. But the meal is a disaster, and the only flame burning is from the candles on the dining table, grotesquely illuminating the hollow faces of seven hungry dinner guests. I can't wait to clear the dishes and slink into the galley, wishing I could crawl into an empty *bulot* shell and disappear. But Olivier takes it all with awfully good humour and follows me, cheerfully scraping the not unsubstantial leftovers into a little bucket, and passing comment that 'per'aps this salmon is a male – I know females taste much sweeter'. And even though he's being cheeky, I'm grateful that he's let me off the hook.

Fortunately Dominic's contribution of magnificent cheeses – a camembert from Normandy as smooth as Charles Aznavour, and roquefort sheep's cheese from the Pyrenees, along with Elly's *tarte tatin*, save the day, and everyone is amply fed. And as they all chatter happily in a language I barely comprehend – but don't care because it sounds like music – I soon find myself feeling quite at home, thinking I could get used to a life on the not-so-high seas. My mood is no doubt enhanced by generous quantities of a smooth red wine – a *canon-fronsac*, 1999, with aromas of plum and orange-peel and earth. It tastes expensive.

'Maybe you are this wine?' I ask Olivier.

'Do you know 'ow I taste?' he replies, with a wicked look in his eye, at which everyone laughs, having picked up throughout the evening there may be something going on between us.

'Well, is it you?' I repeat, flushing slightly. 'It has great depth of flavour. It would have to be pretty close.'

'Maybe closer than you think,' Olivier replies, settling back in his chair and flicking away a baguette crumb from his cashmere sweater. 'Read the label more carefully.'

And there I see it – in ornate script on the label, the words 'Chateau Vray Canon Boyer'. Boyer being Olivier's surname.

But of course. His family own a vineyard too.

It couldn't be a more perfect match. Both Olivier and the *canon-fronsac* are full of character and rich in flavour, although still well-balanced, and as smooth as silk. Neither is excessively woody, unlike some wine – and unfortunately some men – I've tried, and both have a sweet finish. Both are clearly very fine vintages, and they're delightfully intoxicating – just enough to put a smile on your face and a little flutter in your heart.

At 1 a.m. the neighbours finally depart, leaving

Olivier and I to clear up. I collect the table napkins slowly, deliberately, not sure what's going to happen next. Candace retired earlier in the evening to the spare cabin, meaning I'll have to take the couch in the main salon, or Olivier will, leaving me his cabin. But I'm wondering if either scenario will eventuate. Electricity has been quietly sparking between us all night, but I'm not quite sure where I want it to go. Or where Olivier wants it to go either, although I've got a fair idea.

Which gets me to thinking – is it natural, this apparent attraction between us? Or is it borne from a sense of mutual obligation? Would we be thinking whatever we're thinking if we'd simply met at a party, rather than on a blind date set up from halfway across the world? As I collect the wine glasses – more confused than ever – Olivier comes over and kisses me tenderly.

'If you are very quiet you can sleep on my bed. On one side,' he whispers. 'You can't sleep on the couch, it is too uncomfortable.'

I look at the couch and try to calculate if it's long enough for me. No, not really. Not unless I curl up like a roulade. So what should I do? I feel very comfortable with Olivier. But I don't want to give him the wrong idea about me – that I'm this loose woman roaming the globe jumping into bed with whoever offers me a comfortable one. Because as innocent as it might start off between us, one thing would most likely lead to another, and I'm an at-least-six-dates sort of woman. Anything less risks being seen as downright tarty.

As Olivier keeps kissing me though – and I'm not stopping him – I can't help but wonder if it would still be considered tarty when such behaviour was conducted on a *péniche* on the Seine with a sophisticated man who wears cashmere sweaters and has his own wine label? And can recite Tolstoy in Russian? In fact, pretty soon I'm not sure what I was whinging about.

'Well,' I say, 'if you are very well-behaved, I'll let you sleep on the other side of the bed. With a line down the middle.'

I smile, relieved at my decision not to make a decision about where all this is going. Just yet anyway. Olivier kisses me again. This time for a little longer. He's a nice kisser, and I yield ever so slightly into his lips. But I'm still nervous.

'I don't want to start something I can't finish,' I whisper.

'It's a kiss, no more,' he says, now gently embracing me.

'Yes, that's true,' I reply, giving in a little more as the kisses flutter to my neck. 'But if you cross over the line in your bed, I will slap you very hard with this last *girolle*.'

The *grande cabine* is tucked into the curved bow with a low ceiling and dark wooden panelling. There's more art scattered about, including a huge pastel of a reclining nude over the bed. Olivier is still in the galley, so I quickly change and burrow under the covers. I'm suddenly glad that my nightwear isn't a skimpy leopard-skin negligee or a silky camisole, but an oversized white man-shirt in soft Egyptian cotton. I'd carefully chosen it for when I was staying the night in a date's home – as several had kindly invited me to save me the expense of a hotel – and I hadn't wanted my ensemble to be too revealing. Although it can still be sexy if I choose, simply by undoing a few buttons and flicking up the collar, and thus creating the little-bit-naughty, little-bit-nice, spank-me-tomboy look.

The cabin is warm and protective like a womb, with a gentle glow from the night-lights of Paris seeping in from the long thin window leading onto the deck, casting the room in an eerie orange twilight. I'm lying perfectly still when Olivier comes in, my back to his side of the bed, and breathing heavily as if I'm already asleep. Olivier quietly reaches over me to turn off the night-light, and I open one eye just a fraction to see if I need to figure out an escape plan – a buck naked Olivier being the trigger. But he's wearing navy-blue silk boxer shorts, so I can relax. Another quick peep reveals he has a trim, lithe body, and a slightly fuzzy chest like a grey mohair breastplate, and all-in-all is – I have to admit – a rather pleasing apparition to have hovering above me in the bowels of a 100-year-old houseboat.

And then the light flicks off.

We lie in silence for a few minutes, the darkness acting like a thick velvet blanket between us.

'Are you sound asleep?' he whispers, and I can sense his whole body lying straight as a ramrod beside me, yet coiled tightly inside, as if waiting to be let out of the starting gates. I know exactly what he's getting at, but I've still not made up my mind where I want this to go. I need more time, and I need more confidence, and I need to ignore the maddening voices in my head telling me that Nice Girls don't have sex with a man they've only just met. Even if he has a chateau in the Loire Valley.

So I take the easy way out. I ratchet up the 'Can't you tell I'm fast asleep?' heavy breathing, and I don't reply.

Early in the morning, with the room still in darkness, I find Olivier wrapping his arms gently around me. When he senses I'm awake, he kisses my bare neck. I don't move, and he runs his fingers softly down the length of my spine – over my shirt. It feels good. He does it another few times, and I'm quite relaxed about it, as if such intimacy is as natural as holding hands, or kissing. But then he grows bolder and works his hand around to my bare tummy where the shirt has ridden up. He finds my bellybutton, and runs his finger around it.

I'm getting nervous now.

Do I really want this to happen – as pleasant as it may feel? Where do I draw the line? Do I want to stay nice? Or have some fun? Or somehow combine the two so that I can have my cake and eat it too? And do I really want to get involved anyway, only to leave him the very same day? I feel like I'm forever jumping out of the way when someone gets too close, like in a game of tiddlywinks.

'How do you say bellybutton in French?' I ask playfully, although I'm really just playing for time.

Olivier tickles my tummy. '*Nombril,*' he says, a little hoarsely.

But I think he got the message, because he moves his hand away and lies beside me quietly, obediently, as the gentle rocking of the boat and the soft cooing of the pigeons on deck conspire to send us off to sleep again.

But not for long. Soon Olivier's hands are back,

roaming towards my bottom. A bottom that I'm very relieved is still clad in black cotton undies – think a little less Victoria's Secret, and a teensy bit more Bridget Jones – deliberately chosen as the last line of defence.

But Olivier manages to find the one bit of bottom where the undies have ridden up a couple of inches, and he stops right there and starts to stroke my bare flesh.

Damn.

I laugh. A little shrilly. 'And what's that called?'

'*Fesse,*' he replies, not moving his hand away.

'Not *derrière*?' I ask, playing for more time, although I know it's running out fast.

'No, this part is *fesse*.'

I carefully rearrange myself on the bed so my *fesse* is harder to reach, but it's quite clear that Olivier isn't going to give up, as much as I'm not going to give in.

Or might this be my Waterloo?

'I'd like a morning kiss,' he purrs, when he runs out of bare bits of posterior flesh to explore.

Now there's two ways I could respond to this. The first that springs to mind is to pretend to have fallen asleep again, and thus avoid any further complications. Easy. Or, I could remember why I'm here in the first place. Olivier is sophisticated and elegant and respectful and sweet, and I can't deny I'm enjoying the attention. And a kiss is just a kiss. Especially in Paris, where it's as natural as dunking your croissants in hot chocolate. So what's the dilemma?

'Okay, Olivier,' I finally murmur, turning to face him. 'So show me how to French kiss. The real deal. Give me a lesson.'

Olivier obliges. And it's nice. Delicate. And somewhat more refined than the Australian tendency of invariably slobbery tongue wrestling. Or maybe that's just the kind of men I used to date. So I allow myself to enjoy the moment, and it's all very lovely being kissed by a Frenchman who obviously takes his cultural obligations so seriously. He was certainly the right man to ask for help in discovering the romantic side of Parisians.

Olivier shifts his position slightly. 'Now for lesson number two,' he whispers.

Oh no, I was hoping this wouldn't happen. Call me naive, or even a terrible tease, but now that push is rather rapidly coming to shove – so to speak – I've decided enough is enough. The spark still isn't quite there to get me over the line, and as much as I'm really very fond of Olivier, for me sex without a real sense of passion is like eating strawberry ice-cream without the strawberries.

'Lessons are over!' I laugh, wriggling out of his reach. 'I've got a train to catch in half an hour.'

Which is a lie, but I can't think how else not to offend him.

And voila, the moment is broken. And once again I walk away from the opportunity to let someone get close to me. Indeed, I'm more convinced by the day that there's something wrong with me – especially as I'd actually like some sex before my *fesse* turns to feta cheese. But perhaps it's as simple as the timing being right. And the man of course. Not that there's anything wrong with Olivier – far from it – but maybe my gut instinct is telling me to hold out for something younger.

An effervescent champagne, rather than a vintage red.
Because I still have a lot of living to do.

MONACO
Slippery little suckers

Sliding into Monaco's sumptuous train station – with
more marble than a pharaoh's tomb – I contemplate
what the local men will be like. Monaco is the second
smallest country on earth, although per capita it has
the highest number of millionaires and billionaires,
which I'm guessing is bound to alter the usual social
demographics. After all, if everyone is so rich, then how
does anyone get to show off? Having a Rolls Royce just
isn't going to cut it if they're as common as diamonds
at Monte Carlo's Rose Ball spectacular.

Still, as much as I've sworn off Men of Means
because so many of those I dated in the past were ...
well ... just plain mean, I wouldn't mind another look.
I've always rather fancied myself driving a pink Roller.
And it might not be such a ridiculous ambition, as my
friend Taci – an Australian living in Monaco – has been
trying to get me a date with undoubtedly the wealthiest
local of all, who probably has Rollers coming out his
bottom and might want to unload a few. But I won't
know until tomorrow if he's going to work out, so I'll
hold off getting a matching coloured fur for now.

Candace and I book into a hotel that doesn't require
the down payment of a kidney, and take a stroll
around the old part of Monte Carlo. I soon discover
that Monegasque architecture is royal icing gone mad

– with so much ornate plasterwork and pretty, wrought-iron balconies painted in crisp creams, soft apricots and whipped-butter yellows that I feel like I'm walking through the wedding section of a cake shop. However, my gut instinct tells me that they're all display cakes, with cardboard frames, so that even though they're undeniably beautiful, it's only superficial, and inside they're quite empty. Soulless even. Which could make for a challenging few days if the same applies to the populace.

After a leisurely lap of the Monaco Grand Prix circuit, which twists and turns right through town, it's getting dark and it's time to eat. Candace and I find a seafood restaurant on the harbour that I'm hoping might offer something local to match up with Taci's date – if indeed he ever materialises – although when I ask the waiter to recommend a fish-inspired national dish, he scoffs at me. Yes, scoffs.

'There is no such ting as Monaco cuisine,' he says, looking rather pleased with himself that he's just spoiled my night.

I stubbornly scan the menu anyway, even though I had indeed read somewhere that Monegasque cuisine is heavily influenced by French and Italian cooking, so doesn't really have its own identity. I end up ordering *poulpes à la genovese,* an octopus dish which sounds a good cross-cultural combination, and therefore paradoxically 'local'. And it's fabulous – quite the most tender I've ever eaten. The bite-sized chunks just melt in my mouth, with a thick pesto sauce wrapping it in flavour. The only off-putting element is all the delicate pink arms with their slippery little suckers, so there's no disguising what I'm eating. Candace looks aghast.

'I can't eat anything that still looks like what it actually is,' she whimpers, which makes me glad I didn't choose Morocco for my 'M' country, where they barbecue up whole calves heads, eyelashes and all.

In the morning we head for Café de Paris – the best people-watching place in town. Or more accurately, it's people watching people watching people. Everyone seems to be on show here, and boy do they flaunt it. The older men invariably have collar-length white hair brushed elegantly back off their smooth sun-tanned faces, and seem to favour burnt-orange trousers, pale blue shirts and matching mohair jumpers slung over their shoulders and knotted loosely at the throat. Their over-tanned wives have huge sunglasses and thick ropes of marble-sized pearls wrapped around their crepey necks, and handbags that most likely cost the equivalent of a small pleasure-boat. I sense there's a lot of Us and Them going on, of which I'm clearly a Them. Although I wish I wasn't, because that means I'll be lumped in with a table of package-deal English tourists beside me squawking like seagulls, their freshly sautéed pink flesh bulging from their viscose clothing like sausage stuffing trying to escape.

Whilst I'm pondering the merits of retailers only selling tight-fitting synthetic clothing to athletic people under the age of twenty-five, I get the phone call for which I've been anxiously waiting. It's Taci, ringing to let me know the latest on my VIP date.

It appears that to access said date, I need to first be vetted by one of his friends – Frank – who'll decide whether or not I'm worthy of an introduction. Now this may seem a little extreme – it's only a date, not a marriage covenant – but I'm not at all offended by such a provision, as potential date #23 is none other than Prince Albert. Yes – that's right. Prince Albert II, Sovereign Prince of Monaco, the head of the House of Grimaldi, and the ruler of the Principality of Monaco! I'm nearly speechless with excitement as Taci tells me that Frank will meet me this afternoon, although I'm already wondering what I'm supposed to say to not only the heir to one of the biggest fortunes in the world, but also a man who's dated dozens of famous and beautiful women, including Brooke Shields, and supermodel Claudia Schiffer, and is now married to a one-time Olympic swimmer who'd swim rings around me. I know I'm way out of my league, but I'll meet with Frank anyway, on the off-chance Albert wants a quick break from his regular diet of Sex Goddesses. After all, even Dom Pérignon gets boring if you drink it every day.

Frank is forty-five minutes late, and when he sneaks up behind me to playfully tap me on the shoulder, I spin around with my very best please-like-me smile. But even as I'm turning I can see his face clouding over, which, given several recent experiences, I presume is because our go-between Taci is quite stunning, and Frank was hoping the same for me. I mean, I'm okay-looking if you don't look too closely, but I clearly don't make the grade in a country where it seems that everyone is so pampered, primped, plumped and polished that they look like something out of *Dynasty* crossed with a car-wax commercial. Still, I try to remain as upbeat as possible, as I don't have another date organised in Monaco, so I'm rather depending on Frank to make it happen. Which it still might, as after chatting with me for a while and realising I might actually have a personality, he finally deigns to meet Candace and me later on tonight to take a second look. However, he's still so ambivalent that I feel like I've been nibbled at by a food critic and quickly spat out as an inedible morsel. So I'm not holding my breath, and if it happens then that's great, but in the meantime I need a drink. Fast. It might help me to swallow my pride.

The Hotel de Paris is imposing, and I'm not sure whether the doorman with shiny gold epaulets is going to let us in, because he's staring at my little black canvas backpack like it's a dog with scabies. But he eventually relents, and Candace and I find ourselves in a hotel lobby so grand we could quite easily be in a movie. A massive chandelier drips crystals like a fountain frozen in time, and a pale yellow flower arrangement the size of a small coral atoll dominates the centre of the lobby, filling the void with the warm scent of utter luxury.

The bar is full, so we hesitate a moment to consider our options, whereupon a man sitting at a small marble table beckons to us. I take it that he's leaving, so we make our way over to him, although it turns out that he's actually gesturing for us to sit with him. I'm not quite sure what to do, but when Candace kicks my ankle to remind me why we're in Monaco, I accept.

I can't quite believe our luck. Our host, Jorge, is very good-looking in a dark, sultry, Mediterranean way, with glossy black hair like a raven, and hands that are soft and beautifully manicured. He's impeccably dressed too, with a navy jacket over a crisp open-necked shirt, designer jeans that appear to be brand new, and expensive shoes – if the little leather tassels are anything to go by. In fact, he's so elegant that I'm rather surprised that he could be bothered talking to us, given Candace and I are a little more Levi's than Lacroix. Jorge has a Spanish accent as thick as olive tapenade, but tells us he visits Monaco so often he almost feels like a local. He offers to buy us a drink, which we accept, because … well, why wouldn't we? When the waiter reappears there's also a silver-handled glass dish with an assortment of delicacies – miniature bread sticks, a sweet chilli dipping-sauce, and black olives individually skewered with wooden forks tied with a cheery little cellophane ribbon. Even the paper napkins are printed with a gold crown above the words 'Hotel de Paris, Monte Carlo'. It doesn't get much more stylish than this.

Jorge is watching us intently through very dark eyes. His brows are neatly plucked, and look like the outstretched wings of a black swan. He's smiling, but I somehow don't quite trust him. He's too perfect, too neat, too controlled. He asks us if we're staying in this hotel, at which I can only laugh. Hasn't he spotted my shoes and their tatty laces? If I could afford to stay here I could afford those $14,000 Manolo Blahnik alligator boots in the front window of the shop up the road. Which I can't. But Jorge keeps pushing us, wanting to know ''Ow many stars your hotel 'as?', which I find kind of creepy. I kick Candace under the table as a sign not to tell him too much, for fear he'll turn up his nose at us like Frank did. However, I'm happy enough to tell him I'm writing about the cuisine and men of Monaco.

'It's about delicious encounters,' I say, a little more cheekily than usual, because I suspect he's not the type to scare off easily. 'So perhaps I can write about you?'

I don't care that Jorge is Spanish, because he looks so at home here. And besides, unless Frank comes good with Albert, then this may be the only date I can manage in Monaco. I instinctively know Jorge is never going to be The One – much like you know a brightly coloured frog is most likely poisonous – but at least he might be a bit of fun to pass some time with.

Jorge smiles broadly and leans over to tickle the back of my neck. I jump, not expecting any physical contact with someone I've known for less than ten minutes, but touching is clearly something that Jorge is good at, because now he's alternately tickling both Candace and my chins, and stroking our noses whenever we say something funny. Or even something quite unremarkable, which is making me increasingly suspicious of his intentions.

'Can I take your photo?' I ask, subtly moving myself out of reach of his touchy-feely fingers.

'Here?' he asks, to which I nod. 'But I have good photos back in my 'otel,' he purrs. 'You can come, after dinner.'

Having a vivid imagination, I have a sneaking suspicion that said photos are going to consist of a) porn, or b) porn. Either way, I don't need to see them, or end up featuring in the next batch. So I politely decline, and take my own photo of him that won't get confiscated in Customs.

Jorge starts handfeeding Candace the skewered olives, which she clearly finds very charming, but I'm still favouring the more creepy interpretation. He's undoubtedly very smooth, but smooth like an oil slick, and not something I'd want to slip on. I can't quite put my finger on it, but there's something not quite right about our handsome Spanish Lothario.

'Do you believe in destiny?' Jorge suddenly asks, his eyes as black as the last olive he's just fed to Candace.

'Of course,' replies Candace, flushing slightly.

'This is destiny,' Jorge says, leaning forward and holding both our hands together gently in his, and continuing to hold them for just a little longer than I'm comfortable with. 'Maybe we find our destiny together.'

I'm not at all convinced that this performance is anything more than a con, but I'm still fascinated that he can deliver it with such sincerity. It's like watching a politician kissing babies.

'What are you doing for dinner tonight?' Jorge suddenly asks us. 'We can go together,' he adds, softly stroking my cheek, 'and after, well, perhaps we'll see.'

I laugh. Perhaps I'm being too hard on him, as whatever his intentions are – and I'm guessing 'perhaps' in Monaco means the same as 'may be' in Brazil – he makes for great entertainment. And dinner's just dinner, and we'll all pay our own way, so heck ... why not?

Back at the hotel I change into my Drop Dead Gorgeous outfit – a slight variation on the Black Widow Spider ensemble, with lycra rather than lace. Well, I thought it was drop dead gorgeous until I came to Monaco – but I can't possibly compete now with silk dresses and diamond necklaces, and alligator boots that would blow my wardrobe budget out of the water. For ten years. I feel like a country cousin in gumboots at a gala ball, and am finally beginning to understand why Frank was so dismissive of me. Still, I plump up my breasts, shorten my skirt, and put on my shiniest lipstick, and as I pass the mirror in the lobby I throw myself a big kiss. Even country cousins deserve to have fun.

Candace and I meet Jorge at Café de Paris, but he seems distracted.

'I am looking for a bank,' he tells us, which starts alarm bells ringing in my head. Doesn't he come here most weekends? Surely he'd know the nearest hole-in-the-wall if he needed cash? Or is he setting us up for some trickery? This is Monaco after all, attracting shammers, shysters and conmen from all over the world.

'So where shall we go for dinner Jorge?' I ask. 'We just want a simple restaurant. And cheap.'

Jorge laughs. 'Cheap? But you are in Monaco.'

And there go those warning bells again. Louder than ever. Or perhaps it's just the bells of Cathédrale de Monaco chiming out seven o'clock.

Let's hope so.

Candace and I follow Jorge down a side street and then down some stairs into the cosy cellar restaurant of Rampoldi's. By the time the bow-tied maître d' has swooped upon us like a manta ray, and we're sitting at a tiny table at the back of the restaurant, surrounded by other diners who all look very pleased with themselves – like the cats who've got the cream – I realise with increasing horror that the concept of 'cheap' in such an establishment is as familiar as an Aldi homebrand face cream would have been to Princess Grace. But it's too late to escape, as Candace and I are pinned against the wall on a velvet banquette, and Jorge is breezily ordering a bottle of wine to kick off the proceedings. It looks like he's been here before – many times – and I'm starting to wonder at whose expense. When the waiter brings us bread rolls with fat curls of corrugated butter, I know we're in deep trouble. When the butter comes out in little individual foil wrappers, you can afford to eat for the rest of the week, but when it comes in curls, you'll need a second overdraft. But it gets even worse. The menus have arrived, and neither Candace's nor mine have prices.

'Does your menu have prices?' I ask Jorge limply.

'Of course,' he replies, scanning the pages intently.

It turns out that Rampoldi's has two types of menus – males get menus with blue ribbons, which are priced, and women get menus with red ribbons, which are not. The implication being that the men have the money and the women have … well … the nous to catch a man wealthy enough not to care that the foie gras she's just ordered costs the same as a face lift. Which no doubt she's ordered too. I've suddenly lost my appetite, and I'm wondering how I'm going to get out of this without melting my credit card. So I decide dishonesty's the best option, and tell Jorge we'll just have an entree, as we're going out later for supper.

'Is that okay with you too?' I ask, hoping he'll get the hint.

Jorge settles back in his chair and keeps surveying

the menu. His eyes aren't so soft now. He's acting like a fox who's charmed a couple of chickens into a corner, and knows he has plenty of time to play with them before he finishes them off.

'No, I'll have steak I think,' he says, smiling smugly. 'The filet mignon with bearnaise sauce.'

It's at this precise moment the word 'gigolo' comes to mind. Of course, it all makes sense now. Wanting to know the number of stars our hotel has, the photos back in his room, his expensive shoes. I do believe our Jorge is a real live gigolo, trawling the streets of Monaco for easy prey. Or a free meal.

But I'm not going to let him get away with it. Not altogether anyway. I'm happy enough to cover most of the bill, because after all he did buy us drinks, but there's no way he's going to walk out of here leaving Candace and me to pay for it all.

Jorge seems to sense our change in mood, for he's a little less friendly than before, and there hasn't been a chin tickle for at least ten minutes. I'm guessing too that he's realised we're not two rich women looking for a toy boy, and that he's been wasting his time. We eat our meal in silence – an enormous filet mignon for him, and delicate little bowls of asparagus soup for Candace and me. Jorge knocks back the wine with gusto, and I'm praying that its fancy embossed label doesn't mean it's going to cost me an arm and a leg. The way I'm going, I'll end up as limbless as a carrot.

Having finished his steak, and being presented with the bill, Jorge suddenly gets up and heads toward the back of the restaurant. I'm horrified, convinced he's going to jump out the bathroom window and leave

Candace and me in the lurch. So we quickly call the waiter over and pay two-thirds of the bill plus the tip – even though our pro-rata share would amount to half that – and advise him that Jorge will pay the balance upon his return.

'Although if I were you I'd be keeping an ear out for the sound of breaking glass coming from the men's room,' I chortle.

The waiter smiles long-sufferingly, as if he's seen it all before, although I think he's rather impressed that we might get out of it quite so lightly. Much to my relief Jorge returns, but when he sees the bill folder still on the table, he glowers, then turns his back on us and starts chatting up a beautiful black woman and her girlfriend who've just squeezed themselves into the table beside us. Candace is outraged Jorge can be so fickle. Not because she was at all interested in him – and besides, she's very happily married – but because she realises that he's been on quite a different agenda than she'd given him credit for. I guess that dating is a numbers game in Monaco, much like in the Monte Carlo Casino. The more you spread your bets, the more likely you are to win. And perhaps get a subsidised dessert too.

After dinner, as Candace and I are walking up the hill to the casino to meet Frank, it occurs to me the food that best describes Jorge is the *poulpes à la genovese* I ate yesterday. Jorge started off being very tender and sweet, although ended up a bit chewy. And he was oily – very oily. His hands were everywhere, touching and feeling, just like the grabby little suckers on an octopus when it's looking for prey. Yep – I got suckered for sure. But it could have been worse – he could have ordered the Krug.

Frank keeps us waiting – again – outside the casino for an hour. When he finally turns up and suggests we join him for a late supper, I accept, hoping to impress upon him how charming and witty I am. I'm still hopeful of scoring the ultimate VIP date with Albert, and this is my last chance. But instead, I end up being quite viciously berated for the next sixty-five minutes, as Frank is adamant that women only come to Monaco to meet rich men.

'Especially Australian women,' he says pointedly. 'And really Bambi, you're no better than a hooker yourself if you let a single date pay for your dinner on this highly dubious trip you've undertaken. Although at least hookers give something back in return. What do your dates get?'

I stab my fork into the palm of my hand to keep from bursting into tears. Frank's got me so wrong. I'm here to find love, not free meals. Besides, I've offered to pay for every dinner date I've been on so far, so I'm hardly a hooker. But what hurts the most is that after meeting Harry and Christian and Olivier, I think I *have* given them something in return. A sense of self. A certain pride that they were noble representatives of their country.

'Really?' sniffs Frank, when I tell him as much.

I leave in a huff. I don't need to meet Albert anyway. And no, I don't pay for Frank's caesar salad like I was going to. If he can make a point, then so can I.

The next morning I tearfully part ways with Candace to travel the next leg of the journey on my own. I'm feeling more lost and alone than ever, and uncertain whether I can keep smiling when I keep getting my teeth kicked in. If I don't find The One soon, I'm tempted to give the whole game away.

But then, as the train slides out of its marble tomb and heads for Italy, I figure it's far too early to give up. I come from a family of achievers, and of fighters, and indeed my family crest reads, *'Vivere est vincere'* – To live is to conquer. There's another great quote too from Max Ehrmann's *Desiderata:* 'No doubt the universe is unfolding as it should.' So I'll ignore the Paulos and the Eduards and the Franks of the world, and just believe there are great things ahead for me. Although I do ask the universe one little favour.

Please hurry things up.

ITALY
The One that got away

Most tourists avoid Naples in favour of Italian cities where they're less likely to be mugged, scammed, pickpocketed, bag-snatched, or find themselves with an unscheduled appointment for a concrete-shoe fitting and a one-way harbour cruise, having pinched the parking spot reserved for the local Camorra. But not me. I've been here before, and I love it. This city is gritty and colourful, and it's loud, and it's real, with paint peeling off ancient facades, dogs scavenging through litter, humans dodging mopeds, horns blaring, and – strung up above me like flags on a circus tent – the entire neighbourhood's washing on display for all to see, whether these are giant mamma-mia cotton bloomers, or teeny-tiny satin g-strings. I adore the public shamelessness of it all. It seems to sum up Italians' relaxed attitude to life. Indeed, I'm looking forward to not one, but two dates in this country, keen to see if either match the Italian Stallion reputation for which the locals are famous. You know, 'virile, macho, passionate'. Pretty sexy stuff. So even if I don't find The One, at least I might have some fun.

But first I've got some time to kill, so I head for the markets to get a sense of why the celebration of food is as critical to Italians as blood is to veins. The pace is busy along Via Toledo, bustling with Neapolitans doing what they do best: looking good. It's not that the men are particularly handsome or the women beautiful, but crisp white t-shirts teamed with blue jeans and black sunnies don't look this stylish on anyone else on the planet. Italians are able to combine simplicity with chic, as effortlessly – and deliciously – as wrapping fresh figs in prosciutto. They also have a certain confidence about them, like they all have a secret lover waiting to meet them somewhere.

Just beyond Piazza Carita the crowd thickens and streams like a school of salmon into the narrower side streets. And here I am, in the midst of this total, glorious, chaos. A sense of order doesn't seem to be all that important to the vendors – with fishmongers in long white rubber aprons plying their slippery-slimy trade beside cheese traders, and butchers cheerfully competing with florid-faced fruiterers selling mountains of succulent tomatoes, plaits of garlic, and *zucchina* a metre long.

'*Belle!*' one stallholder shouts right in my ear, to which I blush with delight and thank him – it being my first Italian compliment – before realising he's referring to the fat purple eggplant he's waving around.

A *tripperia* displays animal bits limply festooned on hooks with tacky plastic lemons – a blanched pig's trotter, sheets of pink dimpled stomach, curly intestines and moist chunks of something that might be lung, but I really don't want to look too closely. In fact, I feel quite ill – it's one thing to have *trippa Napolitana* served up on a plate with a nice tomato sauce to disguise it, and quite another for it to be presented as an anatomy lesson.

A *panetteria* is far less confronting, and overflows with pasta of every shape and size imaginable – *anellini, fusilli, cappelletti, maccheroni,* and *candele casarecce* as long as my arm and looking indeed like candles at a formal dinner party. Cellophane bags hold multicoloured spirals of pasta, with some in the red, white and green of the Italian flag. Then there's also the mouthwatering variety of infused oils – *crema di porcini* (porcini mushroom cream), *burro al tartufo* (white truffle butter) – and other treats to add to pasta that are bound to sing 'Ave Maria' with every mouthful.

I wander around deliriously until midday, when the stalls start to shut as quickly as a clam sensing danger; they will stay that way for the next two hours. But that suits me fine, as I'm off to have lunch with Elene – a real life princess – in her palace.

I met Elene several years ago in her once noble-man's palace now converted into a boutique B&B – the Palazzo San Teodoro. I'm staying there for a few days to recharge my batteries. I figure hunkering down in a nineteenth-century Neoclassical palace, with Venetian chandeliers and views over the Bay of Naples, is the perfect pick-me-up. It's the only grand accommodation I'm indulging in for the entire trip, and after twenty-eight days of non-stop travelling, and an extraordinary twenty-seven dates, I think I've earned it.

Elene is the sort of princess who doesn't have any real authority, given the Italian monarchy was abolished in 1946. But although not formally recognised, she still retains her title, and many privileges. As does her brother – Pasquale – with whom Elene has set me up on a date tonight. I'm quite beside myself with excitement at the prospect, and tempted to contact Frank in Monaco to tell him that *someone* thinks I'm worthy enough to meet a prince.

Of course, I'm not really expecting anything to happen between us, and indeed, the more famous or wealthy someone is, the less pressure I put on myself to win their affections. It's simply not worth the humiliation. I've learned my lesson recently that to catch the eye of such a man, you usually have to be very beautiful. And let's face it – I'm not. I could probably turn a few heads down at the local bocce club, but dazzling a prince? Hardly.

Still, that's not to say I won't put my best foot forward, so I spend an hour trying on different outfits – agonising over short skirt versus long, too-much cleavage versus too-little, and how much bling to wear to suggest I've got some class, versus too much to suggest I don't. I end up wearing a short black skirt, a peep of cleavage, killer boots and a dramatic faux-pearl necklace. No, too showy – make that a teal pashmina flung elegantly around my neck. I'm exhausted before I even walk out the door.

Elene has invited me over for a Campari in her apartment to kickstart the evening. Pasquale is there too, sprawled comfortably on an oversized sofa. He's in his mid-forties, with glossy black hair, and smooth olive skin that suggests he looks after himself. His face is finely sculptured with dark features and a composed smile, reminding me of Italian Renaissance paintings depicting life in the royal courts. His eyes too are vaguely familiar – the intelligent, ever-watchful eyes of a royal falcon out hunting for rabbits in the foothills behind Naples. He speaks impeccable English, with a warm, smooth Italian accent, like Frangelico liqueur. I'm a little disappointed though. I'd been hoping Pasquale would be wearing a shirt monogrammed with HRH, or a solid-gold signet ring – anything to indicate he's a prince. But instead, he's casually dressed in an open-necked shirt and jeans, and stylish Italian shoes. Indeed, far from being snooty or lording it over everyone, he doesn't appear to take himself too seriously. He is even bordering on the cheeky – as Erica, his sixteen-year-old niece, heads off in a giggle of girlfriends to party in a back room of the apartment, Pasquale spreads his arms wide and looks mortally wounded.

'And where's my invitation?' he asks, smiling now. 'I can still dance you know.' Erica blows him a kiss and disappears, so I take the initiative. 'Well, you'll just have to party with me,' I say, wondering when I got to be quite so brazen. He is a prince after all.

Still, my own cheek pays off, and we're soon heading off to find a restaurant, chatting like old friends, and before long I've even forgotten that he's a member of the most privileged institution in Italian society. Which is just as well, as the butterflies in my stomach were quite spoiling my appetite.

Pasquale has offered me a choice of any food I'd like, but as the last thing I want is to be seen as an opportunist – Frank's words still ringing in my ears – I pick pizza. Naples is pretty much the birthplace of pizza, it reputedly having being invented way back in 997 a little further north, and then commercialised in Naples in 1830, arguably making it the first fast food on the planet. Besides, it's got a nice ring to it – *The Prince and the Pizza*. A little like *The Princess and the Pea*. Perfect.

Even so, the pizzeria that Pasquale chooses – Pizza Re, on the main esplanade overlooking the Bay of Naples – is not your average pizza parlour, but more like an exhibit in a Milanese home-decorating show. Black-and-white photos hang on the walls to match their checkerboard black-and-white tiles and the glossy black ceiling. Funky lighting brightly illuminates the small – almost private – rooms, with ours leading directly onto the busy kitchen, where four chefs are getting down to business dressed top-to-toe in black-and-white uniforms. Only the Italians could be so colour-coordinated.

'There are only two real *pizze* in Napoli,' Pasquale explains, scanning the menu. 'The rest are more recent imposters. So I suggest we have margherita, which is tomato, mozzarella and basil – the colours of the Italian flag. And marinara, which is not seafood like you might expect, but tomato, olive oil, oregano and garlic. It was traditionally prepared by "la marinara", the seaman's wife, for her husband when he returned home from fishing trips in the Bay of Naples.'

We watch from our table as the *pizze* are made just metres away from us on a thick marble slab, with the two lumps of dough being mercilessly pummelled like they're in the hands of a Calabrian masseuse, until they're so thin they almost rip, before being finished off with a quick low aerial flip. Then the *pizze* disappear into the oven, and before long delicious smells come curling out. The end result is skinny *pizze* with char-speckled crusts, and just a delicate layer of topping. In fact they're so light-on that they really only serve as a starter, so Pasquale orders one of the more substantial 'imposters' – the *mozzarella di bufala con prosciutto crudo*. Buffalo mozzarella is one of the region's most popular cheeses, so along with the *pizze,* I'm killing two culinary birds with one stone. We wash it all down with a bottle of local wine – an *aglianico* from Campania – a very dark, smooth red with hints of coffee and smoke and leather.

As we eat, I'm back to being very conscious that Pasquale is a prince, and am careful to follow his lead in eating the *pizze* with a knife and fork – whereas back home I use my hands – and also to hold the wine glass by the stem and not the bowl, which I sometimes do when I'm being lazy. I don't want him to think I'm a *trappano* – a Neapolitan term for somebody with bad manners and poor education – but that I'm elegant, sophisticated and can hold my own with the best of them. Not that Pasquale seems to be judging me at all. Indeed, he seems very egalitarian.

Which gets me to thinking what sort of food he matches. I'm even tempted to nip up to Milan which is famed for its *brodetto de rana* – frog broth – because after a couple of Camparis and the red wine, I'm thinking that if Pasquale is a prince, then there's a slim chance he was once a frog that got kissed, and was turned into a human. Coincidentally, Pasquale tells me that one of his ancestors was Count Giambattista Basile, who had a collection of fairytales published in 1634 called *The Tale of Tales*, or *Entertainment for Little Ones*, which included the first versions of 'Cinderella', 'Sleeping Beauty', 'Hansel and Gretel' and 'Snow White'. Apart from impressing me no end because being a writer of children's books myself, I know how hard it is to get published, I speculate that this means that the whole frog thing might have legs after all.

As I gently press Pasquale to tell me what it's like being a prince, he lets slip that he's also a hereditary count. In fact, the Conte di Torrone, courtesy of being a direct descendant of this literary Giambattista chap.

'So which do you use more frequently – prince or count?' I ask, rather jealous that the only titles I get to choose between are Ms or Miss.

Pasquale shrugs and tops up our glasses. 'Neither,' he says, 'it's not important. Although of the two, I care most about my title of the *conte*, because it's older, and has more of a story behind it.'

This impresses me too. A man could be forgiven for feeling rather smug having a princely coat of arms with a knight's helmet and more heraldic flourishes than a silk Versace scarf, but Pasquale doesn't appear to be the type to show off. Indeed, his conversation is frequently punctuated with comments that suggest the concept of Us and Them rarely darkens his door. He tells me he'd like to be popular with everybody, from 'other princes, to our waiter', before warmly asking young Nico, as he tops up our wine, how he's going with his new baby.

Talking of which, I ask Pasquale if he's ever been married.

His eyes cloud over a little, as he lightly touches on the 'two stories' of lost loves in his life.

'But they're behind me,' he says resolutely, 'and now it's time to look ahead, and hopefully start a family.'

'With what sort of woman?' I ask, barely believing I'm getting quite so personal with a prince, and hoping he might like the long leggy lanky types. With Australian accents. And somewhat 'mature'.

Pasquale thinks for a moment, his normally smooth brow furrowed. 'I'm forty-six, so a woman around thirty-five is about right.'

Damn.

'A woman young enough to still breed, but old enough so we have things in common,' he continues, which strikes me as very practical, but perhaps a little clinical. But that's just coming from a middle-aged woman whose eggs are getting more coddled by the day, and who may no longer be able to offer such choices.

'And what about you, Bambi?' Pasquale suddenly asks. 'What sort of man are you looking for?'

I'm not sure what to say. I wasn't expecting him to ask such a question, because in my experience men are rarely comfortable talking about women's personal issues. Especially when they can talk about football instead. And although I'm grateful that he seems to care, I'd feel awkward telling him that after years of broken dreams, all I want now is a man to hold me, to love me forever. It suddenly sounds a little ... well ... soppy, as if I should be far more sophisticated about it. So I sit there dumbly, a slight flush on my face, and twist the table napkin tightly beneath the table.

'I don't really know,' I say limply. 'I always seem to pick the wrong men.'

'Well, maybe you will marry a prince,' he says warmly, at which I blush madly and stick my face deep into the dessert menu.

I manage to turn the focus back onto Pasquale's life as a prince. A life of privilege where he has a private chef to 'cook me whatever I want', travels frequently overseas to opening nights of the latest hot New York artists, and acts as a 'bit of a cultural ambassador' whenever he's needed in Naples for theatrical events, film festivals or the opening of anything that requires something with a little celebrity status. And given we're talking about culture, I cheekily ask him whether Italy's men deserve their reputation for being 'womanisers', and am surprised by his frank admission that he doesn't see infidelity as a problem.

'At least not a problem for the one that has a mistress. Only a problem for the wife,' he says, shrugging his shoulders. 'But he can honestly say that his *soul* has never been unfaithful, just his body. When he is with another woman it is only sex.'

'And if the woman cheats on *you*?' I dare to ask.

'I am getting crazy.'

I can see this conversation getting tricky as I'm not a great fan of double standards, so I duck for cover with my favourite question. Besides, as much as I've learned about his more public persona, I still haven't reached the emotional core of him.

'To which animal do you most relate?'

Pasquale doesn't hesitate. 'A lion. It's strong, but also protects its family. It's loyal, and loyalty is very important.'

Which makes me rather wonder if it was to him I'd just been speaking about infidelity. But no matter, despite some quirks, I like Pasquale. Although I'm not sure if that's because of Who he is, rather than who he is. I mean, even though through my father, who was a very highly ranked naval officer, I've met all sorts of important people at various official functions – admirals, generals, ambassadors, state premiers and the odd prime minister – I'm still a little starstruck when it comes to serious VIPs, and a prince is undoubtedly in a whole league of its own. And it must show, as Pasquale laughs, and holds my gaze for several seconds.

'I am a very private person,' he says. 'But I show my secrets to those people who are special in my life. Maybe if I ever come to Australia, then I will show you some of these secrets.'

For a moment I wonder if Pasquale is flirting with me. But then I remember he's Italian, and that's just what they do.

'Well, if that's the case, then the food I'm going to match you with is a *tartufo*,' I say boldly. 'It's got several layers – like you – and when you get to the middle there's a little core of extra special sweetness. It just takes a bit of digging to find it. I reckon if I had enough time with you I'd get there.'

No sooner than these words are out of my mouth, I kick myself. Pasquale is, after all, a prince, and might not take kindly to such familiarity from a mere commoner.

But he laughs warmly. 'Well, we'll see.'

The twinkle in his eyes gives me tingles right down my spine.

As the night progresses from *pizze* to panna cotta, Pasquale's eyes twinkle ever brighter – soon competing with the safety lights on the yachts in the marina across the road, and although I never get to his *tartufo* core, I can still taste his many layers of sweetness which encircle it. And when he finally walks me home through the pitch-black streets of Naples, and lingers with me for a moment outside the Palazzo San Teodoro, I hug him tightly, feeling privileged that he let me in, just a little. That he shared with me that even though he's a prince, it doesn't mean that he gets it all his own way. That love doesn't happen just because you've got castles and cooks and monogrammed slippers and peacocks in your garden.

Which depresses me somewhat, because if *he* can't get it right, then what hope do I have with only castles in the air, and sparrows?

Two days later I'm due to have a date in Rome with Stefano, who was introduced to me via Karen, a friend of Catherine's in Amsterdam. I remember her introductory letter well:

Stefano is a naval architect. He is highly
educated, well-travelled, attractive and
charming, charming, charming.

Which had sounded positive, but it wasn't until
Stefano's own email that I really became intrigued.
When someone asks for a photo, 'one of those taken
without being aware. It is important to know people
with all the twenty-four senses ...' you know you're
onto someone special. Indeed, I hadn't realised there
were twenty-four senses, and after counting the five
I knew on one hand, and then adding in a few rude
ones, I'd given up. But perhaps Stefano will educate
me further.

Stefano's most recent email had left me in a bit of
a lather too. I'd told him that the day after our date I
was going to the Vatican to research my 'V' country,
whereupon he'd responded with, 'Just as well you are
going to see the priest at the end of our time together
...' which nearly made me fall off my chair.

As I wait at the train station for Stefano, I try to strike
an attractively nonchalant pose such as Sophia Loren
might adopt in a photoshoot for her signature perfume,
but I'm too nervous. Before I can quite perfect the look
I'm after, Stefano arrives. He's very tall and slim, with
pale olive skin and fairish hair, starting to recede ever
so slightly, but which makes him appear attractively
professorial. He's definitely more northern Italian
than the swarthier southerners, with a face that's long
and handsome – not handsome in a classical way like
Michelangelo's *David*, carved from marble, but more
malleable, friendly and interesting. His grey-blue eyes

sparkle behind cute frameless glasses, and he has the most enormous smile spreading right across his face, sporting a fabulous set of huge white teeth that must use up half a tube of toothpaste every week.

'You must be Bambi,' he says energetically. Warmly. 'Are you ready for your adventure? I'm taking you first for lunch, and then tonight for dinner. And then you'll have all of tomorrow for your date with God. Yes?'

Oooooh, yes!

Stefano has arranged for me to stay in the heart of town, at a friend's apartment conveniently situated on the floor above Stefano's office. On the way there by taxi to drop off my bags, I barely notice the busy streets surging around us, so enthralled am I already by my Roman. There's something very special about Stefano, like he's a great big jack-in-the-box bursting with vitality and good humour. I already like him. A lot.

We alight on Via Tomacelli, one of Rome's most elite shopping strips, and pass through massive wooden doors into an airy lobby, where a flimsy wrought-iron elevator – not much larger than a telephone box – is our precarious transport up to the fourth floor. I somehow squeeze into the elevator with my suitcase and my laptop, and Stefano standing – oh – just a heartbeat away. We ascend the first few floors in silence, and I keep looking at him sideways to make sure he's really real. And that I'm really here too.

'This is a very good start for a first date,' Stefano finally says with a big grin, upon which I notice we're grazing elbows, and I get a tingle right through my body. I'm almost relieved when we reach our floor, as the tingle has become so intense there's a real danger of me igniting, in which case I could well cause Rome to burn to the ground, once more.

After I've dropped off my bags we head out again, Stefano loping beside me with long, even strides, and me sneaking in several more furtive glances. He looks like an advertisement for Armani, with his immaculate black suit, black cashmere scarf, and black jacket flapping around his legs. He's style on steroids, and I'm thinking I might need to take something too, like valium.

We're having lunch at TAD Café, where casual ottomans in rich shades of plum are scattered about on pistachio-toned floors, within a courtyard hung with dozens of designer pendant lights.

'I didn't believe Karen when she tells me about your trip,' Stefano says of our go-between, as we tuck ourselves into a corner.

'Which bit? That I'm travelling the world to learn about food? Or to see if I can find any romantic male stereotypes?'

Well, I didn't want to give away too much in my cover email. Like I'm looking for love. He'd probably never have agreed to meet me.

'For both I'm suspicious,' Stefano replies cheerfully, 'I think there is another reason behind it. Women say one thing and mean another. Besides, I don't know if I'm so typical, but you will have to find out for yourself.'

I smile, warming to this man as fast as cocoa in a microwave. If he's already picked up that I might have ulterior motives – as honourable as they are – then that's exactly what I'm after. I no longer want to be taken at face value by any man with whom I have a relationship, but want him to dig a bit further, right down to the very core of me. Even to discover parts of me that I don't yet know exist. And I do believe that Stefano, with his playful and intelligent sense of curiosity, can do just that.

As the busy café buzzes about us, and the smell of fresh figs teases one of my twenty-four senses, I'm becoming acutely aware that I like this man more than anyone since Mark. I know I've only just met Stefano, but I already feel an extraordinary connection with him, like the universe has thought to itself, 'Oh heck, I've tested you enough, here's The One. On a platter. Now will you quit bugging me?' I've never quite believed in love at first sight, but right now I'm willing to be proven wrong. There's just something about him – everything about him in fact – that speaks of warmth and intellect and integrity and … well … downright sexiness.

And then suddenly I notice it. The Ring. A shiny gold band on his wedding finger.

Damn, damn, damn. How could I have missed that? I was so busy being a moth drawn into the flame that I forgot all about due diligence. It's quite one thing to date a married man for purely research purposes, but quite another to fall head over heels for him. Damn.

'You're married?' I say lightly, trying not to sound like I care, and somewhere in the back of my mind it's suddenly making sense why he's put me up for the night with his friend John.

'Yes,' he replies without a twitch, 'but I was curious. I am broad-minded always, and open to suggestion.'

And he leaves it maddeningly at that, which means I still don't know if a) he's happily married, b) in the throes of a hideous divorce and about to be single, or

c) single and just wearing the ring to throw annoying Australians off his scent. I'm hoping like crazy it's c), but just in case it's not, I decide not to ask anything more about his family – wife, kids, pet terrapins, anything. Because then I can simply ignore the fact that I've just met the most amazing man – who seems to tick all the boxes, and then some, and even reminds me a little of my father with his impressive naval involvement – but that he's off limits. And this way maybe I can get to the end of our date without feeling like a hungry dog having a bone dangled in front of it.

As we sup on a gorgeous lunch of pumpkin and green poppy seasoned celery cappuccino – a soup topped with such delicate pale green froth that a barista would be impressed – and cod pancakes with green tomato cream, I'm determined to find out as much about Stefano as I can. Just for me. Blow the book – it's about time I had a real date.

Stefano tells me that he's not just a naval architect but also an aeronautical engineer – which impresses me no end because he'd have to be seriously smart – but then he cheerfully tells me that in the US aeronautical program he failed the sexual harassment test. Three times.

'What? How?' I ask, horribly disappointed, not having picked up he was a sleaze.

'In one test they watch people's body language,' Stefano tells me. 'They send pretty women into the room and see how they react. But if a woman walks past, of course I will look. I am Italian! So finally,' he adds, with a laugh that comes from somewhere very deep and warm inside, 'I got special dispensation due to my culture.'

And I can't help but chuckle too. Only the Italians.

'So, Stefano,' I say, a little breathlessly, 'just what *are* the twenty-four senses you mentioned? I can't think of that many.'

Stefano sits back in his chair and looks at me with his bright, all-seeing eyes. He has so much energy I can feel its pulse from the other side of the table. It's so uplifting to find someone of such keen intelligence, and who's playful with it, not like many men I've known who were smart but cruel. The barrister who said I had a brain the size of a peanut. The film-producer who said I was a 'fill-in' between real girlfriends. The IT boffin who said my carefully prepared paella looked like someone had thrown up on his plate.

'Textures,' Stefano says. 'Cool, soft, smooth, warm. Sun on face, salt on skin. Music, a blackbird outside your window. To smell *tartufo*. The list can be even longer depending what makes you feel alive.'

Oh dear, I'm liking this man very much. Shiny gold ring or not.

After our meal comes the question of coffee, which is a tricky one, as caffeine does to me what LSD does to chipmunks. I love it, but even a cappuccino gives me such a heart-racing high that it takes me twenty-four hours to stop doing somersaults on the roof. So my rule is none after 10 a.m. or I'll be awake all night. I look across to Stefano who's sitting there like some delicious chocolate-dipped biscotti.

Decisions, decisions.

'Yes,' I say, crossing my fingers under the table. 'I'll have an espresso. Double. Thank you.'

Stefano has an afternoon meeting, so I spend the rest of the day bouncing around the back streets of Rome like someone's wound my gears up to full spring, then let me loose. I'm not sure if the heart palpitations and light-headedness are from the coffee, or from the thought of seeing Stefano again, but either way, by early evening I'm still a bit manic, and having trouble deciding what to wear that will best impress Stefano. I end up choosing the Black Widow Spider outfit, as after all, wasn't it the Italians who invented the colour black? And then when the doorbell rings, after I've changed and then changed back again, I take a deep breath and just hope I've got it right.

When I open the door, Stefano looks me up and down, nodding approvingly. Not in a chauvinistic, patronising or judgemental sort of way, but – I suspect – from a more generous place in his heart. A place where men don't see women as mere decoration, but as – well – women. Which I've got to say, does wonders for an ego somewhat deflated after some of my recent dates. And only makes me more enamoured of him.

Damn.

Stefano and I head down in the elevator, but we haven't even got to the first floor when I feel one of the press-studs in the crotch of my lace bodysuit go 'pop' and it's undone. I wonder if it's an omen. I'm careful not to catch Stefano's eye, as I don't want to give him the faintest impression that I fancy him, for that would surely send him running. No – I'm going to play it cool. I know I'm reneging on my deal to be more open and honest in my dealings with men, like I'd tried with Eduard, but look where that got me. Nowhere. And

Stefano's ten times more gorgeous, so I have to get it right. To be gentle. 'Softly softly, catchy monkey', as my Mum would say, and she won my father over, so it's worth a shot. Then, once Stefano's fallen madly in love with my winsome charms, I'll crank up the pace a bit.

We catch a taxi, leaving behind the busy streets of Rome, and meandering up a long and winding road beneath a handsome avenue of towering ancient oak trees.

'I am taking you to one of the best views of Roma,' Stefano says in an accent as luxuriant as cashmere. 'It is on one of the Seven Hills. I think you will like it.'

'Pop' goes the second press-stud.

We drive through the grand wrought-iron gates of the Cavalieri Hilton, where we enter a ballroom-sized marble lobby with huge white-on-white floral arrangements, and sculptured fish gargling water into granite basins filled with white roses. We are then ushered upstairs into a restaurant with a broad *terrazzo*.

'We are not eating here,' Stefano says, leading me outside. 'But we have a drink with a nice view.'

For a moment I'm speechless, as 'a nice view' hadn't prepared me for the spectacular sight below. Night has fallen and beneath its velvet mantle Rome is all lit up like a firefly convention. Before me are two of the seven hills and the softly illuminated dome of St Peter's Basilica arching majestically into the blackness above. Buildings well familiar from history books glow golden-yellow, and the tail-lights of cars stuck in traffic on Via Flaminia – once an ancient Roman road – look like a procession of red-eyed centaurs. It's so beautiful that I have to suck back in a little spurt of tears so as not to smudge my mascara. Stefano seems pleased at my reaction. He leads me back inside where we sit on huge white couches, and as if on cue a waiter brings out two champagne flutes on a silver tray.

'The best sparkling wine in Italy,' says Stefano. 'It's like French champagne but better.'

It's a 2005 *prosecco di Valdobbiadene* from the north of Italy, just below her boot cuff. The drink is fragrant, elegant with a delicate nose of peach and apple, and it's going to my head so fast that I've already given up the thought of writing any notes tonight. In fact, I couldn't care less if I just wrapped things up right now and never had another date in my life. Apart from with Stefano.

'Pinot *grigiou* is like a woman,' I hear Stefano saying through the haze, and I realise I've missed a great chunk of conversation whilst I've been spinning about in my own little universe, complete with exploding suns and spiralling galaxies.

'It only grows if taken care of,' he's saying. 'No care – no reward. It's like a princess. I think perhaps you too, Bambi, are a princess.'

Now I've been called a princess before – by Harry, who thought it was cute – but with Stefano I'm not quite sure what he means. In Australia 'princess' is a term reserved for spoilt little misses who can't even hoist their Louis Vuitton totes onto a train rack for fear of snapping a fingernail. Unlike me, who's already hauled my Samsonite with a wobbly wheel through seven countries. I'd hate Stefano to think I was pathetic. Or precious. Or even worse – stupid. For me, being thought of as stupid is tantamount to a beauty pageant contestant being called ugly. After all, never having thought of myself as beautiful, I had to have something about which to feel proud, and being reasonably smart was about all I thought I had.

Stefano must see the horror on my face. 'What I mean is you deserve to be treated like a princess,' he says gently.

I suddenly want to cry, for a thousand reasons, and all of them to do with the emptiness from which I've been trying to escape, and the love I'm so desperate to find. So maybe I *am* a princess after all, if even the tiniest grain of perceived criticism bruises me so deeply – like a pea twenty mattresses down.

I'm saved from bursting into tears by the arrival of Alex the waiter, who presents us with a plate of appetisers, then patiently explains each offering, giving me time to collect myself.

'Here is a *crème brûlée di fegato di anatra*. Crème brûlée of goose liver,' Alex purrs. 'It is to be eaten with a gold spoon.'

At first I think I've misheard him, but then I see it – a gold teaspoon, tucked in beside a small white dish crowned with a delicate caramelised glaze. A gold spoon. Oh yes. Silly me to be confused. Of course a crème brûlée of goose liver must be eaten this way.

Stefano leans back nonchalantly into the embrace of the couch and smiles. 'Silver or stainless steel oxidises and affects the taste,' he tells me. 'It must be pure on your tongue so you think of nothing else.'

Speaking of which, I'm not thinking of much else either, as with every little beguiling trick Stefano pulls out of his neatly turned sleeve, I'm becoming even more infatuated. But, to bring me back into the Now so I don't make a complete idiot of myself, I try the best I can to focus on Alex's ongoing culinary commentary.

'Here we have *spigola dorata fritta su letto di rucola e olio al basilico*,' Alex says, the words rolling off his tongue like an acrobat at the Circus Maximus. 'And this is *alici con zenzero e salsa al lime*.'

The dishes Alex is presenting don't just sound good, they look good too. The *spigola dorata* is a delicate piece of fried sea bass with a single curl of rocket wrapped around its shoulders like a feather boa, and the *alici con zenzero* are anchovies individually threaded like dollar signs onto wooden skewers, and drizzled with dark syrupy oil. I cross my legs carefully to preserve my third and last press-stud – as a mishap now could prove extremely embarrassing with such a short skirt – and eat the morsels one by one, so as not to mix the flavours, each of which is worthy of a gold medal, let alone a gold spoon.

'I'm overwhelmed,' I tell Stefano, who – again – seems pleased at my reaction. Not, I suspect, because it makes *him* look good for having organised such a treat, but because it's making *me* feel good.

'*Buon appetito*,' he winks at me, and as we sip the rest of our *prosecco* whilst the lights of Rome blaze away beneath us, I feel a little dizzy, like I'm floating, lost somewhere between one of the world's most ancient centres of civilisation, and a place in the clouds where Venus – Goddess of Love – surely resides.

After the appetisers we head for the famous Trastevere neighbourhood with its gorgeous medieval cobblestoned side streets. On Via dei Genovesi we duck our heads beneath the lintel of Osteria, a cosy little restaurant buzzing with locals, where the owner greets Stefano warmly. The air is heavy with the rich scent of garlic and grilled meats. Stefano has booked a table right beside a glass partition into the kitchen, where we can see the four deep-fry tubs and eight burners going full bore, and the six cooks in white aprons at a stainless steel workbench madly chopping and peeling and mixing and whisking with barely a moment to draw breath.

'What would you like to eat?' asks Stefano, handing me a menu written in Italian, which I'm happily unable to read.

'I'm in your hands. You make the decisions,' I reply, a little breathlessly.

Stefano looks at me for quite some time with a cheeky grin playing on his face. 'Okay, I will for now,' he says, 'but you will have to make some decisions later.'

I nearly fall off my chair. Decisions about what? Eating dessert? Having sex? Not that it really matters what he means, because I'm happy for him to make the call for pretty much everything in the next few hours. And I mean everything. The only decision I can foresee me having to make is whether or not to get on a train tomorrow and leave him behind.

Our wine is a *falanghina* from Campania – a nicely floral white with a vanilla finish. 'It's a bit *frizzante*,' I say, showing off about the only thing I remember from a wine appreciation course I did before I left Australia in order to impress my dates.

'Yes,' Stefano replies, 'like life.'

Now Jens was good, and Olivier was better, but Stefano is making them both look like first graders in the School of Charm. And he delivers it with such warmth and sincerity that I'm deliriously believing every word he's saying. Although there is one question I should ask him before the evening progresses any further. Just so I can avoid any embarrassment or heartache or knuckle-chewing later on. So I bring out my question-naire as if it's a frightfully official document, and one to which I don't have any personal attachment. Which of course I do.

'So what's the deal on infidelity?' I ask Stefano, feeling my ears turning pink. 'Are affairs acceptable in Italy?'

Stefano smiles knowingly, and looks right into my soul.

'Men compartmentalise,' he replies. 'They put things in boxes. Sex. Love. Trust. It all can be kept separate.'

'And so does that work for Italian women too?' I ask, hoping it cuts both ways. In which case there'll be less chance of finding myself with a bowl of minestrone over my head if Stefano is indeed married and his wife tracks us down.

Stefano leans back in his chair. It's the first time I've seen him quite so serious, and I'm guessing I've hit a nerve. 'Not so much,' he says. 'A woman has to have the whole package, she's not so happy with different boxes.'

Now perhaps I'm a wishful thinker, but such a com-ment leaves me with the very strong impression that Stefano – perhaps having juggled those boxes once too often – is indeed separated. Which means that maybe – just maybe – there's a chance of him and I hitting it off, and who knows where that may lead? Indeed, the more I find out about Stefano, the more hooked I become.

He sails, he cooks, he game fishes, he skis, he travels extensively. He thinks in a past life he was a Viking. He thinks in a future life he'd like to be a woman. Not because he's weird, but because he's the sort of man who wants to experience everything life has to offer. He's *la dolce vita* personified.

'A fish,' Stefano replies, when I ask him the animal question.

'Why?'

'Because I am free to explore new depths, and places that have never been discovered before.'

I nearly choke on my wine. He's not only exciting, he's dangerous, and I'm starting to fantasise about him leaping over the table, kissing me passionately, ripping off my clothes, and … well … discovering places that have never been discovered before. And yes, there are still a couple left.

My thoughts are interrupted when the waiter sets down a large plate, neatly laid out with thin slices of meat, translucent like the finest handmade lace, scattered with small brown shavings of unidentifiable origin. It smells absolutely amazing – like earth and poetry and hot summer nights – and I bend my head to the plate reverently to inhale it deep into my lungs.

'This is sea-bass carpaccio with truffles,' Stefano explains. 'You eat first with the nose, then with another four or five senses to appreciate all the dimensions.'

The lacy carpaccio is so delicate it falls apart as I lift it. The taste is subtle, and only slightly fishy. The flavour of the truffle is exquisite; however, it's quite impossible to accurately describe it – perhaps somewhere between the rich black soil of an enchanted forest, and heaven.

Maybe this is a good match for Stefano.

Another plate arrives – oysters, prawns, clams and an octopus carpaccio in such incredibly thin slices and not a chewy sucker in sight, I'd never have guessed what I was eating. It's sweet and delicately flavoured, helped along by a drizzle of fragrant Sicilian dressing.

'I had some great octopus in Monaco. France too,' I say, blissfully wiping a dribble of oil from my chin.

'French is shit,' Stefano responds, grinning.

More dishes arrive – seafood linguini with smoked cod-roe, a bowl of *fettuccini e porcini*, and a salad of baby fennel and blood orange. I try to protest that there's already far too much food, and with even more to come I'm worried that it will be more than my press-studs popping.

But Stefano won't have a bar of my remonstrations. 'You don't have to finish it, but I want you to at least taste all the flavours of Rome,' he says encouragingly, sliding yet another portion onto my plate. 'This is homemade spaghetti with garlic, oil and red pepper.'

'It sounds hot – perhaps this is your food match?' I suggest, emboldened by my second glass of wine.

'Well, it doesn't look that good,' Stefano says as he looks at me unwaveringly with those hypnotising eyes. 'But it's *very* good, and you only know it when you taste it. When it's in your mouth you can appreciate the full flavour.'

Things are getting steamier by the minute, and it's not just coming from the pots bubbling away in the kitchen. Stefano seems to be a consummate flirt, and I'm thinking that tonight might be the night to finally flick off that annoying

Miss-Goody-Two-Shoes-Keep-Yourself-Nice-Party-Pooper from my shoulder, and go for it. It's been six months since I was with Mark, and quite frankly I'm missing the sex. I love sex, and I used to have lots of it. But now I feel like that last chocolate in the box, blotchy and crazed and brittle on the outside, and dried up inside. Not having sex for 183 – and a half – days simply isn't healthy for a red-blooded woman.

So what the heck, let's see where some flirting gets me.

'So what Italian food works as an aphrodisiac?' I ask, this time not shifting my gaze when he catches my eye.

'Spaghetti,' he replies, after some consideration.

I laugh, hardly thinking that anything as limp as spaghetti could be a turn-on.

'Why?'

'Because you can eat together, each starting at the other end and eating it to the middle, and then seeing what happens,' Stefano says, not breaking his gaze either. 'But it's not a food so much that's an aphrodisiac,' he adds, 'it's a place and a state of mind.'

Then he looks at me even more intensely. 'And do you know that the hypothalamus in the brain controls urges for both sex and food? If you like food, you must like sex too.'

Stefano says this just as I'm halfway through slurping down a triple strand of garlic-infused spaghetti, and clearly enjoying it. Ah, now I understand why he's been watching me all evening with a knowing little smile on his face. Indeed, I've been gobbling food like there was no tomorrow.

How embarrassing.

Once the plates are cleared, Stefano suggests we have an espresso to finish off, which I decline as I'm still having heart palpitations from the double at lunchtime. 'Maybe for your book I'm an espresso,' Stefano suggests.

'Why an espresso?' I'm thinking that's a little too bitter for him.

'Because it is quick to drink, but intense and very good,' he replies, whereupon I get the unsettling feeling that he's been reading my mind like a Romani gypsy, which means he's probably picked up on the bodice-ripping table-top fantasy. Oh God.

By the time we get through an after-dinner liqueur – an amaretto that tastes like liquid almond cookies – I've pretty much convinced myself that Stefano isn't married. If he were, surely he wouldn't have been quite so charming, quite so suggestive, quite so generous – because yes, he absolutely insists on paying for dinner despite my protestations. Just as he had for lunch. I know he's Italian and such behaviour comes with the territory, but if he were married surely he'd have held back a little? And surely he wouldn't be inviting me to go somewhere else for a nightcap?

But he does, and of course I say yes, because married or not, I don't want the night to end. Ever. And just flirting is fine. Surely?

Beneath a nearly full moon we stroll arm in arm through the empty streets of Rome, strangely quiet on a Thursday night, with the normally exuberant fountains in the piazzas turned off, and a few sheets of newspaper dancing in the breeze like pagans at an Easter festival. And as we walk I ponder again why I like Stefano so much. I don't think it's just because he's exceptionally charming, and warm, and smart, and funny. It's something more – something that transcends the superficial and obvious. Stefano, it seems to me, grasps life like there's no tomorrow, squeezing from it every sweet ounce of juice. And I'm enormously attracted to such a quality, because I too am a great believer in *carpe diem* – seize the day. And I also believe that you can add so much flavour to your life if you're just willing to add a few extra ingredients to the recipe. A pinch of positivity, a spoonful of good humour, a good slug of courage. And with Stefano so piquing my interest, it's not just sex I'm fantasising about now, but a vine-clad cottage in Tuscany, with – heck, let's go for broke – Antonietta, Paola and *bambino* Stefano tumbling about under my feet.

As the slightly ferocious dolphins in the Fontana del Pantheon seem to lick their lips at me as we pass by – or that could just be all the wine I've drunk – it suddenly occurs to me that I might be feeling all soppy about Stefano because I've finally found a man from whom I don't feel the urge to run away. Or in whom I keep finding petty faults like he's too short, or too chubby, or too handsome, or too nice. And why should I? Stefano seems to me about as perfect as they come, and as the bright lights of the Piazza Navona up ahead flicker warmly in the purple gloom of night, I dare to hope that perhaps there's another life for me, at the ripe old age of forty-seven. Because … well … because I think I've finally found The One.

Vineria Botticella Café looks welcoming, with part of its front window stacked with backlit bottles of liqueur, looking like stained-glass in an old church. We pull up tall stools right beside the bar, and Stefano orders a round of semi-frozen *limoncellos*, which he insists I try for my 'education'. *Limoncello* is made from the macerated skins of lemons grown in southern Italy, and is the second most popular liqueur in the country, regarded as an excellent digestive. Even though it tastes like lemon candy, it has an alcohol content of around seventy-proof, which is enough to put hairs on your chest. Or perhaps feathers, given it's the same bright yellow canary colour as Tweety Bird. And although I know I shouldn't have it if I want to keep my wits about me and not let Stefano know I'm starting to fall for him in a big way, I'm on a roll. So I finish it off, then follow it up with a *sogni di notte* cocktail, for no other reason than it translates as 'dreams in the night'. And I can see why, for it's a very sexy drink, with an under-the-covers silky smooth flavour of vodka, coffee liqueur, amaretto and cream that sends naughty shivers down my spine.

But I have a problem with drinking. The first two or three drinks usually make me feel as happy as a pig in a truffle patch, but then I start to go downhill rapidly, beating myself up for what I perceive to be a million inadequacies – too tall, too thin, too pointy, too dumb, too eccentric – so with each sip I take I'm getting increasingly pessimistic that anything's going to happen with Stefano. And let's face it, why would anyone who I think is so amazing be interested in me? Seriously? It's just not a great fit, like asking Giorgio

Armani to wear a homebrand tracksuit. Comfy perhaps, but a bit baggy around the bum. So if I'm to be kind to myself, the sooner I back off the better. If I get any more cracks in my heart, I'll just bleed out. Besides, if he *is* married, forget it.

'I recently went to a restaurant in London with incredible food,' Stefano says, flipping me the business card from Nobu, a famous Japanese eatery. 'I'm going there in three weeks.' He pauses casually. 'You should come.'

'To the restaurant, or to London?' I ask playfully, still happy to flirt. After all, it's not over 'til it's over.

'Both.'

'You're inviting me?' My heart flips like a pizza in the making.

'Yes.' Stefano looks at me intensely with those bright blue-grey eyes, as if challenging me to a duel.

I'm not sure how to respond, especially after the hard time I've just given myself. An avalanche of thoughts hurtle through my mind, which I'm utterly unable to process. So I just sit there gobsmacked, pretending to study the labels on the liqueur bottles behind the bar, and trying not to pass out.

But Stefano seems to be waiting for an answer, so I desperately search my mind for some throwaway line that will show I'm interested, but not too interested.

'I think I'll be in Russia then. I'll check my itinerary and let you know.' I sound appropriately nonchalant, but the moment these words leave my lips I realise I've probably just made the biggest mistake. Have I learned nothing these last few weeks? Yes, Eduard had taught me it's not so smart to show your underbelly too fast, but nor is it smart to play it too cool, as it can be mis-construed as disinterested, or playing games, which will surely only end in tears. My tears.

But perhaps all is not lost, as there's still tonight, and as we walk back to the apartment through the deserted streets, I'm becoming increasingly deranged with desire. Indeed, I'm tempted to throw all caution to the wind. After all, didn't the Romans also invent the phrase, *'Carpe di notte'* – seize the night?

So I take a big breath.

'It's nearly morning,' I say, as we reach the heavy wooden door to the apartment block, 'so it's almost silly going to sleep.'

Well, it's not quite as bold as I'd like, but this way nei-ther of us gets embarrassed if he's simply not interested.

Stefano doesn't reply, but looks at me intently. 'I have something I want to give you from the office,' is all he offers me by way of hope.

We ascend in the elevator, so close that our bodies are touching. Stefano doesn't move away. My heart is practically leaping out through my bodysuit, and my last press-stud is in grave danger of chucking the game in. I'm sure the temperature has just gone up ninety degrees. As we enter Stefano's office I'm wondering what he has in mind, and find myself strangely recep-tive to a bit of a boardroom-table frolic. Something I would never normally do, but hey, what's normal about tonight? But no, he's far too gentlemanly for that. Instead, he gives me a large box of Baci chocolates, and a beautiful travel diary. 'So you won't forget me too quickly,' he says. Then he walks me up one flight of stairs to his friend John's apartment, which has me thinking Stefano may make his move there. Not that I'm thinking all that clearly, as my brain is practically exploding, with all twenty-four senses on full alert.

I don't know what happens next.

Well, actually nothing happens at all.

There's not even a kiss goodnight, apart from a polite peck from Stefano on each cheek. No passionate embrace at the door. No lingering farewell or softly spoken *buona notte*. Certainly no ripping off of clothes. Nothing. Nought. Zip. Zero. *Niente.* Stefano simply leaves me at the door with a smile and a sparkle from those cheeky eyes, and he's gone.

Oh.

I feel like a pan of popcorn that has got to the point where it's about to go pop, then someone kills the heat and it's all over.

What happened? Or more to the point – what didn't? Was I too forward, or too cautious? Too serious – or too light-hearted? Or just too damned useless at ever making anything in the romance department go right for me? I let myself into the apartment and pull off my boots, then curl up on my little bed with its fancy wrought-iron bed-ends. I feel abandoned and confused and ugly, and incredibly empty. And before I know it, I'm crying, trying to muffle my sobs under the eiderdown so that John won't hear me from the next room.

It seems that there won't be any vine-clad cottage in Tuscany after all.

A text message comes through at dawn. I'm half dead

from lack of proper sleep – having spent the night plagued by nightmares of being trapped in a garbage compactor after being deemed to be well past my use-by date – so I can barely even find the phone let alone read the screen.

I eventually make out the letters swimming before my eyes.

Good morning Princess, the dream is over but it has left something that last forever in our soul. Sorry to not personify the real Italians, but I introduce you to Stefano.

I respond, although not particularly eloquently as I'm feeling somewhat numb.

Thank you, you are so special.

I slowly tap out the letters. He might not be a typical Italian, but who wants to be just another square peg in a square hole anyway? His reply is quick.

Just close your eyes, I will be your espresso.

I answer far more flippantly than I actually feel.

Yes, you are my *doppio espresso*, short and intense, refined, robust, sweet, and full of flavour. And you kept me up all night!

I'm not game to add that like an overdose of caffeine, he gave me such a rush I was on the verge of having a heart attack. If we're still going to meet up in London,

I need to keep a few cards close to my chest. He texts back straight away.

Well, it's best to sip espresso at the end of your meal, when the flavour lasts longer in your mouth.

I reply, frustrated yet exhilarated.

Now you are just teasing me.

His response?

No, I am tasting you …

VATICAN CITY
Soul food

After such an extraordinary date with Stefano, I'm exhausted, both physically and emotionally. I'm even wondering if there's any point in continuing my journey, now that I've found The One and he clearly doesn't feel the same way about me. Why keep torturing myself? I'm feeling so sorry for myself that I stay in bed for as long as I can, wrapped in my doona like a cannelloni, having fitful dreams of wearing a bridal gown sewn from old rags, and standing on the end of a jetty above a swirling, muddied river. I wake myself up just before hurling myself in, and decide to get to the Vatican as quickly as possible in order to keep myself distracted, and then to hightail it out of a city that now exhales the memory of Stefano from its very foundations.

Vatican City is the smallest country in the world, a walled enclave within Rome just forty-four hectares in area, with a floating population of around eight hundred – mostly men. I've chosen it as my 'V' country simply because of the challenge of finding a date in this location. I'm clearly not going to find myself a husband here, but I'm still curious to see whether there's any such thing as a romantic male stereotype in such a rarefied atmosphere, or whether his passion has been reserved for God.

I step over the painted white line that separates the Vatican from Italy proper, and find myself in a vast piazza bound by colossal Tuscan colonnades, four columns deep, and a central Egyptian obelisk towering twenty-five metres up to heaven. I feel like I've stepped back in time several thousand years, and that any moment I'll be surrounded by dancing maidens in white togas strewing petals upon the ground and chanting Latin at me. But as I join the snaking queue outside St Peter's Basilica, the mood is far from frivolous, and indeed, the pious solemnity of the Faithful in Waiting has already started to seep deeply into my very being, like syrup into a *crespelle*.

Once inside, I'm completely overwhelmed. There's a reverent hush so thick you could bottle it, and even though I'm not at all religious, I feel like a fraud walking in here on a mission to find a man rather than God. Angels and cherubs carved from creamy marble hold up busts of holy men and popes, and I swear they're each slowly turning their heads upon their cold stiff necks to look at me – condemning me for bringing into their sacred space such an impertinent project. I stop near an altar, my heart tight in my chest, as I suddenly wonder what on earth I'm doing. Perhaps I should have taken on Vietnam or Vanuatu instead, and not some holy place where if I'm deemed to be unworthy, I risk God striking me down with an almighty lightning bolt hurled at me clean through the mosaic cupola.

But then as I bow my head in shame, I notice the floor. The marble slabs look like food – here a caramel-and-chocolate gelato, there a swirl of crushed plum sorbet. To my left, a thick slice of Greek *halva*, to my right, marble cake. It's oddly mouthwatering, which I'm not sure was ever the interior designer's intention, but it means that even if I don't find myself a date, I'll at least have fulfilled my mission of trying out the local food. Well, sort of. But still, it's my other mission – finding a local man – in which I'm more interested, so I keep my eyes carefully averted from the heavens so as not to attract unwanted attention from You-Know-Who, and try to figure out how I'm going pull off such an audacious plan.

Eventually I head for one of the many confessionals scattered about, hoping to wangle my way in and have the full attention of a priest who won't be able to escape too easily. A guard eyes me suspiciously as I loiter outside an elaborately carved redwood booth, whereupon I smile broadly and ask him if I have to be a Catholic to go in. '*Si*,' he replies sternly, then follows me around for the next ten minutes watching my every move, which makes me wonder if he can actually tell the difference between Catholics and heathens. Do we style our hair differently? Wear pearl necklaces instead of rosary beads? Have a blazing X scorched into our foreheads? Whatever the giveaway, I'm not willing to create a scene, so I opt for plan B, which is to engage a roaming clergyman in simple conversation, and see what I can learn about him. I'm never going to find anyone born and bred here, but a transient citizen is the next best thing. And it shouldn't be too hard, as there are plenty of priests here, of all colours, shapes and sizes, so I can pretty much take my pick.

I plunge myself into the churning flood of people in the Basilica, feeling a bit like I'm bobbing for apples, and after a few depressing laps where it seems that men of the cloth are either bald, fat, old or have small forests growing out of their ears, I soon spot a priest who couldn't be more perfect. He's young and fresh-faced, with a wide, friendly smile full of huge white teeth like smooth granite tombstones, and wearing a black cassock with a clerical collar. He's leading a group of tourists around, to whom he's chatting in a light American accent, which suits me just fine, as there won't be a language barrier. I nickname my priest 'Gabriel' for the time being, and discretely tag along behind the group, feeling rather pleased I've avoided having to settle for a crusty octogenarian. Gabriel soon stops in front of a large iron door with a heavy metal grill, adorned by a stone-faced pope coldly ignoring a weeping woman prostrate at his feet. So much for Christian compassion. Gabriel asks the group if they know where this door may lead to, upon which there's a respectful silence.

'A tomb?' one asks eventually.

'The Pope's office?' asks another.

Gabriel smiles. 'The janitor's closet,' he says, opening the door and revealing the tools of trade within. 'Even the Vatican needs a place to put the brooms,' he chortles.

Gabriel continues on cheerfully, giving a frequently humorous running commentary about each statue or artefact we pass. I'm most impressed that he's able to maintain his enthusiasm for them despite there being countless dozens scattered about in every nook and cranny, all of which start looking pretty much the same after a while. Seen one pope, seen them all really.

But Gabriel is clearly devoted to his task, and I happily follow him around for the next hour, wondering how such a lovely young man could have turned his back on the 'real' world and entered the solemn environs of the Vatican, and all the deprivation that must surely come with it. When he's finished the tour, I gently take him aside and ask him if he'd be willing to answer a few personal questions. At first he's startled, but then relaxes when I promise not to reveal his real name, or publish his photo. And fair enough – I guess when you're in the God business you have to be squeaky clean, and this way if he inadvertently lets slip about getting stuck into the communion wine when no-one is looking, he won't get into trouble.

We find a place outside in the sunshine where we both gradually defrost after the coldness of the Basilica, but I'm suddenly tongue-tied. I mean, how interesting can a priest actually be, if he never dates girls, wears what's effectively a nightshirt during the day, and talks to someone Upstairs when there's no scientific evidence He actually exists? Which, come to think of it, makes Gabriel a lot more interesting than some of the men I've met this trip.

I soon find out that Gabriel is twenty-three years old, was raised in Atlanta, and is a seminarian, meaning he won't be a priest for another three years. I also discover that he studies not just theology, ecclesiology and philosophy, but art history, architecture and literature, the latter to keep himself in the physical world – to help ground him. He's a musician as well, composing and conducting his own music, and is a 'sometimes opera singer', at which I get a rather naughty image of him singing the 'Hallelujah Chorus' buck naked in the shower. Well – he *is* rather cute. And then I find myself asking a question that probably most people would love to ask of a priest or clergyman, but would be far too polite to. But not me.

'How do you cope with celibacy?'

Gabriel doesn't miss a beat. 'Being celibate is beautiful because it's such an intense sacrifice, and I feel closer to God for doing that for Him. It's my gift.'

'But you're so gorgeous!' I exclaim and pat both his cheeks warmly, which rather startles a group of Japanese tourists filing past. 'You're too lovely to be alone in that way,' I add, although as the words come out I realise such tactlessness could well remind Gabriel what he's missing out on. The last thing I want is to have him sitting on his cold little bed tonight chewing his knuckles.

'Yes, it can be frustrating,' he replies brightly, 'but life is much less complicated this way. No girlfriend dramas!'

Gabriel flashes me a toothy white smile, although I notice his eyes don't reflect quite the same enthusiasm. Indeed, I think I may have raised an extremely delicate subject. To lighten things up I ask him the animal question, but it seems to have the reverse effect, as this time his whole face clouds over.

'I'd *like* to be a dog,' he says pensively. 'I'd like to love, and be loved. To care, and be cared for, But that's not the reality of priesthood. It's really rather lonely.'

Gabriel sighs heavily, although then pulls himself together to continue on bravely. 'But what I think I actually *am* is an eagle. An eagle is like a shepherd looking over his flock, with its wings outstretched protectively. It's his job to look after others, rather than himself.'

I'm quite moved – no other date has shown such vulnerability. I put my arm around Gabriel's shoulders, and give him a little hug that's designed to say, 'Well, you may not be a dog, but you still deserve a cuddle.' At first he jumps at the physical contact like I've splashed him with cold water, but then he relaxes and smiles warmly back at me, as if I've touched not only his body, but also his heart.

As the somewhat melancholy bells of St Peter's start pealing, I remember I have to be on a train in less than an hour. It's time to scoot. And as I fondly farewell Gabriel, I think how truly blessed I was to have stumbled upon not only such a refreshing and spirited representative of the church, but also a man who's really rather delicious.

And I've just thought of the perfect food for him. The Vatican has no such thing as a national dish, and comparing him to Communion bread and wine is sure to earn me a one-way ticket to hell. But Gabriel's favourite food in the Vatican café is angel hair pasta served with shrimps, garlic and virgin olive oil, and that will do nicely. Conveniently, it's an Italian-American dish, and there's no doubt that Gabriel is just as angelic, warm, mellow, sweet and rich of soul. And yes – the virgin olive oil bit works too.

SWITZERLAND

A tasty side dish

It's a nine-hour train trip to Zurich, so I pass the time by thinking how cross I am with Stefano. Mostly because before I met him I was coping reasonably well not having had sex for six months. But when someone waves a fresh *doppio espresso* under your nose – with all its deep chocolate flavours and delicious velvety bitterness – you can't help but want it. And if you don't get it when you want it, then you can't help but start obsessing about it, so that it fills your every waking thought.

Curse him.

As a distraction, I eat three of Stefano's Baci, trying to make each one last as long as possible as I relive every moment of our date. But I just end up making myself feel even more miserable, so I send him a text.

The problem with espresso, is that too much is bad for you, but when you have just a little, you want more.

Stefano doesn't answer right away, so I'm convinced I've already disappeared from his life, which makes me doubly miserable. But a few hours later, my phone makes a friendly beep.

Yes, you are right. It is always better to not take an overdose. The effect can be unmanageable.

And then, just as I'm wondering if there's a defibrillator on the train I can use, another text arrives.

When you taste your espresso remember, the first sip is joy, the second happiness, the third pleasure, the fourth folly, and the fifth ecstasy. Then let your mind pick ... and call me!

I'm truly not sure whether this is Stefano's way of leaving things open for a rendezvous in London, or whether he's just tormenting me, but I decide for the time being I don't want to be a masochist, and switch off my phone to focus on my next date with Ali in Switzerland. Who knows, he may be able to take my mind off Stefano once and for all.

I wasn't going to include Switzerland in my trip, given I already had Scotland all scoped out for my 'S' country, but my friend Jessica in Brussels insisted that I meet Ali – a paediatric heart surgeon – who, although of 'Persian' or Iranian descent, has lived here since he was a child. So I reckon he can be a bit of a side dish. Besides, Jessica warned me, 'he has a reputation of being a serious ladies' man, and is very handsome, so watch out!'

So of course I had to meet him.

After arriving in Zurich, I wait outside the train station for Ali, hoping he won't be too handsome, or too smart, or too much of a ladies' man. Because then he may be disappointed with me, like Frank was. And on top of Stefano, I'm not sure I could take any more rejection. A silver Alpha Romeo pulls up to the kerb with an extremely good-looking man calling out to me through the sunroof. He has a rich, deep voice, as smooth as alpine honey, and his smile is broad and welcoming. I get a little thrill that he's quite so gorgeous, and am thinking my luck has finally turned.

But not for long.

The minute I'm in the car, Ali slouches back in his seat and looks a bit grumpy, and I can't help but feel that yes, he *is* disappointed. He's probably been fantasising about a mystery woman travelling the world dating men, and that coming from a Land-Down-Under, she'd be madly glamorous. Like Elle Macpherson.

Which I'm not.

Which puts me in a bit of a pickle. Ali had invited me to stay in his apartment, and I'm guessing that now he's regretting the offer, which has me wondering – again – why I've put myself into a position where I question the very point of my existence. Really, what *was* I thinking embarking upon such a crazy trip where I was bound to be checked over like emmental cheese on the production line? And having little holes poked into me?

However, after a shower I take a deep breath and join Ali in the sitting room, where Vivaldi is playing full blast. I'm wearing my Drop Dead Gorgeous outfit again – having given the lace body stocking a miss because I don't trust those press-studs any more – and slapped on some glossy lipstick. Upon seeing me, Ali warms up considerably, and offers me a glass of wine.

'You look nice,' he says. It sounds like he means it. Which is just as well, as otherwise it would have been a long night.

If Ali's living room is a reflection of his personality, he's got loads of it. Raspberry-red walls are covered with paintings, including several of his own acrylic abstracts, and a huge painted mandala from Thailand. A stunning lamp with seven giant tulip lights sprouts from the floor. There's a whole wall of shelves crammed with CDs from Madonna right though to Mozart, and equally as many books written in five different languages.

'But I actually speak seven,' Ali informs me, which makes me even less confident I'm going to have anything at all in common with him. But I'll still give it my best shot. I am after all a successful businesswoman, fearless globetrotter, and although not quite up to date with cardiac surgery, I still know quite a lot about the workings of the heart – at least romantically – so I'm sure I can cobble up something to talk about.

As we make our way to the restaurant through the pretty woodlands behind Zurich, Ali chats easily about some of his greatest passions, which aren't all that dissimilar to my own. Travel, food, and – well – not men like me, but women.

'Definitely women,' Ali's quick to assert.

Alter Tobelhof is a Tudor-style building with a cosy, ski-lodge atmosphere, and full of locals – a colourful mix of Swiss German, Swiss Italian and Swiss French

– an interesting blend that gives Switzerland its rich culture, along with the Romansh people. Ali and I are seated at a corner table upon which the waitress sets up an elaborate contraption – a stainless steel frame with a burner in the base, and a hinged hotplate above.

'It's for the *raclette*,' Ali explains, 'one of Switzerland's most famous national dishes.'

I'm delighted, as even though Ali is about as Swiss as a Persian rug, at least the food will be the real deal. Our first dish is *trio raclette*, three different types of cheese – garlic, pepper and a mild gruyère – which will be cooked on the hotplate once it's all fired up. In the interim Ali has ordered a red wine from Valais, and when it's poured he raises his glass and looks at me smoulderingly, his dark brown eyes boring right through me. He's got a heavy five-o'clock shadow, his black hair is as lustrous as a mink, and he's the sort of playboy handsome that spells trouble in capital letters.

'*Prost,*' he toasts cheerfully, and I'm beginning to think we just might get through the night after all.

When the waitress brings in a cotton bag full of small boiled potatoes, Ali enthusiastically shows me how to eat them. Mash up a few on my plate, add salt and pepper to taste, then tip the hotplate at an angle so the melted cheese just slides off and goes *gloop* all over the potatoes, covering them thickly like a sticky blanket. With the addition of gherkins and pickled onions it's very tasty, although with so much cheese it's as rich as a Swiss bank account, so I'm going to have to take it easy or that heart attack I dodged in Rome will surely catch up with me.

As I'm watching the next batch of cheese spewing

out little yellow lava flows, I'm thinking that this dish may be Ali. It's very rich and smooth, and sizzling hot. And I mean sizzling, which becomes even more appropriate when Ali reveals he's had his fair share of girlfriends over the years, and – I strongly suspect – sees himself as a bit of a stud. He even describes a procession of past lovers in terms usually reserved for residents of a royal game park – 'exotic, lithe, green-eyed, magnificent and gazelle-like'. It sounds as if he's the Head Gamekeeper. But far from rolling my eyes at such boasting, I'm delighted to have stumbled upon what may be the ultimate romantic male stereotype. And an Alpha male to boot. Still, I don't want to pry too much, in case he thinks I'm aiming to be another notch on his belt. I'm relieved then, when he makes it abundantly clear that I'm not his type anyway.

'My past girlfriends were all very attractive,' he says, which lets me off the hook beautifully. Indeed, I'm learning that there's a certain liberty that comes with being an Ugly Duckling, because people let their guard down, and give away all sorts of secrets they'd never think of revealing to someone they fancy. So with renewed confidence I start grilling Ali shamelessly about his love life, and soon find out that the kitchen plays an important role in his seduction techniques. Whether it's to cook a fabulous meal and impress a woman to the point that 'she gets so turned on she just throws her pants down on to the floor, and that's it', or others to whom he can 'just give burnt popcorn and they will think it's sexy'.

But it's not just the kitchen that brings results. Ali confides that there's a little gesture he uses to win women over, and he shows it to me without a hint of self-consciousness. He clicks his fingers, and then points decisively toward his imaginary 'prey', with his head slightly bowed so that he looks up through his amazing eyelashes – long and thick like a camel in the Iranian desert.

I laugh. It's a bit over the top, like something that Fonzie from *Happy Days* would do. Although I concede, coming from Ali it is indeed very sexy. Cocky, but sexy.

'And what's it mean exactly?' I ask, a little hoarsely.

'It means ...' and he repeats the move, which I assume means, 'I want you. Now.'

'And it works?' I query, wondering why the room has become so hot.

'I can get any girl I want,' he replies, looking for all the world like a sleek black panther.

'Really?' I ask, trying not to sound unconvinced. I mean, he's very attractive and speaks seven languages, but *any* girl? 'How do you spell it?' I ask, with just the teeniest hint of sarcasm.

'Click. Done.' Ali says, shrugging his shoulders. 'I click, it's done. She's there.'

'Click. Done. That's all?'

'Yes.'

Ali fascinates me, and I'm desperate to know what makes him tick. He's quite the most narcissistic man I've ever met, but it's oddly forgivable with him, because he really is a hot package. He's got the looks, the brains, the career and the lifestyle. He knows about music, art, literature and interior design. And cooking, which he proves by demonstrating how to eat a fondue, another of Switzerland's national dishes. It's basically a big pot of melted, bubbling cheese, into which people with a clearly suicidal lack of concern for their cholesterol levels use long three-pronged forks to dunk various ingredients, such as chunks of ham or bread, mushrooms, gherkins, and fresh fruit, and then try to get it into their mouths without scalding their chins from the long strings of molten cheese that stretch halfway across the table.

After eating so much fondue that I feel like a block of Swiss cheese, it's time for the animal question. I'm very curious as to how Ali will answer. Will he say lion, which would suggest power? Or stallion, which would suggest virility? Or peacock, which would suggest vanity?

'Black panther,' he growls gently. 'It's predatory and potentially aggressive, but it's also obscure and laid-back. And very cool.'

I laugh. A panther is exactly what I'd thought when he was demonstrating his 'click – done' seduction technique. I can easily imagine him all lean and dark with eyes gleaming in the night, prowling through the jungle on soft feet so his prey can't hear him coming. They wouldn't stand a chance.

After dinner we make our way back through the pitch-black woodlands, with only the odd glow-worm flying past to give us any sense of space or dimension – like a comet in space. At Ali's place the lights are dimmed and the music is pulsing seductively, and I can sense the black panther is restless. Over dinner Ali had made it clear he wasn't interested in me, but now we're back in his den I'm not so sure, especially as I'd read somewhere that panthers are opportunistic hunters.

I don't want to hang around and give Ali the impression that I'm up for a bit of random naughtiness, as even after nearly popping like popcorn in Rome I'm still a 'good girl' at heart, so I quickly head for my bedroom, where I wedge my suitcase firmly against the door. Just in case the panther decides that a Bambi makes a tasty after-dinner snack.

In the morning I find Ali in the kitchen, padding about in bare feet and brewing up fresh coffee. My God, if he was gorgeous yesterday, then today he's just ridiculous. He's wearing grey-and-white army camouflage pants and a baggy grey t-shirt, and his hair is sticking up in a just-out-of-bed look that's seriously hot. I'm suddenly very pleased that our go-between Jessica is flying in today, and will be staying the night with us, as another twenty-four hours under the same roof may have proved too much for me to resist. Then again, I'll be facing stiff competition from Jessica, as she's single and fancies Ali, so it's anyone's guess how the night will pan out.

Ali has arranged to take Jessica and me to a Marseilles Night, which is being held under the grand grey stone arches of a railway viaduct, below which trestle tables are magically set with crisp white cloths, and silver candelabras drip wax like stalactites in a secret grotto. Romantic French music is bouncing around the arches like a drunken Cupid, and waiters pass around tasting glasses of French wine. It's hardly very 'quadri-cultural', but as it's just a side dish, anything goes.

After taking a sip of one of the reds, Ali is clearly impressed. 'Ahh. This wine is as good as sex,' he says, eyes sparkling.

I try it, and find it to be nice, but as good as sex?

'Ali,' I snort, 'if you think this is as good as sex, then you've been missing out on a lot.'

'Bambi,' Ali responds, rolling his eyes at me, and slapping both hands hard against his chest. 'Do you know who you are talking to? And besides, I said as good as sex, not better than. Nothing is better.'

The second wine smells of toasty peach and pear, and is unbelievably smooth, with a soft vanilla aftertaste.

'*This* wine is nearly as good as sex,' I laugh. 'Although it's probably too smooth. Sex should be a bit rougher.'

Good grief, the wine must be getting to me, because that's far more risqué than my normal party patter. And I'm certainly no dominatrix. But I'm feeling safe now that Ali and I have got over the first night. Besides, with Jessica here, nothing untoward can happen, so I may as well have a bit of fun with him.

A waiter brings us a platter with six fist-sized oysters nestled on a cosy bed of stringy black seaweed.

'I'm not sure if we should eat these,' I tease. 'Ali might find the combination of two women and oysters too much to resist.'

'I don't need oysters,' Ali replies, looking insulted.

The bouillabaisse is served, upon which I close my eyes and fill my nostrils with the unmistakable scents of the ocean – so fresh I can almost hear the cry of seagulls. The aroma is so thick and sweet that it's practically a meal before I raise a spoon to my lips, and the flavour is outstanding – smooth and elegant, rich and luxuriant, although with quite a God-almighty kick from the cayenne pepper. Which gives me an idea.

'This is you Ali,' I blurt out. 'Bouillabaisse with cayenne pepper.'

'Me? Fish soup? First I'm a side dish, and now I'm a soup?' Ali scoffs. He doesn't look pleased.

'It's a compliment,' I reply, not bothering to explain myself, so he can just sweat on it. I'm enjoying not being quite as enthralled by him any more. When he's taking himself so seriously, he's really quite good to tease. And I'm clearly out of the running anyway, as Ali has just admitted he's dating a South African woman, with whom he's clearly besotted, sending her text messages every ten minutes and carrying on like a lovesick teenager whenever she responds. Indeed, I'm getting an insight into the softer and more vulnerable side of our host – making me suspect that in the right hands, Ali the Panther may just be Ali the Pussycat.

After main course there's an impressive cheese platter, and still more wine. My rather addled brain estimates that's five glasses I've had already. Maybe six if you count four half-glasses. I don't know. I'm not much good at maths – especially when I'm tipsy. But it doesn't stop there, as next it's a sticky wine, which is so delicious that I don't particularly care that I'm getting more sozzled by the minute. Jessica and Ali aren't holding back either, and when we get back to Ali's place well after midnight, we're all so upbeat that we hunker down in the living room and keep right on drinking.

'This is much more civilised,' Ali tells Jessica, as he spreads himself across an enormous leather couch, like a panther basking in the sun. 'Bambi just went straight to bed after dinner last night,' he continues. 'Two minutes and voom, she was gone.'

'What were you expecting?' Jessica laughs.

'Well, I thought maybe …' Ali replies, his words trailing off in an uncharacteristic display of uncertainty.

'But you'd made it clear you weren't at all interested in me,' I squeal good-humouredly. 'And I'm not going to sleep with you just because it's convenient for you that I'm in the next room.'

'Well,' Ali says, looking hurt, 'I have to tell you something. I lay in bed for ages and couldn't sleep.'

'Why?' I hoot. 'Not because of me?'

'To tell you the truth, yes.' Ali replies, and I can't tell if he's embarrassed or proud. 'I had a hard-on for three hours.'

Jessica and I erupt into peals of laughter, although in a way I'm oddly flattered. After all, it's better to be looked over than overlooked, and every woman likes a bit of attention, even if it is by a panther with more kills than Bagheera.

'Poor Ali,' I tease, 'I didn't know. I'm sorry. But maybe if you'd clicked your fingers, I'd have been there in a flash.'

It's Ali's turn to laugh, and he does his seductive little move before pouring Jessica and me another glass of wine. And I can't help but think that if I was in a bar somewhere, and there he was clicking his fingers and making camel-eyes at me, I mightn't think it was so silly. And who knows what might happen?

At 4 a.m. I announce I'm off to bed, as I'm about to collapse with exhaustion – and most likely five too many drinks. But when I come out of the bathroom, Ali is in our bedroom with Jessica, who's laughing loudly. I'm startled. He's wearing no more than a pair of blue boxer shorts, and an enigmatic smile. His hands are on his hips, and I try not to look, but I can't help noticing his beautifully toned body, and dark skin the colour of wet desert sand. He's hairy too, but not overly so, with a sexy fuzz down his arms and across his neatly sculpted chest, with a curly little patch on his belly before it disappears behind his short-fronts.

My God he's hot. Matching him with cayenne pepper was a serious understatement.

'You have a very hot body, Ali,' I say calmly, 'but why are you in our bedroom with only your boxer shorts on?'

'I don't know. I'm still awake,' he replies, before disappearing again, leaving me to finish getting changed.

I'm about to jump into bed when I sense a strange silence coming from beyond my door. Something's up, so I wander down the hall and poke my head through the open door of Ali's bedroom, only to find he and Jessica standing very close together and talking in whispers. The room looks like Aladdin's cave, with deep-red walls and a huge bed in the corner with no legs, just a base and mattress. Several Balinese stone carvings mounted on the wall hold gently flickering tea lights, and two larger candles beside the bed are casting dancing shadows on the wall. The air is thick with a heady mix of incense and sexual tension, and I quickly back off, realising I've barged in on something to which I'm clearly not invited.

'Oops,' I say, 'see you in the morning.'

Ali and Jessica slowly turn to look at me. Then Jessica laughs throatily.

'Ali thinks we should all stay in here,' she says.

'I beg your pardon?'

'Ali thinks you and I should stay in here and sleep with him. Together.'

My mind is foggy and I'm finding it hard to grasp exactly what she's saying. Indeed, the longer we stand there, the more I feel like I've been caught up in an audition for an erotic movie. Although with daggy ol' me hanging about in my man-shirt – which I quickly button up a little higher – they're risking one completely out-of-place cast member.

'You and me? With Ali?' I eventually squeak. 'You mean a ... a threesome?'

'Yes, why not?' Jessica replies matter-of-factly. 'He's never done it, you've never done it, so why not?'

'Um. And whose idea is this?' I say, not that it really matters, but I'm just trying to buy some time.

'Ali's. But why not?'

'No, I don't think so,' I reply, my mind starting to spin. 'I told Ali I'm not interested in sex just for the sake of it. Never have been, never will be.'

And although I mean it, I still can't seem to walk away. So we all stare at each other for a few moments, as the red walls seem to close in like a giant womb. Then Ali comes over to me. I can just see his black eyes in the half-light. He's smiling in a sort of black-panther-prowling-in-the-night sort of way.

'Come on,' he purrs.

'No, I don't do that sort of stuff,' I say, my voice coming out a bit strangled. 'I'm shy, I can't.'

Ali starts unbuttoning my nightshirt. Very slowly and softly. And I'm not stopping him.

My God – am I actually going to do this?

Jessica laughs in the shadows, and moves towards the bed. Ali gets to the last button, and kisses me on the neck.

Oh, what the heck.

I awake to dawn pushing softly against the red gauze curtains of Ali's bedroom, colouring everything inside with the molten glow of a steel furnace. The candles are still flickering in their stone niches. The smell of incense hangs in the air. I recognise it now – Arabian spices, and a hint of musk. My eyes struggle to focus. Someone's foot is pressed against my face. It's brown and smooth with fuzzy black hair on the ankles, and neatly mani-cured toenails. Ali's. I focus on the ceiling and try to get my bearings, and realise that my head is at the foot of the bed, and I'm only half covered by the doona. I see another foot across the other side of the bed. It's pale and its toes have light pink nail polish. Jessica.

Oh. My. God.

I wait until I'm sure Ali and Jessica are asleep, and then grab my shirt – still crumpled in the door-way – and tiptoe to the bathroom, fervently hoping I don't wake anyone up before I have time to collect my thoughts. And perhaps call a taxi and get myself the hell out of here. I sit on the loo with the lid down, and press 'replay' in my mind, although I'm rather wishing I could erase any recent memories. That way I'd never have to deal with the horror of what I've done.

Yes, I was drunk, but not overly so. I knew what I was doing every step of the way. I was in control. Well, that is, when I wasn't out of control and doing cartwheels – and God knows what else – across the bed. But still, I can't believe that I've just indulged in a *ménage à trois*. That's definitely taking my research a little too far.

Oh. My. God.

As my heart pounds like a performance of the Swiss Army Drum Corps, I decide not to continue beating myself up. It's not like I did anything too kinky, and my attentions were focused on Ali rather than Jessica, which means I haven't suddenly changed camps. So why worry? I should simply look at it for what it was – a fun night. Slightly wild for sure, but fun. Besides, I'm here to find out what turns men on, so why not find out what turns me on too?

Still ... Oh. My. God.

By the time I'm showered and dressed, Ali and Jessica are up too, eating toast and apricot jam in the living room. Ali is wearing only his camouflage pants, and in the cold hard light of day he's still drop dead gorgeous, so that as horribly embarrassed as I am, I'm still rather thrilled that if I was going to be so naughty with anyone, it may as well be with him.

'Well, that was interesting,' I say as calmly as possible, not wanting to make a huge song and dance about it, for fear of just making it worse.

Thankfully they both seem to be totally cool about the situation, and we eat breakfast like nothing's happened. I feel a bit bad about Ali's girlfriend, but then again, it's all Stefano's fault. He got me to the point of nearly exploding like a pan of popcorn, and then took the heat right off. So what's a girl supposed to do?

After breakfast, Jessica and I prepare to head off on the next leg of our journey, and I say my goodbyes to Ali, kissing him lightly on both cheeks.

'Yes, you are definitely the bouillabaisse,' I say. 'Complex, exotic, loads of flavour, richly textured, and with truckloads of spice.'

Ali nods, clearly happy with the match, and as we drive away, he clicks his fingers, points at me, looks up through those amazing eyelashes, and smiles.

'Told you so,' he says triumphantly.

Damn.

LIECHTENSTEIN
Say 'cheese'!

I originally thought getting a date in Liechtenstein would be a breeze. After all, the entire country is only 160 square kilometres in size, meaning I shouldn't have far to go to bump into someone suitable. But then I had that unsettling online experience with men clad in black rubber, and with bottoms better suited to alpine marmots, and I worried that even if I found a date, the event might be too X-rated to share with anyone but fans of *Fifty Shades of Grey*.

But Ernst came good, and even better, he seems to be quite a catch – being a member of parliament, prominent lawyer and published author. It wasn't until a week before I left Australia that I found out he was married, which although rather stymieing my original hopes of meeting The One (or at least, Another One), didn't worry me too much, as he's still a man, still a local, and still – hopefully – a fitting representative of his country. And even if he's absolutely charming, there most certainly won't be a repeat of the whole Stefano – is he? isn't he? – fiasco over whether he's married. I've learned my lesson that no matter how much fun it is to flirt with danger, it usually bites you on the bum one way or another.

I also have a date with the owner of the pensione in which I'm staying, who's been sending me flirtatious emails ever since I asked if he knew of a man for me, and he offered himself.

```
Yes, I am happy to meet you. I am good-
looking enough, except I am a bit too heavy
for my height, but that just shows that I
love food. I am a true Liechtensteinian.
Let's meet for dinner.
Kind regards,
Martin
```

I tried to tell him I didn't have that much spare time because I was only going to be here for one evening, and had already organised a date with Ernst, but Martin had already thought of that.

```
Wink wink. Nudge nudge. You forgot the
night. lol.
```

Cheeky devil.

Driving into Liechtenstein from Switzerland is simply breathtaking. A vivid slash of green valley carpets the base of blue snow-capped mountains with sides so steep I'm surprised the cows can keep their footing. As we approach they look at me curiously through thick black eyelashes, their floppy grey ears twitching at the odd dragonfly buzzing past. Brass bells hung around their necks tinkle melodiously as they make their way carefully along well-trodden paths behind A-frame houses with time-blackened wooden shingles, and window boxes exuberant with red geraniums. There's a castle perched further up the hillside, although it's solid and sensible and lacks the fairytale beauty of most European castles, which makes me wonder how romantic the local men are. I don't have a clear picture of a stereotypical Liechtensteiner, but I'm thinking he'd be earnest, hardworking, domestic, neat and friendly, with occasional hilarious bouts of leather-slapping when he's drunk too much of the local red wine.

Once in Vaduz, Jessica and I wend our way up to our hotel, which looks like a ski-chalet on an old-fashioned chocolate box. It's here that I'll meet Martin to discuss the logistics of our date.

An extremely large man is tightly wedged behind the reception desk. He'd have to be 140 kilos, with grey curly hair and a little grey beard, and rimless spectacles. He looks like a middle-aged version of Santa Claus – well before he discovered that eating the cookies left out by every single child on the planet was fattening.

'Hi,' I say, 'we've got a booking for one night, and

I'm also meeting a chap called Martin.'

'Yes, we have a date tonight,' he replies with a dead-pan face.

I'm not sure what to say. I don't mind Mountain Men, but men the *size* of a mountain scare me. I'd worry that if we got intimate I'd be squashed flat, not being particularly robust myself.

'Um,' I say, before recovering my composure and flashing him a smile, because he has kind eyes and an open face, and that's all that really matters. 'Great,' I continue. 'Although it can't be dinner, so would break-fast suit?'

'So now you've seen me you don't want to date me any more?' he replies gruffly, at which I'm totally lost for words, because no, that's not the reason at all. But then he sighs heavily.

'Okay, let's make it lunch,' he says, 'in my restaurant. Now.'

The restaurant is closed between dining sessions, but Martin generously organises the chef to open the kitchen so I can try out the national dish of Liechtenstein, 'the way it should taste'. I'm delighted at the opportunity, but also wary, as the dish to which he's referring is *käsknöpfle* – grated noodles topped with a trio of cheeses and onion fried in butter – and quite frankly I need to eat more cheese like a cow needs rollerskates. I'm also aware that the dish was originally created by poor peo-ple combining all their old cheeses – which had turned sour – and cooking it. Hardly an appetising thought. Still, I follow Martin's lead in tucking a napkin into my collar in readiness for the feast ahead. But I should have donned a gas mask too, as I can smell the meal before it's even out of the kitchen. It absolutely stinks, like really whiffy socks on a cross-country skier after a three-day marathon. I poke at the sludgy contents of the bowl disconcertedly, before Martin assures me it tastes much better than it smells. So I take a leap of faith that he's not pulling my leg in some quirky tradition of tormenting tourists – like the deer's blood in Germany's Jägermeister – and take a bite. And it's great. Indeed, I'm soon tucking into it with gusto, the melted cheese stretching into thin strands as I eat it, and then snapping apart and springing back into my face. The dish is surprisingly light – at first – although after half a bowl it's far too heavy and rich to continue, and I have to admit defeat, just taking the occasional nibble so as not to offend Martin.

But Martin's clearly made of sterner stuff, for he polishes off the whole serving like a baleen whale sucking in krill. I'm beginning to understand why he has a problem with his height-to-width ratio.

As we eat, Martin talks cheerfully of his life in Liechtenstein, and although I discover he has two young daughters about whom he's clearly crazy, he carefully avoids mentioning a wife, so I'm guessing he's single, or unhappily married. Which might explain why he's been quite so flirtatious in his emails.

Sadly, I don't have much time to get to know Martin because my 'real' date with Ernst is looming, but if I was to sum him up I'd compare him to *käsknöpfle* with apple sauce, for although somewhat bland in appearance, it surprises with its richness of flavour, and an underlying sweetness tinged with a not-distasteful sourness. It's forthright, honest, heartwarming and has a certain confidence about it – like it knows it's homely but that's not going to make it take a back seat in the restaurant. And he's as resilient as sticky cheese too, as when I apologise that I don't have the time to get to know him any better, he looks at me intently and tugs at his beard.

'Well, there's still the night,' he says poker-faced.

He had emailed a similar comment to me too. I don't know if he's serious, but I make a note to wedge my luggage against the door before I go to bed. Just in case.

I've invited Jessica along on this afternoon's date. As long as she doesn't get me into trouble like she did with Ali, she'll be a great asset if I get stuck for words with such a distinguished man as Ernst. We're meeting him at the frightfully smart Park-Hotel Sonnenhof, although he only has time for a drink or two, so I'll have to talk fast.

There's a pretty driveway into the stately grounds of the hotel – a turn-of-the-century white stone chateau warmed up by lemon-yellow awnings and cascading purple geraniums. The drawing room could be in someone's private home with its bookshelves lined with pale-green linen-bound books, huge blonde-leather couches with plump rolled cushions, Persian rugs scattered everywhere, and antique coffee tables in an eccentric mix of shapes and sizes. Ernst is already here, lounging comfortably on an oversized armchair in sumptuous red brocade. He looks right at home – all he needs is a smoking jacket and he'd be Master of the Manor. He's a very handsome man, about fifty years old, with a neat little beard, and such twinkly blue eyes they're almost sending out sparks. He's wearing a navy-blue blazer over a dark turtleneck sweater and grey slacks, and looks about as stylish as they come. Indeed, he'd give those Italians a run for their money. Ernst greets Jessica and me warmly, and promptly buys us a drink before I can offer to do the same for him.

'*Zum wohl,*' he toasts enthusiastically, 'it means "to health". And now tell me what on earth I'm doing here meeting two lovely ladies from the other side of the world?'

Ernst is very charming and easy to talk to, even though the more he divulges, the more I realise what a high-powered man he is. He was the first person in Liechtenstein to study commerce law in New York, and to get his law degree there. He was once an eminent politician but is now semi-retired, although he still has his finger in a dozen pies, including the renowned Liechtenstein Symphony Orchestra, boy scouts, law, banking and economics. He even plays a 100-year-old Austrian harp, both professionally and privately, for which he's earned the nickname Harp Daddy. And he also acts.

'Yes,' Ernst says, clearly enjoying himself. 'I was the First Knight in the musical of *Dracula*. I look quite fetching in chain mail and body armour, if I may say so myself. Oh, and I'm hand-building a huge underground cellar at my home,' he says proudly, almost as if that's his greatest achievement of all.

'What for?' I ask, trying not to let my mind wander to that Liechtenstein website with people in dungeons doing rude things to each other.

'Absolutely no idea,' he replies heartily, 'but why not?'

By now I feel comfortable enough to press Ernst to divulge more about his private life, and soon learn that as well as having a clearly creative side, there's a romantic – or at least sensual – side to him.

'Ankles are an erotic sign. I knew immediately she was my woman when I saw her ankles,' Ernst says, referring to his wife with whom he's very happy, even after having six children together.

'Six children. Imagine that!' he laughs. 'I was prac- tising Family Planning, but I was so diligent that rather than just doing it once a week, I was doing it twice a day!'

I love the fact that Ernst is being so frank with me. He may have a beard, but he's not hiding behind it, as I suspect many men do. Still, as up-front as he is, I'm not sure how he'll take my next question, given he's clearly highly intelligent and may think it beneath him.

'And if your personality was an animal, what would you be?'

'What?' he laughs so loudly that he startles the wait- ress. 'That's a great question! But gosh, I'm so many I can't choose.'

'Perhaps a chameleon if you are so many?' I suggest.

'No,' he answers decisively. 'Not a chameleon. I don't hide myself.'

Hah – I was right.

'Maybe an eagle, or an albatross,' he continues. 'An eagle is free and powerful, and an albatross ploughs the world above. Both are creatures of substance, but still independent, and sometimes solitary.'

And so the conversation continues, with Ernst coming across as an open book, and certainly one with many chapters. I'd love to have the time to read it in full, because although I've met many lawyers in my time who've taken themselves far too seriously, Ernst seems very relaxed in his own skin. Well, when he's not jumping out of it that is, being so full of energy. Before long the three of us are chatting like we've known each other for years, and even vowing to keep in touch once we've departed. Which means a lot to me, as with every date I go on, I put my pride on the line. But it's people like Ernst who teach me that there's a whole world out there of delicious men. And whether or not any of them turn out to be The One, my life has more flavour already.

'Or maybe I am a bull,' Ernst continues enthusiastically. He's not finished yet, and his eyes are shining ever brighter. 'They're very strong, down-to-earth and not very flexible. They're fast and quick and sturdy.'

'And a food?' I ask. Well, I may as well get good mileage out of him now that he's all warmed up.

'A potato,' he says, after a moment's consideration.

'A potato? The humble spud?' I laugh. 'No way!'

'Oh yes,' he replies cheerfully. 'A potato has many varieties, all of which have a distinctive taste, and this is me with all my interests. A potato is useful, and it feeds the world.'

I still don't think Ernst is a boring old potato. He's far too open-minded, colourful, visionary and sharp-witted to be plonked in the same category as Sam Spud down at the village green, with his knee-length breeches and his traditional flat black hat. Silk smoking jackets are far more Ernst's style. But it begs the question whether or not Ernst is a typical Liechtensteiner.

'No,' he responds definitively. 'Liechtensteiners can be very narrow-minded, almost as if they are hemmed in like the mountains either side of them. I'm not like this.'

I have to agree. There doesn't seem to be anything hemming Ernst in. To him life is a journey, not a destination. There may well be a horizon for which to aim, but then there'll be another. And another. And along the way, I suspect he'll extract from life every ounce of marrow that it offers.

I'd love to stop and chat forever, but Ernst soon jumps up to leave, having cheerfully overstayed by more than an hour.

'It's been a pleasure. Or two,' he says, kissing us both warmly on our cheeks, his beard tickling me rather deliciously. He's such a rich and heartwarming personality that it's been like breathing in an entire bowl of *käsknöpfle*. But without the calories. And if he wasn't married, I'd be hanging around for a month or two on the shameless pretext of taking glockenspiel lessons.

Jessica and I have a five-minute break before we're due in the restaurant to meet our next two dates – organised at the last minute by Martina from Liechtenstein Tourismus, who is clearly on a roll. As I'm reapplying my lipstick in the bathroom, and wondering where those bags under my eyes came from –

so large I'll be charged excess baggage on the next flight
– I once again think how crazy it is to be meeting such
an exhausting procession of men. It's like speed-dating.
It's true that I'm meeting loads of interesting people,
but it's becoming increasingly frustrating to have to
keep on moving and not have the chance to really get
to know them beyond a fairly artificial dynamic. I have
to sum them up in just a couple of hours, when really it
would take months to get to know them properly. Like
starting a three-course meal, and never getting to dessert. So as a result, I'm always left feeling a little hungry.

The rest of the evening is a bit of a blur – a procession of more pre-dinner cocktails, and a fabulous dinner
in the hotel's one-Michelin-star restaurant, presided
over by one of the country's top chefs – Hubertus Real.
The parsley cream soup is a masterpiece, elegantly
presented in a fine porcelain demitasse, with the soup
such a startlingly bright green, topped with a deep
layer of froth as light as air, I feel like I'm ingesting the
misty-morning breath of dragons. And with the odd
medieval castle dotted around these parts, it seems
perfectly appropriate. The soup itself tastes absolutely
exquisite, with an intense parsley flavour tempered delicately with cream. It reminds me of Ernst, because like
him it starts off reasonably subtle in flavour, but then
develops a warm and deeply complex character. It's a
dish with tremendous personality, and certainly one of
the more memorable taste sensations of the trip.

We finish off with late-night drinks at Café Wolf,
which is a fitting end to my stay in Liechtenstein,
given its legends of werewolves roaming about the
forest. Coincidentally, it's a full moon, which makes

me wonder if it won't just be Martin waiting up for me tonight back at the pensione. Although by the time Jessica and I drag ourselves back to the hotel at 2 a.m., I figure any self-respecting werewolf will have gone to bed. Martin too. I hope.

I get through the night with no scratching at the door from either man or hairy beast, but in the morning I still feel a whole lot worse for wear. Two nights of drinking is taking its toll, and I decide to back off for the next few days, given I'm still not even halfway through my mission, and I'm beginning to wonder how I'm going to find the fortitude to visit the rest of the countries on my itinerary. As I nurse my throbbing head back down the valley towards Switzerland, I'm seriously tempted to call it all quits, and head home to Australia where I can just eat Vegemite on toast without being all philosophical about it.

But of course I won't, as I've never been one to leave a job unfinished, and so I'll continue with my gruelling schedule, inspired by a quote from mountain climber and author Barry Finlay: 'Every mountain top is within reach if you just keep climbing.'

Well if it doesn't kill you first.

HUNGARY
Cereal killer?

I don't know much about Hungarians, but fortunately

I'm sharing a couchette on the train to Budapest with a pretty bottle-blonde who's happy to share her views on the local men.

'My last boyfriend tells me, "You are the one,"' Hajnalka says plaintively, 'then a week later I found him in bed with another woman.' She looks pained, then brightens up as she adds, 'But most Hungarian men are very attractive, interesting, charming and amorous. They make you feel special and are very passionate. The only problem is it's hard to find one who will stay true to you. If they find something better, they just move on.'

It sounds like a bit of a lucky dip, but it's faintly more promising than some online descriptions I'd found, including one suggesting that Hungarian men were 'hairy and rude', and 'pervasively sexist'.

But I had still decided that I'd have more luck finding The One here than my only other 'H' options – Haiti and Honduras. All that voodoo business freaks me right out, so I'd rather risk 'hairy and rude' than having six-inch nails jabbed into my effigy if my dates there decided they didn't like me.

I'm staying on the Pest side of Budapest, which is the 'lively pulsating urban half' of a city commonly regarded as the Paris of Eastern Europe. And deservedly so, with its imposing avenues of grand five-storey buildings, some adorned with enormous statues of musclebound men wearing no more than skimpy marble loincloths as they hold aloft mighty stone columns – the strain showing on their grey faces in little rivulets of white tears. There are church spires everywhere, many with quaintly bulbous bases like oversized spring onions, and the Triumphal Arch is big enough for a herd of giraffes to pass through. Indeed, much of the architecture is so exaggeratedly huge that I feel like I'm Alice in Wonderland after being shrunk down to the size of a teacup. It's all very imposing and beautiful, give or take the occasional mortar-pocked wall from the Soviet tanks back in '56, like scars that have never quite healed. I suspect in more ways than one.

My destination this morning is the famous Great Market Hall – the largest and oldest indoor market in Budapest – where I'm hoping to get some culinary inspiration for my two Hungarian dates. The Hall is a Neo-Gothic splendour that looks more like a church or a convent than a place to get your spuds. There are also pastries galore, candies, meat, fruits, fish and spices, most of which have been so painstakingly arranged into perfectly symmetrical mounds that I wouldn't dare upset the balance by buying anything. But as colourful and impressive as it is, there's nowhere near the same spirit as most other European markets I've visited, with their crazy shouting and flipping fish and the odd stray onion rolling cheerfully down the aisles – that delightful chaos which is surely the very soul of most markets. Instead, the stallholders here are earnest and business-like, and when I ask a butcher if I can take a photo of him with his racks of bright-red smoked sausages, he half smiles and rubs his fingers together, intimating that he wants to be paid, and frowning at me when I back off. In fact, I'm finding that no-one here is particularly friendly, and smiles are rare. Maybe it's the language barrier, or maybe they don't like tourists coming to gawk. Which is fair enough I suppose, as the Mongols, Turks, Habsburgs and Soviets have been invading for over eight hundred years, and perhaps the locals are just sick of it. But there's something else in the grey faces that I see here – something tired and heavy and a little hopeless, which I'm guessing is more to do with them only having recently – in 1989 – crawled out from under the shadow of communist rule. And then, with years of socialist sloth and corruption effectively bringing the country to its knees, they've spent most of their lives just trying to survive.

I turn my attention to more cheery locals – the radishes and eggplants, tomatoes and cucumbers, and a bewildering variety of peppers – or paprika. These range in colour from almost black to bright red, through to pale green and yellow. And even milky white, which I think is very tricky of them, because they look so innocent, although I suspect they're not. Once bitten, twice shy. I just hope there's a colour-coded warning system for paprika when I'm eating out here, so I don't end up burning off whatever tongue I have left after that fiery little incident in Brazil.

But it's the salamis that really catch my eye, and perhaps for all the wrong reasons. Because – well, quite frankly – they look a lot like what you'd see in the men's sauna room at a UN convention – long and thin, short and fat, wrinkled and tight, white and grey, red and brown, speckled, freckled and downright scary. I blush as a stallholder catches me out staring at them, and I scurry away quickly to hide my shame at the goose stall a little further up. Although, I wish I hadn't, as now I'm confronted by whole plucked geese hanging ungracefully from their beaks on butcher's hooks, their big dimpled feet with their pink webbing delicately folded like bat's wings.

As I'm thinking that I should perhaps have avoided Hungary after all, and risked my body parts in Haiti, my attention turns to the locals doing their weekly shopping. The women aren't overly attractive en masse – at least, not like the Dutch, or even the French – and seem to favour bottle-blonde hair or unnatural shades of red, which looks a bit odd on heavily Slavic features. The young dress provocatively in miniskirts and net stockings, with their – often clearly fake – breasts brazenly on display, whilst the older women look like they've just given up. The men have strong, broad and handsome faces, and a high proportion have moustaches or neat little goatee-like beards. I don't normally like facial hair on men – like they've got something to hide – but it suits the Hungarians, who look all the more masculine and confident for it.

After the market I'm on the hunt for goulash – a meat, potato, barley and paprika soup or stew, traditionally eaten by Hungarian cattle herders or stockmen. The dish is more mainstream these days, and it seems that every restaurant serves it, but I opt for a stylish venue – the Cyrano Restaurant Bar – simply because of its fabulous decor that's right out of a Gothic fantasy, with embossed black velvet curtains, and an extraordinary four-metre-deep black feather chandelier. Now, I should have known that there's a direct correlation between feather chandeliers and menu prices, but by the time I discover that the *gulyasleves* is a day's wage for the average Hungarian, I'm already tucked into my table with two waiters at my elbow, and another at the door – presumably in case I cut and run.

Still, when the goulash is eventually brought out in a crisp white bowl, I don't care about the cost, as the aroma is irresistible. It's sweet and spicy all at once, and oddly comforting, like I've stepped back in time and am sitting around a campfire with a bunch of friendly stockmen, one of whom is playing folksongs on a double flute. At first the goulash looks like plain tomato soup, with swirls of oil and fat on its surface, but when I plunge my spoon in, I discover there's a whole world beneath of flavour and texture that's both rich and luxurious. It's a real stick-to-your-ribs kind of soup, and I can feel it warming my soul with every mouthful.

I finish the bowl off in no time at all, wondering whether my date with Andras tonight will be half as delicious. After all, I worked up quite an appetite with all the effort it took to secure a date with him. There were no less than four 'middlemen' involved. First of all a workmate Elly, her mother Eveline, Eveline's friend Gabrielle, and Gabrielle's Hungarian cousin Zsuzanna, who led to Zsuzanna's friend Andras. Quite an odyssey in itself before we have even got to the date. And it promises to have a tasty conclusion, if an email I received from Andras earlier in the week is anything to go by.

Hi Bambi,
This is Andras - your date in Budapest!
  I've taken the liberty to offer you my humble abode and some home cooking. Be

not afraid, my friends claim I'm a great chef, and none of them have died. Yet. :)

I'm going to prepare for you the famous *paprika's csirke*. It's a chicken stew served with a small gnocchi called *galuska*. A side dish would be a cucumber salad. I'll also get some good quality Hungarian red wine.

Tell me if this 'plan' suits your needs. :)

Cheers,

Andras

Andras is the first date to cook me a meal in his home, so I'm taking along some treats from the market, and a really good bottle of *tokaji*, wine from the region of the same name, to show my appreciation. I'm very excited to finally get a behind-the-scenes glimpse of a local on his own turf.

If I ever get there that is. Andras lives on the Buda side of Budapest, which necessitates me catching a tram across town and over the mighty river Danube. But once onboard, I can't find the ticket machine, and everyone just looks at me blankly when I ask for their help. So here I am on the tram wondering what the punishment is in a socialist country for travelling without a fare, and hoping I'm not going to be dobbed in by that surly old woman opposite me with a face as wrinkled as an overbaked potato, and hands like gloves full of marbles.

I get to my stop without being arrested, and Andras is waiting for me with a welcoming smile. He's around thirty years old, and over collar-length hair is sporting

a white tie-down cap like rappers wear. His army camouflage pants are rolled up at the cuffs to show bike
tights below, and his red t-shirt is designer-grunge. It's
all very 'student-cum-gangster-cum-biker', and I feel
like I'm back in my uni days, although his neat beard
and impressively bushy sideburns are definitely more
'60s than '80s.

Andras greets me enthusiastically, and I'm relieved
that he speaks such excellent English, as quite frankly
all the *jsz*'s, *szia*'s, and *férj*'s are starting to do my head
in. Indeed, if I were to try to speak Hungarian myself,
I'd most likely end up dislocating my jaw. Andras leads
me back to his apartment in a very old building, with an
elevator that only works if it's called from the ground
floor, and has me wondering if perhaps that's another
reason everyone looks so grumpy in Budapest.

The apartment is the smallest I've ever seen.
Immediately past the front door is a kitchen about
the size of a tea towel, containing a teeny-tiny oven, a
teeny-tiny sink filled with dirty dishes, and a teeny-tiny
fridge that also acts as a workbench. I feel like I'm Alice
again having just consumed an Eat Me cake, and am
growing bigger by the minute. The hallway isn't so
much a hallway as a storeroom, stuffed with overflow-
ing bookshelves and three bicycles. The sitting room
also serves as a study and bedroom, with a very large
double bed in the corner. There's no space for a dining
table or chairs – just a stack of brightly coloured cushions and a rug, which makes me wonder where we're
going to eat dinner. But with the walls painted a fresh
orange-pink to impart a lovely homely atmosphere, and
cheery jazz music playing on the stereo, what it lacks in

area it more than makes up for in personality.

I've already decided that Andras isn't going to be The One, both because of his age, and the fact that I've never had much success dating men with facial hair, of which he has a fair bit. Kissing a beard or a moustache makes me break out into a rash, and invariably ends up in unstoppable bouts of sneezing. But I'm only too happy to be here, and whether he turns out to be a typical Hungarian or not, only time will tell.

And I don't have to wait long. I'm standing in the kitchen with Andras as he starts preparing the meal, when he suddenly turns to me and wags his finger.

'I must just tell you one thing about me,' he says almost apologetically. 'I am not a typical Hungarian man at all.'

'In what way?' I ask, amused that so many of the men I've met protest they're not typical – although I'm guessing they are.

'Well,' he says, carefully laying out all the ingredients on a chopping board, 'Hungarian men are jerks most of the time. They are unreliable. And they have a big macho attitude.'

'But not you?'

'No, not me,' he snorts dismissively, 'I prefer to keep to myself and smoke pot.'

'So you're not interested in girls?'

'Oh yes, of course,' he's quick to clarify. 'Although the problem with Hungarian girls is they can be beautiful, but they have no sense of style.'

Hah, and this coming from a man wearing army pants and tights.

As Andras prepares the meal, he gives a running

commentary on his progress, and pretty soon I'm wondering if I've got myself involved with a chef, or a psychopath.

'First you chop two chicken fillets,' he says, fastidiously trimming off the excess fat and skin before painstakingly cutting them into bite-sized chunks. 'You don't need to chop them, but I have a dark need – I like to chop. Then you take an onion and a clove of garlic, and you chop them too. I like to chop, did I tell you that?'

By the time he's peeled, seeded and cut the tomatoes with the skill of a surgeon – or Jack the Ripper comes to mind – I'm backed up hard against the front door, evaluating whether I could escape quickly if the need arose, although that faulty elevator could cause some problems.

'Then you take a paprika,' Andras says cheerfully, 'the official Hungarian paprika which is sweet. You can get this in orange or yellow or green, but I like orange because they are prettier.'

Just as I'm starting to relax again – rationalising that if he was a psychopath or homicidal maniac, he would have made his move by now so as not to have to prepare enough food for two – Andras turns around and waves his knife around in the air, a small strip of chicken skin jiggling disturbingly from the blade.

'If I was a serial killer,' he says, 'I would be very good at it. Professional even.'

'Why?' I ask as calmly as possible, feeling for the door handle behind my back.

'I like cutting things up as you can see,' he explains cheerfully, 'and I am very neat.'

I wonder how the Hungarian police will break it to my parents that I've been murdered. And they've only been able to find a few bits of me floating down the Danube, like discarded sushi. But fortunately Andras decides he's done enough chopping for the day, and tosses the knife into the sink and out of harm's way. I heave a sigh of relief, and vow never again to watch films such as *Silence of the Lambs* and *Saw*.

While the meal is cooking, we head into the living room for pre-dinner drinks and nibbles. I'm hoping Andras doesn't offer me the bed to sit on, just in case things turn weird, so am relieved when I get 'the best cushion of the house', a velvet hippy thing with huge pink-and-green flowers. We sit on the floor and tuck into a large platter of antipasto, each item of which Andras goes to great lengths to explain to me, including the *kolbász*, which is Hungary's traditional smoked sausage. It's bright red and looks dangerously hot, being thickly encrusted with flakes of dried chilli. It even smells hot, which has me checking that the water jug is close at hand, just in case I need to stick my tongue in it.

'This is from a special kind of pig called a *mangalica*,' Andras explains, nibbling on the sausage with apparently no immediate ill effects. 'It's a very ugly pig, covered all over in wool.'

I'm rather taken aback. A woolly pig? That's a first for me, and rather puts me off the *kolbász*, as the thought of eating a fluffy little Babe is far from appetising.

'You have to be careful with Hungarian sausage,' Andras says. 'They can be extremely hot. Hotter than a hot day in Acapulco.'

'A hot day in Acapulco isn't very hot,' I reply

good-humouredly.

'It depends who you are with,' Andras says with a wink.

'*Egészségedre* – to your health,' Andras toasts as he pours out the *tokaji*, with which he's delighted.

My conversation with Andras is all over the place – or rather *he* is all over the place – but in a delightfully energetic and enthusiastic way, and I find myself growing quite fond of him, albeit in a big-sisterly fashion. I've always liked eccentrics, and Andras is no exception. He tells me he has a cactus called Oscar, and two other plants called Louis and Frigina. He even names his bicycles, and calls them his 'mistresses'.

'So which one do you give the most attention?' I ask.

'Always the one that I'm riding.'

Smart answer.

I discover Andras studied English literature as a major at university, which would explain why his English is so good. But I suspect he's also been heavily influenced by American sitcoms and TV dramas, and perhaps even the cartoon networks, as his conversation is littered with expressions such as 'okey-doke' and 'right-on', and when he's excited about something he speaks in capital letter, such as, 'KAPOW!' and 'BANG!'

He's also 'addicted to addictions', such as smoking, TV, sport, cycling and speed. 'And yes,' he says, 'I'll happily admit I'm a bit of a pothead.'

'That's okay,' I reply, 'I'm a fare-evader, so if we get caught, we can share a cell in the gulag.'

Andras tells me that his father died when he was just one year old, which means that he was pretty much raised by women. 'That is probably why I get along so well with them,' he says.

Although apparently not indefinitely.

'I've had twenty-five girlfriends, no – twenty-six,' he says glumly. 'And honestly, I'm tired of it. Girls are a bit tricky, so I'm not going to bother any more trying to find The One. I'm just going to leave it all to chance.'

I know how he feels. Sometimes I think I should just give up looking too, and let fate take its course. But then I remember that time is ticking away, and that use-by date is looming, so I can't afford to be complacent.

It's 11.30 p.m., and we've only just started on the main meal. But it's worth the wait. *Paprikás csirke* is one of Hungary's most famous dishes – chicken simmered in a paprika-flavoured sauce with loads of garlic and onion, and topped with sour cream and lemon juice. It's served with *galuska* or *nokedli*, which are little buttery pasta dumplings, and *uborkasalata* – cucumber salad in vinegar, garlic and more paprika. We eat sitting on the floor and balancing the plates on our knees, and at my very first bite of the chicken I can see why it's so popular, with its silky smooth, creamy, texture, and a mildly sweet, aromatic flavour.

'Fucking A!' Andras hoots in delight as he takes a mouthful. 'I'm a genius. It's even better than I thought it would be.'

We slurp our way through the main meal, and finish off with a fat slice of *Esterházy torta* I brought along. It's a dessert of chocolate buttercream sandwiched between six layers of almond meringue. It's so fluffy and light that it reminds me of a ballerina in a powder-puff tutu.

The night is drawing to an end so I ask Andras my animal question. I'm curious to see how this apparently confident, certainly hyperactive, and charmingly quirky man sees himself.

'An eagle,' he promptly replies. 'An eagle because it has freedom in flying, and can watch what's going on below without having to get involved. And it's proud and creative.' Andras pauses indecisively. 'Or maybe a cat. They just love being stroked. That's really all they want in life.'

This is the first hint of vulnerability I've seen in Andras, and suggests that his bluff and bluster is mostly about covering up his insecurities. But I can relate to that. I spent years acting like I was confident and sassy, so I perhaps came across as a bit of a rambunctious wildflower, when really I was just a simple wallflower at heart. And these days? Well, perhaps more of a dandelion head blowing about in the breeze, its future exciting, but uncertain.

Before I head home, Andras asks me what food I'm going to match him with. I can tell he's hoping he's made a good impression, and I'm only too happy to help boost his ego. When you're a little lacking in self-confidence – like that wallflower I used to be – a bit of fertiliser goes a long way.

'Probably tonight's *paprikás csirke*,' I reply, 'because you're equally as rich in flavour, quite sweet, a little spicy, and certainly as complex.'

'Yes, that's me,' Andras replies, clearly delighted, and purring like that cat who's just been stroked. 'I too am as sweet as a love, and as hot as passion.'

And on that note, I take my leave, and get out of there before he feels the need to start chopping up anything else.

Before I leave Budapest, I have a last-minute date with Attila the Hun. Yes, really. I was supposed to meet another man yesterday for lunch, but when he had to cancel, he kindly found me a substitute – Attila. I thought this was a joke, because I studied Attila the Hun at school, and can't quite believe there is a modern-day version. I mean, what mother would name her child after a ruthless barbarian known for tearing his victims limb from limb?

But incredulity soon turns to delight as I realise that I've now got a second date in Hungary, so I can get a better idea if Andras is typical, untypical or just plain eccentric in comparison. Brilliant.

I'm meeting Attila in Menza, a very smart restaurant in the fashionable part of town. He's extremely friendly and open from the word go, and I can tell it's going to be a fun night. He's a handsome man with strong Slavic features – thick black hair, dark eyes and a broad nose. He's stylishly dressed in a shirt with wide pale pink-and-white stripes, a light blue jacket, and has a thick gold chain around his neck. As he cheerfully leads me upstairs to our table, I'm taken by the walls papered in dramatic retro gold-and-olive chrysanthemums, and funky gold lampshades. It seems that not all of Budapest is in the doldrums after all. Indeed, it's so gorgeous here that I don't even care what the meal might cost me, as I'm a bit ahead on my budget, having only eaten bananas and Baci two nights earlier on the rare occasion of having a date-free night.

I don't challenge Attila on whether that's his real name – with a name like Bambi who am I to question its veracity? But he explains to me anyway that Attila is as common a name as John, and speaking of which, he actually looks a bit like John Travolta when he was younger – a rugged manly look with a confidence that I find very attractive.

Attila tells me that he's instructed the waiter – Ákos – to impress me.

'Impress me?' I ask, confused.

'Yes, for your research. I asked him to impress you with all the good food of Hungary.'

I've got to say, I like this man's style. A lot. He has a decidedly calm yet authoratitive way about him, which is making me feel very relaxed, and even a little light-headed.

Or maybe that's the *pálinka* – a type of fruit brandy – that Ákos serves with a dramatic flourish. It's usually flavoured with pear, plum or peach, but in this case it's quince and, according to Attila, the most special *pálinka* you can get. It's very good, with an elegantly bitter, citrus-like spiciness, and really quite smooth, although I wouldn't want to drink too much of it, or else I'll be going *pálonka* headfirst down the stairs on the way out.

It soon becomes apparent that this Attila the Hun is no marauding tribal leader, but a loving family man, as is demonstrated after he takes a brief call from one of his children.

'I always take their calls,' he apologises. 'It's a different ring tone to everyone else. Not even my wife has a special ring tone. I must always answer in case they need me.'

I'm very impressed. I knew Hungarians were supposed to be family oriented, but Attila has a real warmth and generosity of spirit to boot.

No sooner than we finish the *pálinka*, a glass of *tokaji* arrives. Attila explains that it's a *szamorodni*, which is different from most wines in that it's made from bunches of grapes that contain a high proportion of botrytised grapes, making it very sweet.

I take a sip and tell Attila that I can't quite describe its flavour.

'Shut your eyes,' Attila says, 'and think of a colour … what do you see?'

'I see yellow fields of grass,' I reply, delighted with his approach.

'Nature. You see nature?'

'Yes. And it's fresh and warm and light, like a summer afternoon.'

'Then that's what it tastes like,' Attila says with a huge grin spreading right across his lovely, friendly face.

It turns out that Attila is a very successful businessman, being the Hungarian General Manager for Red Bull energy drinks. He calls it the 'the nectar of youth', so much so that he's back to going to nightclubs, and feels younger than he has in years. Yes, I can just see him on the dance floor having got all fired up on it. Indeed, Hungarians are known for the unusually large amount of 'personal improvisation' in their dancing. The mind boggles.

Ákos serves up the entree, which I smile bravely upon, wondering how on earth I'm going to eat it. Or else politely refuse it. It's goose-liver puree, and frankly I don't subscribe to eating a product created by force-feeding a ten-week-old goose with litres of grain and fat via a tube shoved twelve centimetres down its throat, whereupon its liver eventually becomes so engorged it can grow to ten times its normal size. No, I don't 'do' foie gras, nor do I do veal – cruel, battery chickens – cruel, factory-farmed pork – cruel, monkey brains – outrageous, or live donkey salami – unspeakable. I'd really rather eat my own lightly sauteed earlobes. I look at the plate containing two golf-ball-sized scoops of *magyar libamájpüré*, and feel rather limp, but both Attila and Ákos are watching me carefully, so I really don't have much choice. In I go, and I instantly feel guilty that it tastes so good – very rich and buttery, and incredibly smooth and delicate – almost opulent. After three more bites I check myself, and surreptitiously push the last of it under the fried onions and rocket, quickly starting up a fresh conversation with Attila, so he doesn't notice what I'm doing.

Somewhat coincidentally, when I ask him what animal best describes his personality, he replies that he's a duck.

'A duck?' I ask, surprised.

'Yes, a duck can swim, but not so well like a fish. A duck can fly, but not so well like a bird. A duck can walk, but not so well like a panther. But it can do a lot of things quite well, which is me. And of course a duck looks after its family, and to me my family is the most important thing in the world.'

Attila pulls out a photo of his wife Magdalene and his three teenage children, and proudly announces he's been happily married for twenty-four years. Magdalene is a kind-eyed, plump-cheeked and homely looking woman, and it's obvious that Attila is still smitten by her. It's refreshing to note that not all the succesful men in the world are driven to only go out with wafer-thin supermodels.

'And what about infidelity in Hungary?' I ask, keen to compare notes with so many other countries I've visited where it's clearly quite acceptable. Maybe he'll break the mould in that respect too.

Attila looks serious and puts his elbows on the table and his chin in his hands. 'It happens of course, but affairs are not okay in Hungary. If it happens, people try to hide it because they are ashamed. An affair is a reason for a divorce. And besides,' he adds, smiling broadly, 'why would we want to cheat? Hungarian women are the nicest women in the world.'

'And who wears the pants?' I ask, recalling that Hungarian men are supposedly a little sexist, which was what Hajnalka had also intimated on the train.

Attila smiles broadly and leans back in his chair. 'My wife is the boss. Absolutely,' he says, his eyes shining with pride. 'She's brighter, smarter and quicker than me, although she's not pushy about it. She says, "I'm okay if my husband is the head of the family, as long as I'm the neck." She controls everything, but that doesn't make me weak, it makes me even stronger knowing she's there to support me.'

I hadn't expected that. Attila is really one out of the box. A strong man who doesn't try to subjugate a woman just because he's a male. This guy is as far from Attila the Hun as sweet hazlenut cake is from sour cherry strudel.

But such a realisation about Attila makes me feel sad too. Sad that I've not met anyone in my life to be there for me like Attila is for Magdalene. At the rate I'm going, I'll be lucky to get twenty-four weeks out of a relationship, let alone twenty-four years.

Fortunately the bean soup arrives just as I'm tempted to start wallowing, so I turn my attention back to being a cultural detective, which isn't hard to do, as the food keeps coming. And coming. We eat *bab leves* – a thick bean soup with smoked ham hock, navy beans, sausage, onion, garlic, potatoes and sour cream. And paprika – of course. Next is a fantastically melt-in-my-mouth beef tenderloin surrounded by a thick serving of *lecsó* – a vegetable dish of baked tomato, peppers, onion and garlic. And paprika – of course.

We drink a rare wine called *kadarka*, from the Villány wine region of Hungary. The deep aroma hits me before I even taste it, and the first sip is heavenly, packed with notes of cherry, orange, dried figs, almonds and black pepper. *Kadarka* is often used for making *egri bikavér* – bull's blood of Eger – Hungary's most famous red wine, with the name originating from the invasion of Suleiman the Magnificent, where it was rumoured that bull's blood was mixed into the red wine to give the attacking soldiers superior strength. Given that Attila runs Red Bull, the connection is perfect.

Attila tucks into the meal with gusto, then looks at me curiously. 'I'll ask you a question now,' he smiles. 'What animal are you?'

Such a question only serves to prove that Attila is a deep and thoughtful man. Only a couple of other dates have asked me this question, and I think it says as much about him as it will say about me.

'You tell me,' I say playfully.

'A fox.'

'And why?'

Attila smiles, and doesn't take his warm brown eyes off me. 'You are smart and curious and like to explore,' he says kindly. 'But you are also shy, and don't want to be in the glare of the spotlight. You are lone, a survivor and very brave.'

My eyes prick with tears at this summation, as it's not lost on me that foxes are often misunderstood and villainised. And often spend their whole lives alone.

Fortunately, I'm saved once again from tormented musings when Ákos brings yet another *tokaji* for me to try. That makes it my sixth glass of alcohol tonight. My head is starting to spin, but Attila convinces me to try the richly topaz-coloured *tokaji aszu*, regarded as one of the top ten dessert wines in the country, with a wonderfully deep flavour of prunes, or maybe raisins, and a syrupy but not too gluey viscosity. It's like drinking sex – deep, close, smooth, intimate, relaxed, mellow and flavoursome. Heavens. Who needs Stefano when I can just drink a bottle of this every night?

After a dessert of potato dumplings – yes, a potato dessert, called *gomboc*, which consists of one dumpling coated in deep-fried breadcrumbs, with mashed potato inside, and rich plum jam in the centre, and the second with a similar filling but a chocolate coating with a fine coconut crust – I'm fit to burst, and feel pretty much like a potato dumpling myself. Indeed, I think I need a little lie-down.

The night is coming to an end, and I'm seriously

impressed with Attila's honesty, gentleness, loyalty, generosity of spirit, romantic nature and appreciation for what he has.

'Socialism has made us a softer people,' he says. 'Under communism I wouldn't have had these same opportunities, but in 1990 we were given the chance of choice, money and freedom. I am still grateful for this. I am bathing in this freedom. I have two hundred reasons to have a big head, but you know what? All that matters to me is my family. That's what makes me proudest.'

And as we finish our drinks and his eyes twinkle merrily, and he and Ákos joke good-humouredly together, I'd have to say that Attila is one of the nicest, sweetest men I've met thus far on my trip. Indeed, he's not so much the Attila the Hun, as Attila the Honey.

But an actual food match for him? The *gulyasleves* – goulash – unprepossessing to start with, but the more you stir, the more the flavours come to the surface. He's homely yet refined, and doesn't take himself too seriously. He's heartwarming, wholesome, deep, soulful and sweet right down to the last mouthful. Delicious.

The next morning I feel low. Really low. Although I only have myself to blame. Last night when I got back to my pensione – quite frankly a little tiddly – I sent Stefano a text. Normally I wouldn't be quite so bold, but the New Me thinks it's about time I stood up to be counted. No more wallflowers for me.

No decent espressos in Hungary. Could come back from

> **Russia early if yr London offer still on, and the coffee still strong and sweet? Bambi**

But this morning I received a text that wasn't at all what I was hoping for.

> **Ciao Bambi. We have had a very pleasant date, but it will be difficult to recreate the same ingredients. I will be in London only Monday, so don't give up on your Moscow encounter.**

I don't reply. Partly because I can't think of quite the right words, but mostly because I can't see through the tears to text back. I just sit on the end of my cold little bed in my pock-marked apartment block, with its dripping tap and a patch of mould on the ceiling that looks like a portrait of Stalin, and I feel unbearably lonely, wondering for the hundredth time what the whole point of this trip is. Sure, I'm meeting lots of other nice men apart from Stefano, but there's an emptiness and one-dimensionality about it all that's eating away at me. I've spent most of my life looking for love, but I've clearly been doing something wrong. And even now that I've changed my modus operandi and have dramatically edited my checklist of desirable attributes in a man – more substance than style, and more heart than hubris – I still can't seem to find anyone who's even halfway to being The One. Stefano was my Great White Hope, and now I've got to go right back to square one. I'm seriously considering going back home to Australia and joining a nunnery.

Or dating a pot plant.

DENMARK
Licorice allsorts

Despite leaving Hungary feeling like my soul has been squished through a noodle grater to make little *nokedli* dumplings, I try to rally some enthusiasm, reminding myself that not many middle-aged women get the chance to travel the world taking little nibbles at men. Besides, I am actually quite excited about what awaits me in Copenhagen. I've always had a thing for Vikings – tall, square-jawed, long-haired and attractively dishevelled. Just my cup of tea. True, they may have pillaged their way across Europe, but I don't mind a man who can throw me over his shoulder and cart me off into the sunset every now and again.

And at the airport I'm not disappointed, although the hair on the younger men is in Rastafarian dreadlocks, and beaver-skins have been replaced with Ripcurl and Billabong hooded sweatshirts. But I can still tell they're Vikings, with their white-blond hair and eyebrows, pale pink lips, and eyes the colour of the deepest ocean depths.

And they look friendly. In fact, I've read that the Danes are amongst the happiest people in the world, and have a great sense of humour. They're also seen as kind, well-mannered, informal, non-judgemental and not at all chauvinistic. Oh yes, and extremely liberal-minded when it comes to sex. Which could make for an interesting time tonight with Claus – date #41.

Heavens – has it been that many already? Catherine in Amsterdam, who knows Claus through work, set us up, and even though he's only in his mid-thirties, I'm hoping that coming from a society with such liberal views, he mightn't mind the age gap. Which I certainly don't, having decided of late that maybe it's best to get them young, and before they get all embittered by the world. Or married.

I've got just enough time before I meet Claus to book myself into the Cabinn Hotel in the centre of town. It's very quirky, with teeny-tiny rooms similar to the cabins of a cruise ship. The shower recess is the whole bath-room, with a circular shower screen you pull around yourself to prevent water splashing onto the bunk beds. The taps are very tricky though, as they're the same for both basin and shower, so when I try to clean my teeth just minutes before Claus is due to pick me up, the shower turns on, soaking the back of my skirt. The Danes may well have invented Lego and designed the Sydney Opera House, but I think their plumbing needs a little work.

After a quick change of outfit so he doesn't think I've ... well ... wet myself, I meet Claus in reception and am delighted. He's about as close as you can get to being a Viking, although thankfully nowhere near as smelly. He's tall, slim and handsome, blue-eyed, and has white-blond hair that's fashionably messed up with gel – punk rocker meets Erik the Good. However, Claus doesn't seem quite so delighted to see *me*, and once again I'm painfully reminded that I don't have firm young breasts the shape of melons, and skin with the radiance of a virgin bathing daily in asses' milk. Indeed, Claus looks so disappointed that I'm half expecting him to start limping and cancel the date on the pretext of a flare-up of an old horseshoe-tossing injury – which Vikings supposedly get a kick out of. But I'm getting used to such reactions, so I smile broadly and decide to make the best of it, vowing to be as witty and charming and playful as possible. Even for an ancient 47-year-old. And it works, because before long Claus relaxes and even becomes quite chatty, as if he's accepted his fate and is going to make the best of it too. He has a lovely soft accent that's somewhere between flat German, and melodious Norwegian – with its sing-songy intonation that sounds like there's a question mark at the end of each sentence. And when he says, 'Oh crap,' when he makes a few wrong turns in the car on the way to the restaurant, it's oddly endearing.

En route Claus talks candidly about Danes, as if perhaps he's trying to justify his initial coolness towards me.

'We stick to ourselves,' he says. 'We have six months of darkness, so lots of people are depressed this time of year. We're cold, and not just physically. We are emotionally cold. It's hard to get to know us because we don't like talking about our emotions.'

Well, I don't know what happened to Danes allegedly being such happy chappies. And Claus is right about being a little unapproachable at first, but frankly I don't think that someone with no emotions would talk so much about not having emotions. Indeed, I think there's more to young Claus than meets the eye.

When we get to the restaurant, we have pre-dinner drinks at the bar, and are soon wearing the cigarette smoke of fellow smokers wrapped around us like silver fox fur stoles. Claus orders me a wine, and himself a Diet Coke, explaining that the only reason he's not drinking is that he has to work tomorrow. Which, given it's Sunday, makes him either a workaholic or a man with no social life. The latter being unlikely, given he's so cute.

'Danish people drink a lot because they actually *do* want to show their emotions,' Claus says, sipping his drink. 'It releases their inhibitions. They want to express themselves in a culture that doesn't encourage individuality and self-expression, and where we're raised to think that we're all equal and no-one is better than the other.'

'Women too?'

'Oh yes,' he replies. 'What's the difference? Men and women are fully equal. Danish women will not accept just being a hausfrau. No way.'

'And what do the men think of that?' I ask, already planning on immigrating here. Not that young Claus is going to be The One – I think I've missed my Viking longboat by a decade or two – but he might have a nice uncle.

'We like strong women,' Claus responds. He sounds sincere. 'We want equal partners. We want a woman with her own personality. Her own ideas. And just because a woman is equal, it doesn't make a man less of a man.'

I think I might have hit paydirt. Men who look like

Vikings, and when faced with a woman who's happy to say boo, don't get all huffy and weird. I'm filling out the visa application tomorrow.

But then there's the other issue for which Danes have earned a reputation, and I take a big sip of wine to give me the nerve to broach it. Because – well – in the cold light of day, and despite my recent shenanigans in Switzerland, I still can't quite shake off my prudish schoolgirl mentality.

'And sex?' I ask, as boldly as I can, so Claus can't tell I'm embarrassed. 'Danes are known for being pretty open when it comes to sex. Does that go for women too?'

'Oh yes,' Claus answers matter-of-factly. 'If a Danish girl picks up a guy in a bar, and takes him home, that's great! It takes the pressure off us. I'd think she was a wonderful girl.'

'So that doesn't make the girl cheap?' I ask. 'If we do that in Australia we're regarded as too easy. A bit of … um … a slut.'

'Why? Sex is natural,' Claus replies, his bright blue eyes boring into me in the way that only bright blue eyes can. 'It doesn't matter who makes the first move. A woman needs sex as much as a man. So why not? And Danes are tolerant too of homosexuals. Pornography. Topless waitresses. It's all okay.'

'So, let me get this right,' I say, choosing my words carefully. 'As a race you're all stitched up emotionally, and don't like to show your feelings, but you're totally relaxed about sex, which is about the most intimate thing you can do. You're cold. But you're hot. I'm confused.'

There's silence as Claus furrows his brow deeply and thinks. He's a real brow-furrower, this Claus, and I sense that he's emotionally mature well beyond his years, with the world weighing heavily upon his shoulders. Indeed, he seems a little melancholy, much like that poor Little Mermaid in the harbour, freezing her bits off with nary a clump of seaweed to keep her warm, in winters that can get down as low as minus five degrees Celsius.

'Well, maybe we have sex because it's a way of expressing our emotions,' Claus finally concedes. 'Sex is a way to show the passion we can't verbally express. And besides,' he says, as if shaking off a little grey cloud, 'it's fun, so why not?'

Yes, why not indeed? So far this trip I've learned that the Cubans, Brazilians, French and Italians make sex as much a part of their daily routine as cleaning their teeth, so why not the Danes too? Besides, they need to do something in winter to stop them freezing to death.

We are shown to our table – punching our way through the cigarette smoke like firefighters – and I'm thrilled that Claus is really opening up to me, and even seems to be genuinely enjoying my company. And the more I get to know him, the more I see that despite his protestations, he's actually very sweet and caring. He has a deep love of living by the sea, 'with its gentle beaches of sand as soft as talcum-powder', which must go some way to lift his spirits, even though he lives in a world where there's only around three weeks of decent summer a year. During this period there isn't even really a night, but a twilight that lasts for six hours. The sun goes down at 10 p.m. and rises again at 3.30

a.m., although in between it's never really dark. Claus spends most of this time outside making the most of it, and 'living intensely, living every moment, because I know it won't last and it will be a very long winter again soon. So I party hard. I mean, really party.'

Claus fixes me with eyes the colour of the sea he loves so much, as if to gauge whether I know how to party. I mean – really party. Which, if he wasn't drinking Diet Coke, and I didn't have things to do tomorrow, I'd be only too happy to prove. Ten-year age gap or not. I didn't get a reputation in my twenties and thirties for being a Serious Party Animal by staying home at weekends drinking Milo.

My *flæskesteg* arrives, and I'm salivating before I even get the fork into my mouth. It's the Danish version of roast pork, cooked with bay leaves and cloves inserted into deep cuts on its flanks. There's loads of perfectly crisped crackling to accompany it, as well as *brunede kartofler* – caramelised potatoes – which are so wickedly sweet that I hardly know if it's a side serve or dessert. It's so delicious that if I ever did immigrate to Denmark, I'd have to put a little metal band around my neck like a cormorant to keep my appetite in check.

As we eat, Claus talks of old girlfriends, broken hearts, new girlfriends, and how beautiful the Danish women are. Indeed, it's becoming ever clearer that as cool as Claus presents on the outside, inside he's as warm as the cherry sauce on Danish rice pudding.

'Once I trust someone,' he says solemnly, 'then I can let them in and show my real passions.'

'So have you been in love?' I ask. 'I mean, really in love?'

He looks pained, and takes some time to answer.

'Yes, with a Venezuelan girl. A few years ago. She was the total opposite to me. She had dark hair and brown eyes, and was full of passion and fire.'

'And she melted that heart you keep so safely tucked away?'

Claus just smiles.

'And now?'

'I have a German girlfriend. But she's not the same. She's like an onion. I can get past the first two layers, but then I can't get any further.'

'So why are you with her?' I ask, to which Claus shrugs his shoulders and smiles.

'The sex is good.'

I admire Claus's forthrightness, and I don't think he's hiding anything too much from me now, having slowly opened like a mussel when it's subjected to a gentle steam bath. Still, I'm hoping to find out even more about him with my animal question.

'Perhaps a tiger,' he sighs. 'It's beautiful and mysterious. It has everything it needs, and the freedom to go anywhere. But it can hide if it needs to. And everyone respects it.' Claus leans forward as if to tell me a secret. 'Being respected is important to me. When I was younger I liked to have status symbols to show that I was successful, but now being respected for who I am, not what I have, is more important.'

Claus's eyes are tender, and I feel oddly close to him. It sounds like we've travelled much the same journey. Substance over Style. It just took me a decade longer to figure it out.

The bill arrives and I try to pay, but Claus generously

waves his hand. 'You've come a long way,' he smiles.

I'm grateful, of course, but it's also nice to think that in a country where men and women are regarded as absolutely equal, there's still a bit of old-fashioned chivalry going around.

But the night's not over yet. Claus wants to show me another side of Copenhagen – 'the fun side' – and has in mind a venue favoured by gays and transvestites. I'm not even going to ask how he knows about such a place, but I'm delighted to put a different spin on the stereotypical Dane. Although, an image of Sweyn Forkbeard wearing a horned helmet with long flaxen pigtails and pink lippie rather ruins my more romantic notions.

Café Intime was first opened in the roar of the roaring '20s, and is still going strong. It's in a stylish old redbrick building with its name in glitzy Hollywood-style lights above the entrance. Inside, there are ceilings crisscrossed by heavy wooden beams, a handsome etched-mirror bar, and coloured leadlight windows. But that's where the conservatism ends, and the chaos begins. The rest of the room is decked out with fabulously kitsch decor – mauve and green and red striped walls, a ceiling festooned with plastic grapes, and a virtual op-shop of mismatched vases and porcelain memorabilia. It's all charmingly bohemian and eccentric, with an indecent yet appealing vibe. 'A place where locals can be lewd without their neighbours finding out,' Claus says knowingly.

A gnarly, bow-tied piano player with a halo of grey hair is at a grand piano belting out traditional Danish songs and toe-tapping *schlagers*. He's surrounded by a colourful assortment of people, from a few gay guys with the sort of exaggerated mannerisms that comes from watching too many Lucille Ball sitcoms, several straight couples, and small groups of younger people having a Saturday night out on the town. I'm disappointed not to spot any trannies or drag queens to add a bit of theatre, so the waiter will have to do, with his heavily studded leather belt and leather pants, and tattoos wrapped around his arms like a Viking comic book. He's joking around with an older bartender, and both are knocking back shots of *akvavit* between serving customers – 'one for you, one for me, one for you' – to the point I wonder who'll be left to serve.

Akvavit is exactly what I'm after. It's Denmark's national drink, and essentially a flavoured vodka, although I'm nearly put off trying it at all when Claus advises that I try one that tastes 'less of petrol'. Good idea. The Krone *akvavit* he suggests is delicious, with hints of licorice, caraway, orange and pepper, although it still burns my throat as I swallow, and once again I'm left wondering why such liqueurs, spirits and 'health' digestifs are quite so popular all around the world. Frankly, I think they're a health hazard.

Claus seems to be really enjoying himself now, and I can finally see the party boy within of which he boasted. As a group of revellers start singing loudly in the corner, he's all smiles, and cheerfully orders me another type of *akvavit* called North Sea Oil. It tastes like chocolate, cough syrup and licorice all mixed together. But mostly cough syrup.

'It's good for you,' says Claus, laughing, as my eyes start to water and I reach for a tissue. No wonder the Danes turned into Vikings if they were knocking this back night after night. It would have put hairs on the soles of their feet.

As we stand at the bar and chat, I'm finding out more things about Claus which have me intrigued. He's certainly romantic, but also pragmatic.

'Falling in love is great, but there's an 80 per cent rule,' he tells me. 'It's better to accept that if you have a good 80 per cent, then you just have to put up with the 20 per cent bad, rather than waiting for the 100 per cent good, and maybe ending up with nothing.'

I'm very impressed. How is it that someone twelve years younger than me has already figured all that out? I wish I could go back to being twenty-five and starting all over again. I would have avoided years of angst.

When Claus drops me back at my hotel, he gives me just one perfunctory kiss on my cheek, although his embrace is very warm.

'We prefer to hug,' he explains. 'A kiss is superficial, but a hug is more intimate, and means we mean it.'

And with that he turns to leave, and I have a nice glowing feeling inside – sure in the knowledge that I've still got what it takes to melt an icicle.

Or perhaps to dissolve licorice, for Claus reminds me Denmark's famous *salmiakki* – salted licorice. It's got an astringent, salty taste at first, and can be a little mouth-puckering. But if you persist, the sweetness soon becomes apparent, and it ends up being really quite tasty. So tasty in fact, I rather wish I was a whole lot younger, and then maybe Claus could ditch the German onion for something easier to get to. Like a big Australian marshmallow.

As I fly out of Denmark, still empty-handed but some-how a little more confident about where I'm headed – at least for the time being – I feel good. Denmark has loads of potential – female equality, handsome Vikings, yummy roasts, great sex – so if by the end of my trip I'm still single, I just might call up Crown Princess Mary, to see if she could do a fellow Aussie a favour and set me up with a nice royal butler.

RUSSIA

Something fishy's going on

I'm halfway to Russia and I'm already nervous. The plane is full of thickset men with bullet-shaped heads and #2 haircuts, and not one of them is smiling. Although, having been fed a healthy diet of Russian stereotypes over the years, I'm lucky they don't have mouths full of sharp metal teeth. I have read that Russian men are 'big drinkers, depressed, aggressive, lazy and deeply sexist', although other posts describe them as 'romantic, sentimental, big-hearted, generous and hospitable'. So one way or another, my dates here will certainly be interesting.

But as the plane dips towards Moscow like a giant snow goose returning home from its spring migration, I wonder if I'll have the energy to even go on a date. I'm exhausted from being nice to people all the time, and trying to keep the conversation going, especially in the odd instance when I only have about as much in common with them, as 'Species: Human'. And I'm no closer to my goal of meeting well, winning over The One, which is becoming demoralising. I haven't even had a string of fabulous affairs to make the whole trip a bit more exciting. Still, here I am, about to land in a country with which around two decades ago we were effectively at war – albeit a cold one – so perhaps sitting on top of ten thousand nuclear warheads will at least give me a bit of a thrill.

My taxi is an old heap with more dents in it than a schnitzel after a few rounds with a meat mallet. A crack stretches right across the windscreen, and where the wipers don't reach, the glass is thick with brown sludgy snow. My seatbelt buckle is broken, and as the driver weaves maniacally in and out of the traffic – clearly a firm believer in reincarnation – I set my teeth grimly and look out the window trying not to feel like a bullet in a game of Russian roulette. Not that the landscape is a great distraction, with row after row of soulless grey apartments, like huge tombstones, interspersed with the fat chimneys of power plants belching out clouds of steam. Electricity pylons straddle the highway and march off into the distance with their legs splayed, looking like giant robots with itchy crotches.

Thankfully the ugly scars of civilisation eventually peter out, and it becomes forest – the bare birch trees with their black-and-white trunks shivering in the snow like huddles of skinny old babushkas in a bathing house. Fresh snow is beginning to fall in gentle drifts and quickly fills in the footsteps of people trudging home from work, obscuring all trace of them as if they never even existed. It's beautiful and stark all at once, and leaves me feeling slightly pensive, like I too am drifting toward nothingness. But before I completely disappear, the taxi deposits me at the rather dated Izmailovo Complex Gamma-Delta Hotel on the outskirts of town, built to house the athletes and officials for the 1980 Summer Olympics. At 330 Australian dollars per night it's outrageously expensive, but at midnight I'm too tired to care, and collapse in an untidy heap in my room, which smells strangely of stale chicken soup.

My first date is with Artashes – a banker – who's meeting me for lunch. But first I have to get halfway across Moscow on the metro to meet our go-between, and there's a slight problem. I'm lost. Hopelessly so. I have a map, but it's in English, so it doesn't correspond with what's signposted – in unintelligible Cyrillic script – at each stop. I need to get off at Novoslobodskaya Station, but by the time I compare all the upside down U's and backward R's, and N's that are sneakily disguised as H's, and B's that are V's, the train has moved on. I ask a woman wearing a large furry cat on her head what station we're at, using the universal language of lots of gesticulating and grimacing, but she shrugs dismissively, so I ride the metro for another hour, in ever-decreasing circles until I eventually figure out where to get off.

But the trauma's not over yet. Halfway up the steep

stairs of the metro I meet a little old lady wearing so many layers of clothing that she looks like a wooden *matryoshka* doll. She's humped over a shopping trolley full of bulging plastic bags, and looks so disoriented and weary that I feel compelled to help, especially as everyone else is stepping around her like she's a discarded garbage bag herself. I gesture to her and smile before pointing up, then down the stairs, hoping to ascertain in which direction she's heading, then I grab the bottom of the trolley so we can carry it together. But suddenly she's shrieking like a steam kettle, and the other commuters are glaring suspiciously at me. Like all of a sudden they care. Now I've heard what happens when mobs take a disliking to a stranger – like a Siberian chipmunk in the midst of a wolf pack – so I smile broadly and back off fast. Even so, as I get to the top step, she's still hurling abuse at me with such fury, I'm sure I'd blush if I could actually understand a word she was saying.

By the time I get to go-between Sam's apartment – two hours late – I'm about to burst into tears. And when he opens the door, I throw myself into his arms like a wife greeting her husband returning from three years on the Western Front. Sam is an Australian living in Moscow, and was introduced to me by my friend Catherine in Amsterdam, who clearly has more international contacts than most diplomats. Sam has kindly offered to have me stay over for the next two nights, and has also organised the lunch date with Artashes, who just happens to own an investment bank. Well, 16 per cent of it anyway, which is still pretty impressive, as it's ranked in the top twenty-five banks in Central and Eastern Europe. This makes him one of the emerging breed of super-rich who've benefited from Russia's recent economic growth built on the back of oil and gas.

'He actually owns a bank?' I gasp, never having met anyone who possessed much more than a bank overdraft, which really isn't quite the same. I mean, I've met very rich people before, and eaten pizza with a prince in Naples, but meeting a man who owns a bank, and could conceivably earn up to twenty million dollars a year – or thirty times that in roubles – is certainly one out of the box. Indeed, I'm beginning to feel that familiar churning in my stomach of, 'What on earth is he going to think of me?' followed closely behind by, 'Oh shit, why haven't I swotted up on the Russian Revolution and Tolstoy?'

But it's too late to opt out, so Sam drives me to an upmarket Italian restaurant with a security guard at the entrance, and a doorman taking coats. Artashes is already there and greets me with a warm and genuine smile. He's in his early forties, and is tall and slim with fine features, and very well-pampered skin – the sort that only rich people have, like they've been soaking in a cocktail of virgin olive oil and juiced silkworms. He doesn't have a whole lot of hair, but that just makes him look more distinguished – like Yul Brynner. His eyes are brown and gentle, with nary a trace of panic or disappointment when I join him, or suddenly remembering he has to catch a matinee performance by the Bolshoi Ballet. So far, so good.

Sam leaves me to it, and as much as I've been fantasising about meeting Artashes, and even half wondering whether Boris or Vladimir would be the better name for our firstborn, I suddenly find myself strangely tongue-tied. It's not that Artashes isn't very receptive and engaging, it's just I feel a little intimidated. Not because he's hugely wealthy, but because I can already tell he's very intelligent, and probably more used to talking about algorithms than my silly little questions about aphrodisiacs. Indeed, he holds a PhD in mathematics from Moscow University, whereas I failed arithmetic in Year Ten. And very smart people have a certain confidence about them, like they understand things that Lesser Mortals don't, and regularly use words with more than nine syllables – in several languages. Still, I figure if I avoid talking about chess, or world economics, or Dostoyevsky's views on religion, he won't catch on that I'm one of those Lesser Mortals. And it seems to work, as we're soon chatting away easily, and he's taking great delight in hearing about some of my dates, especially Andras in Hungary, and his penchant for chopping.

'In Russia you must be careful too,' Artashes says cheerfully. 'We have the eighth highest murder rate in the world.'

As Artashes says this, he ever-so-casually looks toward the door of the restaurant, then picks up the menu and scans it distractedly before ordering his favourites – *pappa al pomodoro* (tomato soup), quail risotto and a bottle of *barolo* Italian red wine. Both the decor and the food is about as Russian as a pizzeria, but I figure I'll get to the borsch and *botvinya* in the next day or two.

'So, let's get down to business,' Artashes says with a friendly wink, which gives me a little shiver down my spine, because I suspect he's the sort of guy to mix business with pleasure.

I discover that Artashes is Armenian, but considers himself a Muscovite as he speaks perfect Russian, and has lived here for five years, setting up his bank. That's local enough for the purpose of my 'cultural' research, and frankly I don't give a fig what nationality he is for my 'romantic' research either – Armenian, Russian, Mongolian, as long as he's cute. And he is. But there may be a slight problem, as Russian women are purportedly amongst the most beautiful in the world.

'Yes, they are beautiful,' Artashes replies when I put it to him. 'Especially the ones with Tartar blood. But I also like Slavic women, with their wide faces and narrow hips.' He pauses, as if in conflict. 'But I like the women in England too, they can be gorgeous. Although all that said, my current girlfriend is Jamaican.'

'Jamaican? That's exotic,' I say, promptly putting aside any silly notions that I could possibly compete with her. She's probably got legs up to her cute little pierced belly button, and skin the colour of a café au lait.

'Well, there is a big problem with women in Russia,' Artashes grumbles good-naturedly. 'There are many gold-diggers. They're looking for rich men to look after them.'

'And that bothers you?' I ask, thinking most men wouldn't mind women throwing themselves dotingly at their feet.

'Of course,' Artashes sighs, 'although some men like it because it's good for their ego. But not me. I like a woman to be my equal, someone I can relate to intellectually. I'm well past the stage where I need to have a beautiful woman on my arm just for the sake of it. Or even an expensive watch, or a Ferrari. That's all very superficial, and actually rather crass.'

I heave a sigh of relief. Artashes is opening up nicely, and I feel confident enough now to ask him some more personal questions. For all he's worth – quite literally – he's turning out to be a remarkably unassuming and down-to-earth guy, and not at all tied up in knots about how rich he is. Still, I reckon I can dig a bit further.

'Okay, if you were an animal, what would you be?'

Artashes furrows his brow and looks bemused.

'An animal? Well, I don't see myself as an animal. But if you really need an answer, it would have to be a predator.'

'A predator?'

'Well, I'm a banker after all,' he laughs warmly, so I know he doesn't mean it. 'Yes, a predator,' he continues, 'but not like a marauding lion with the scent of blood in its nostrils. Maybe more of a dog. Something a little more docile. In fact, I want to sell my share of the bank and take up photography, or art, or writing. And it doesn't have to make me any money, because I'm not motivated by that. Or power.'

We're interrupted when our tomato soup arrives, although it's not any old tomato soup – much like Artashes, who's clearly not any old expatriate. It's served in a big round loaf of highly glazed bread with its insides scooped out to make a cavity for the soup. It smells heavenly, and it tastes deliciously rustic – like I've fallen into a Russian fairytale, tucked away in a little hut deep in a birch forest, and surrounded by squirrels. I'm very impressed by such a creative presentation, which leads me to ask how Artashes would impress a girl on a 'real' date. He looks nonplussed.

'With flowers?' I prompt, having seen a number of young men in the metro bearing single long-stemmed roses.

'Flowers? No!' Artashes breaks into huge grin and starts laughing. He clearly thinks this is terribly funny. 'Flowers? Are you serious?' he hoots.

Now it's my turn to be perplexed. 'Yes. Why? What do you do?'

'Nothing. Not really,' he replies, chuckling again. 'You must understand that in Russia successful men are in high demand. They don't have to do much to impress a girl.'

Well, I'm glad I'm not Russian. I like getting flowers. And chocolates. And taken out for the odd dinner. The thought of a man doing nothing more than sitting on his wallet – full of self-importance but empty on sentiment – is rather offensive, and I'm wondering if I got Artashes all wrong. But he must sense my disappointment, as he hastens to explain himself.

'I'd much rather have a relationship that isn't based purely on financial security for the woman, and for me a kitten to play with when I feel like it. I like a mind, and a challenge.'

Okay, so he's not a creep after all.

Artashes is in the middle of explaining that 'even though communism has gone, everyone is still watching everyone', when the door of the restaurant suddenly flies open, and he visibly jumps. After two hours of me watching him watching the front door – like a snow hare in its burrow with a pack of coyotes outside – I jump too.

'Do you have a bodyguard?' I ask nervously, although it turns out it was just the wind catching the door.

'What's a bodyguard going to do?'

'Well, aren't they supposed to protect you?'

Artashes laughs, and turns his chair a little so he has a better view of the front entrance. With growing apprehension I notice we're now the second-last diners in the restaurant, and the doorman keeps looking over at us with a bit more attention than is normal.

'People get murdered here even with bodyguards,' Artashes says. 'Bodyguards don't help if someone really wants to get you.'

'So people get murdered here?' I squeak. 'Over business?'

Artashes laughs. 'All the time.'

I dig so hard with my spoon into the soft sides of the bread bowl, that tomato soup splashes all over my shirt, rendering me in much the same mess as if I'd been hit at close range with a Kalashnikov. Which, in the present circumstances, is somewhat unnerving.

'Why do they get murdered?' I whisper, wishing the doorman wasn't now on the phone in deep conversation. Doormen are supposed to watch doors, not tell assassins the coast is clear.

'Why?' Artashes says, lowering his voice a decibel or two. 'Because there's a very tight intermeshing of government, criminals and big business. There are enormous interests at stake. You can't make mistakes.'

'But aren't you scared?'

'No,' Artashes replies. And I believe him. 'You watch your back. You adapt your lifestyle. For example I would never take the subway, where I'd be an easy target if someone wanted me. There are simple rules, and you follow them.'

He looks towards the door again. His body language is reasonably relaxed, but he's certainly more alert than the average guy eating tomato soup in an Italian restaurant. Unless of course he was in Naples and deep in Camorra territory. But as slightly unsettling as the situation is, I'm actually rather enjoying it all. I feel as if I'm in a James Bond film, especially as the only remaining couple in the restaurant look suspiciously like undercover agents, and the clearly fake-blonde waitress keeps filling our wine glasses from a bottle I'm sure has been switched. Even our water tastes a bit funny.

Fortunately, just before I excuse myself from the table and climb out the bathroom window, the main meal arrives and I can focus on my food. And of course on Artashes, who I've decided is nice. Really nice. I have concluded that he's way too sophisticated for me though, and I'm guessing that I'm not his type either, for exactly the reverse reason. Not that I don't hold my knife and fork properly, or know what 'perestroika' means, but as unpretentious as Artashes is, I'm guessing he'd want to hang out with someone a little more – well – glamorous, rather than someone who wears flannelette pyjamas to bed. Polar bear–printed to boot. Still, there's an easy warmth and genuine conviviality between us, and I'd like to think he's enjoying himself as much as I am. Which I believe he is, as even though it's now late afternoon, and the waiters are starting to set the tables for dinner, Artashes makes it clear he's in no rush to go anywhere. So we stay put, talking animatedly about our shared interests of art, travel and writing, until I'm feeling that perhaps I'm not such a Lesser Mortal after all. We eventually finish up just as the dinner guests are starting to arrive, whereupon Artashes offers to drop me back at Sam's.

'The driver will be wondering where we have been,' he smiles.

At first I think he's referring to a pre-booked taxi, but no – Artashes' personal driver is sitting cold and hunched in a huge black BMW with dark tinted windows, and a scattering of brown cigarette butts outside his window, like felled trees at Chernobyl. I'm horrified to learn he's been there for five hours, as it's near freezing outside, and already dark. I smile in apology, but it looks like he's used to it, and he opens the doors for us with a resigned shrug of his beefy shoulders. On the way to Sam's, Artashes gets two phone calls, and I notice with intrigue that they're on two different mobile phones. He keeps the calls short, and winks at me, pointing discreetly towards the driver.

'I don't let him know too much about me,' he whispers, 'It's better that way.'

When Artashes drops me home I'm suddenly glad nothing's ever going to happen between us, even on the extremely unlikely chance he might half fancy me. Although he's got it all – style, humour, intelligence, warmth, creativity and a gentle confidence – it would be exhausting dating him. We wouldn't even be able to go for a walk together without him jumping into a side alley every time a Lada backfired. Which happens a lot in Moscow.

Back at Sam's apartment I meet his live-in Russian girlfriend Alla, and also her mother Galina, who's staying here over winter because where she comes from in the north temperatures can plummet to minus forty-five degrees Celsius. I'm in luck, as tonight Galina is preparing a Russian favourite – *blini* with caviar. I'm glad it's not the real caviar, from Beluga sturgeon. Because I've just learnt that overfishing has so depleted their stocks, they're no longer killed, but given a caesarean section without an anaesthetic and their roe either scooped out with a special spoon, or squeezed out through the wound. Like freaking toothpaste for heaven's sake. Then they're stitched back up, and returned to their ponds where they might survive getting sliced open another three to four times over several spawning cycles, before they succumb. I'm horrified, so I'm glad Sam has only bought lumpfish and salmon caviar, which is extracted a little more humanely. Well, if you call killing something in order to eat its tiny unhatched babies 'humane'. Either way, that's another two things I'm adding to my list of never eating again. Well – once I get home anyway.

Galina painstakingly makes dozens of *blini* – or crepes – so thin and pocked with tiny air bubbles they look like lace doilies. She favours dipping these into melted butter, and spooning homemade strawberry jam over them. Other options are fillings of honey, smoked salmon, cheese, or mushrooms, with arguably the most decadent being caviar. Galina shows me how to lay a *blin* flat, spread it with sour cream then a big spoon of caviar, roll it up, fold it in half and then eat it – trying not to drop the sticky little eggs all down my front.

'*Priatnago appatita*,' says Galina.

'Good appetite,' Sam translates. 'And *za tvoyo zdorovie*, a toast for good health,' he adds, pouring out a little tumbler of vodka. 'But you must always toast *to* something, not just for the sake of it. So we'll toast to the success of your journey, Bambi, and to the minimum of weirdos you meet along the way.'

'Thanks, Sam,' I reply, 'but it's already too late for that.'

The *blini* with caviar are delicious. So delicious I have four in quick succession. The red salmon eggs are almost pea-sized, and go 'pop' in my mouth with a refreshing burst of salty sweetness. The black lumpfish caviar is a little too gelatinous and fishy for my liking, but the two together create such a unique combination of flavours and textures that I want to get down and do the Cossack dance with no clothes on.

But I don't.

However, I do decide that these are the perfect match for Artashes. A *blin* on its own is refined, delicate, gentle and polite. It's simple, yet sophisticated, and has both style and substance. But it's the variety of fillings that make it really colourful and interesting – rich or sweet, salty or savoury, every mouthful is a delightful surprise to excite the tastebuds. Just like Artashes.

I stay in Moscow for another two days, another two dates, and enough borsch (beetroot soup), *shuba*

(layered salad with beet topping) and *vinegret* (vegetable salad including beets) to give myself quite a scare after one particular bathroom stop. Well, bright-red poo is hardly normal, so I'm halfway to a medical clinic before I realise it is all the beetroot I've been eating. Phew.

On my very last day, I head off for a spot of sightseeing – a luxury I haven't afforded myself the last five weeks, given my frantic schedule – and soon I'm standing in front of surely one of the most gobsmacking manmade structures ever built.

St Basil's Cathedral was commissioned by Ivan the Terrible in the sixteenth century to commemorate a military victory, but he couldn't possibly be so terrible if he thought up a masterpiece like this. Eight huge onion-domed spires jostle for attention in the sky – decorated exuberantly with green-and-yellow diamonds, red-and-green pyramids, blue-and-white stripes, green-and-gold spirals, red-and-green tiles, and a little solid gold onion topping the ninth and tallest spire. The French diplomat Marquis de Custine once commented that it combined 'the scales of a golden fish, the enamelled skin of a serpent, the changeful hues of the lizard, and the glossy rose and azure of the pigeon's neck'. I couldn't have come up with a better description myself, and I stand here for a full ten minutes just marvelling at how completely over-the-top it is.

But then I experience something even more spine-tingling, as the huge bronze bell in a little church at the other end of Red Square starts to ring very slowly, in deep, rich, golden tones. I just stand here letting it wash over me, when it occurs to me that if sound too had a flavour – like my men – then this would be old honey. It rings every thirty seconds, each peal finishing just before the next, and it soon fills Red Square with an overwhelming flood of serenity. And now a cheerfully tinkling little bell starts up, pealing at a much faster pace than the first bell – if this sound had a flavour, it would be champagne. A middle-toned bell rings too, pealing at a pace in between the two others. It's melodious and warm, and if it had a flavour it would be chocolate syrup. They all join together in a heart-lifting melody – a cocktail of love – and soon Red Square is filled with its magic, and I just can't believe how lucky I am to be here. Bugger the men. If I can drink in experiences like this for the rest of my life, then my soul will surely be adequately nourished.

But it's not just Red Square that has teased my senses – there have been so many 'flavours' in Moscow I'm about to explode – the taste of honey-and-pepper vodka, the feel of caviar popping in my mouth, the grumbling of fat babushkas, the smell of freshly baked *borodinsky* bread, the sight of strapping young soldiers goose-stepping at the gates of the Kremlin. There's a famous Russian phrase, 'Appetite comes with eating', and I concur, for now I'm hungrier than ever to taste what the rest of the world has to offer.

So bring it on.

SCOTLAND
Guts 'n' glory

With appetite come hunger pangs. At Heathrow

Airport on my way to Scotland, all I can think about is that botched rendezvous with Stefano. Meeting up with him again – for either a polite meal or a full-on carnal cornucopia – would have made this whole trip worthwhile. Well, perhaps not quite *all* I'd hoped for, but at least something to make me feel a little less of a complete failure. But Stefano's long gone, and now I'm wondering if he ever really meant it about meeting him in London. Perhaps he's just a player like so many other men in my life. Perhaps he's not a *doppio espresso* after all, but just a mocha chocolate.

Still, the show must go on, so I'm glad I've got a few dates in Edinburgh to keep me distracted. And I'm quite excited about it, as if the Scots are anything like they're depicted in the movies during the 'days of yore', then I'm half expecting to meet a tall, well-built man with long, fiery red hair, dressed in a kilt, and given to standing on cliffs on misty mornings playing his bagpipes. Of course, these days he's unlikely to be as dramatic, but I'm hoping he'll still have a few *Braveheart* tendencies – warm, sentimental, fiercely loyal, stubborn and rebellious – any of which would make for an interesting date.

However, I'm not quite so optimistic about the food, given the Scots' propensity to deep-fry anything that will stand still long enough. They also seem to favour foods with rather suggestive names, such as 'border tart', 'cock-a-leekie', 'festy cock', 'Glasgow roll' and 'softie', which has me wondering if the locals constantly have sex on their minds. In which case I might be fending off my dates with the butter knife. Although I suppose I should be safe with a 'softie'.

My first date with Hamish – purportedly 'Scotland's foremost divorce lawyer' – is a delight. In his early fifties and with silvery hair, he's the spitting image of a slightly younger Sir Anthony Hopkins, and has a wit as dry as the bottom of a whisky glass at a Scottish buck's night. Speaking of buck's nights, I soon discover Hamish is hoping to marry his girlfriend next year, so sadly he's out of the picture for me. However, I have another date tomorrow night with one of his colleagues at his law practice, and it's not just another dime-a-dozen lawyer. Lorne – #47 – also happens to have recently been named the sixth most eligible bachelor in Scotland. So if there was ever an opportunity to say 'Hoots mon!', this is it.

The next morning I decide such a momentous event calls for a haircut, especially as I've begun to resemble a shaggy Loch Lomond goat. However, when the stylist starts darting in and out of my shoulder-length locks with a razorblade and slicing out great chunks of hair, I begin to have serious misgivings. Which are not unfounded. By the time she's finished with me, my hair is all different lengths – from short, to really short, to a Highlander's bum fluff. I look like I've been attacked by a whipper snipper, and I don't know whether to laugh or cry. I walk the streets of Edinburgh fretfully, pulling my hair hoping it might lengthen like one of those dolls that 'grow' the hair tucked away inside their skulls. But I just give myself a headache. I'm seriously considering cancelling our date because I feel so ridiculous. But then my phone rings. It's Lorne.

'It's yer Scottish date,' he says, in an accent as broad as the River Clyde. 'Let's meet at th' Tigerlily bar in George Street. But hoo will ah recognise ye?'

I'm contemplating fessing up to the botched haircut so Lorne doesn't get a fright when he sees me, but decide that if I act like there's nothing wrong, then he might just think that it's normal for Australians to look like convicts. Especially given our penal colony heritage.

'I'm tall and dark, and will be looking a bit lost,' I say as cheerfully as I can.

'Och, ah'm tall and dark tae, and ah always look lost,' he replies.

I get to Tigerlily early. It's a handsome Georgian townhouse in the smart part of New Town, with four levels of French windows through which a warm red glow emanates, as if behind them very high-class Ladies of the Night are entertaining the local gentry. A girl standing at the top of a short flight of steps looks down suspiciously at my hair as I approach, as if perhaps I'm lost and really want to be at Filthy McNasty's further up the road. She's holding a clipboard that must have a list of Beautiful People upon it, as she looks at me, then at the list, and then back at me again.

'Are ye oan th' list?' she coolly enquires, subtly repositioning herself so that the door is blocked.

'No, but I'm meeting a friend.'

'Name?' she asks haughtily.

'Lorne. Lorne Cousins,' I reply, hoping she'll recognise his name, and let me in with a fawning apology.

''Er name's nae doon,' she says, scanning the clipboard intently, like a catalogue at a Sotheby's jewellery auction.

'It's a he,' I say limply, wishing my hair didn't make me look like my great-great-great-grandfather was shipped off to Australia after stealing a loaf of bread. Which – by the way – he wasn't.

'His name's nae doon either,' the girls says without smiling.

I'm scared of Door Bitches at the best of times, but a Scottish one seems scarier than usual. Maybe it's her guttural Lowlands accent, or her ten-centimetre stiletto heels, but either way, I somehow have to get inside before Lorne arrives, so that I can compose myself. So I do what any self-respecting 47-year-old would do under such circumstances – I grovel, and Door Bitch eventually begrudgingly lets me in.

Once inside, I can see that it's no up-market brothel, but an über-cool bar. The back wall is shimmering with tiny retro mosaic mirrors, juxtaposed by a dramatic Venetian etched-glass mirror. An enormous moulded PVC chandelier above the bar looks like a luminous brain coral, and a motorised glitter ball the size of a small meteor sprays fragments of light onto walls pasted with silver flocked wallpaper. It's fun, it's stylish, and it exudes a certain sophistication I wasn't quite expecting from Scotland, given that I was born in Paisley – a little further west of Edinburgh – which was described to me by my mother as the singularly darkest period of her life. Quite literally, with cruel winters, and 3.30 p.m. sunsets plunging the moors into a deep purple emptiness, and bossy nannies who fed my three older sisters bread and dripping. We left when I was two years old, when my father got his next naval posting.

And even though I've never been back to see for myself, I've always visualised Scotland with belching smoke stacks and ugly knitting mills. Certainly not etched-glass mirrors and glitter balls. I'm so glad to discover how wrong I've been.

The young men lounging up against the bar are also a nice surprise. Most are tall, slim and handsome, and appear to be quite comfortable paying up to ten pounds for cocktails with delightfully Scot-inspired names such as 'Lily's New Knickers'. I'm guessing that they're part of a privileged social minority, and not at all representative of the 'real' locals, but I'd still rather be here than at Filthy McNasty's.

After our rendezvous time has come and gone, I'm wondering whether Lorne has stood me up, or if Door Bitch has warned him to make a run for it. So when at last he arrives and makes a beeline for me – as I'm the only single middle-aged lost-looking woman in the room – I'm very relieved. He smiles broadly and is immediately warm and welcoming, and, even better, he doesn't seem to notice anything odd about my whipper-snippered hair.

Or is perhaps too polite to let it show. Lorne is in his early thirties, with boyish good looks and a fresh face with just-out-of-bed hair, and shiny pink cheeks from the biting winter chill outside. He's wearing an olive tie and hound's-tooth sports jacket, and neatly pressed trousers. I'd been hoping for a kilt, but at least his jacket is evocative of misty Scottish moors filled with genteel hunting parties flushing out grouse and pheasant. And his accent is even more delicious than it was on the phone. Indeed, it's positively sexy, and I wouldn't be surprised if he made the eligible bachelor list on his dulcet tones alone.

We have a glass of wine at the bar, which is now slowly filling up with Beautiful People – whom I suspect had no problem with Door Bitch – before heading off on foot to our next destination. We're on the smarter side of Edinburgh, with elegant grey houses standing side-by-side like neatly arranged Scotch Finger biscuits, and through whose windows I can see grand chandeliers and paintings of horses and hounds gracing the walls. I feel oddly at home here, and experience a pang of regret that I haven't spent more time in the country of my birth.

Lorne ushers me into the Stac Polly, a little restaurant below street level and down a steep flight of stairs, opening up into a dungeon-like space of rough stone walls and low ceilings. It could be gloomy if it wasn't for the rich tartan furnishings that give it a cosy ambience, along with tables dramatically set with huge, single, Scottish thistles. So huge in fact, that when we're seated at a tiny table for two, I have to peer around it like a hare on the moors, to see if Lorne's still there. He is, and insists I try some of the more traditional dishes, including an entree of haggis, *neeps* and *tatties*, and for main course the Loch Duart Scottish salmon. Lorne orders the Barbary duck, although tells me he prefers to shoot his own. Now, I knew Lorne was a bagpiper, but being a hunter too is a real coup, as it seems I've bagged the quintessential Scottish 'hero'. And a very cute one at that. The night is going from good to better.

Lorne orders a special aperitif – a ruby-red kir mixed with Highland spring water – and raises the glass to toast me.

'*Slàinte mhòr* Bambi, an' welcome tae Scootlund. Ah hope ah don't let ye doon as a perfect Scoottish gentleman.'

I'm trying to appear as nonchalant as possible, but my heart is beating faster than the drum roll finale at the Edinburgh Military Tattoo. That accent is doing something to me that would make me a fortune if I could bottle it, and sell it as an alternative to amphetamines. Still, as we nibble on neat little squares of bread delicately topped with smoked salmon, I manage to ask Lorne how he got to be voted the sixth most eligible bachelor in Scotland.

'Is it true it had something to do with playing the bagpipes for Madonna?' I ask. If that's the case, it means I'm just two degrees of separation from knowing one of the greatest pop stars of all time.

'Aye,' Lorne replies, and the more I hear his voice, the more it sounds like a melody right from the bubbling, swirling streams of the Highlands. 'Ah started playing th' pipes when ah was jist a wee laddie, an' loved it sae much ah've played ever since. My parents were neighbours of Paul McCartney an' Linda, in Mull of Kintyre. After Linda died, Paul arranged a memorial service, an' asked me tae play th' pipes. Then Stella McCartney asked me tae play at her wedding, an' Madonna was there an' heard me. Then a wee while later she contacted me, tae see if ah'd like tae go on tour wi' her for six months in th' Re-invention Warld Tour of 2004. Sae I did.' Lorne shrugs his shoulders as if he still can't quite believe it himself. 'An it war magic,' he continues, his eyes lighting up at the memory. 'Ah'd come up through a trap door wi' swirlin' smoke all over th' place, an' then move right across th' stage along a conveyor belt as ah played th' pipes. An' then ah'd have a wee dance with Madonna before goin' doon another trap door.'

It's a great story, and most people would probably leave it that. But not me, because there's another question I just have to ask. I don't think it's because of the alcohol content of the aperitif, but perhaps the sea air is getting to me, because I wouldn't normally be quite so … well … direct.

'And did you wear underpants? I heard Scotsmen don't wear anything under their kilts.'

'Och, aye,' Lorne replies with a fresh-faced smile. 'Ah had tae. Ah was up high on stage, and jiggin' about an' such, soo ah haed to keep meself nice. An' besides, thare was a safety issue.'

'A safety issue?'

'Aye, ah was on a conveyer belt, sae ah could hae had a nasty accident if ah'd fallen doon.'

I'm saved from getting too strong a visual on this when my haggis arrives. And whereas last night with Hamish it had been encased in two parcels of crisp filo pastry – so I couldn't really tell what I was eating – this is a little more in my face. Although thankfully still not the pink, pudgy, lumpy business quivering on the plate like a little alien foetus, as I'd half expected. Instead, the dish is presented in three neat elliptical mounds – the white being the *tatties* or mashed potatoes, the golden-yellow being the *neeps* or mashed turnips, and the mottled black-and-brown being the haggis, which Lorne cheerfully tells me is made from 'th' bits of a sheep tha' wouldn't pass muster on their own, like its heart an' liver an' lungs, an' usually encased in th' sheep's wee stomach'.

Fortunately there's no stomach today, so it looks less like a half-cooked Martian and more like the stuffing out of a roast chicken, with a crumbly breadcrumb texture. And it's delicious, with a deep, rich flavour, like very fine minced meat mixed with herbs, onion and oatmeal. It's both sweet and savoury, and far more refined than I'd have expected. Much like I'm finding Scotland as a whole – to my great delight.

'So tell me more about your piping, Lorne,' I say, before telling him that at the age of eight, my mother gave me a set of toy bagpipes to encourage my 'Scottishness', and then promptly banned me from playing them in the house because it sounded like I was throttling a donkey. Slowly.

Lorne smiles broadly. 'This is so refreshing; most people just ask me aboot Madonna. What colour is her bathroom? What does she eat? It's so nice not to talk about it, it gets so repetitive.'

'But I'm not interested in Madonna, I'm interested in *you*,' I say, at which Lorne's chest puffs up with a young man's pride, and he launches into the sweetest tale of his love affair with the bagpipes, starting when he was just six years old with his grandfather's set. I'm moved that he's carrying on such a noble tradition, and one that can stir the soul so profoundly within just a few moments of its haunting, ancient melody. If this doesn't make him the quintessential Scottish romantic, I don't know what would.

The Loch Duart salmon arrives. It's delicately sweet and almost buttery, with firm pink flesh that falls apart in neat flakes. Lorne picks quietly at his Barbary duck, bemoaning the fact it's not as good as a wild mallard or teal from the mudflats or lochs down south. Coincidentally, when I ask him a little later how he'd impress a girl on the first date, he doesn't hesitate.

'Ah'd take her duck shootin',' he replies enthusiastically, 'but ah'd have tae make sure ah took a dug this time.'

'A dug?'

'Yes, a dug that knows hoo to retrieve, as th' last time ah took a girl shootin' th' dug was young and couldn't find th' wee duck, sae the girl and ah had to go into th' marsh oorselves an' find it. Not very romantic. Ye need an experienced dug.'

He leans back in his chair shaking his head with the memory of a retriever dog that wasn't quite up to it, before asking me to ask him what his best chat-up line is.

'Best chat-up line?' I laugh.

'Aye, ah was asked by *The Scotsman* newspaper for this Sunday's edition. Ah came up with something off th' cuff, but maybe ah should use it in the future?'

'Okay, so what is it?' I reply, thinking how delightfully unassuming and honest Lorne is. I can't think of many men who'd give away their trade secrets.

'Yer eyes tell me everythin' but yer name,' Lorne says proudly.

I'm struck dumb for a moment, but then I can't help myself. 'Oh Lorne, but that's dreadful,' I whisper, 'Please tell me that you'll never use that on anyone. Ever.'

'Okay,' he replies good-naturedly, 'but there's an

even worse one. It goes like this: Where are yer bruises?'

'What bruises?' I ask, confused. Until I realise that's the whole idea.

'From when ye fell doon from heaven,' he says triumphantly.

Oh dear. Lorne may indeed be one of the most eligible bachelors in Scotland, but I think he's got a bit of work to do on his presentation skills.

I'm now sufficiently emboldened by alcohol to ask Lorne what other Scotsmen wear under their kilts. Or don't.

He laughs. 'Weel, traditionally they used not tae wear anythin', but then when underpants were invented they helped with th' cold draughts, not tae mention th' wee midges in th' Highlands.'

'And now?' I ask, thinking those wee midges would have to be very brave to tackle a Scotsman's – well – tackle.

'These days it's fashionable again not tae wear anythin',' Lorne continues. 'It's called a True Scotsman. The younger men especially like it, tae show hoo tough they are. Unless of course they're a Highland dancer or an athlete, and then they're recommended tae wear them so as not tae scare th' spectators.'

The mind boggles. I think I need another drink.

'Okay Lorne, if you were an animal, what would you be?'

'Weel, perhaps a stag,' he replies thoughtfully. 'It's sensitive an' proud, an' a wee bit wild without being predatory. An' it's handsome too,' he adds, laughing at his own cheek, before looking serious. 'Besides, it's a symbol of Scotland, an' I'm proud tae be Scottish.'

Although most men I've met on this trip have been quite nationalistic, to Lorne a sense of national identity seems to go far deeper than just draping the Scottish flag around his shoulders at a football match. He appears to live and breathe all things Scottish, including playing its very soul through his music.

'In fact,' Lorne suddenly says, his blue eyes sparkling with excitement, 'Ah'm handin' in my resignation on Monday. Ah'm goin' tae Los Angeles to try my hand as a professional bagpiper. Ah want tae follow my dream. I love playing th' pipes more than anything in th' warld.'

'Even more than being a lawyer?'

'Och aye,' he says emphatically. 'Ah want tae do somethin' that makes me happy. Being a lawyer is a job. Ah want a passion.'

It's in this moment that I see in Lorne such a bright and shining spirit I'm almost dazzled by it. It's the optimism of youth, yet also the wisdom of years, and reminds me we all need to follow our dreams and carve out our own path in life, whether that be in the form of a little bubbling brook, or a crashing, cascading river hurtling down the mountainside. And I do believe that Lorne's path in life is going to be the latter.

I wonder if I'm brave enough to do the same.

I try to pay for dinner, especially as I've heard that 'Scots are so tight that they only breathe in'. But not Lorne. He generously insists on taking it on, although I note with some amusement that he carefully studies the bill.

'They haven't given us anythin' fer free,' he says, somewhat disgruntled. 'I told th' manager yer writing a book, so yer'd think he'd at least throw in a wee whisky.'

I try to disappear under the table as Lorne calls the waitress over and tells her as much. I'm mortified, especially when the manager – Roger – then comes over to our table, and looks me over grumpily as if evaluating whether I'd make a good venison sausage.

'So ye want a free whisky?' he grunts.

'Well,' I say, feeling my face flush, 'I'd love to know more about Scottish whisky, so I can understand it better.'

'Do ye even like whisky?'

'No, not really.'

'Weel, ah'll tell ye what,' Roger replies gruffly, although I think he's thawing out a little. 'I'll give you two tae try. One is th' classic Scottish whisky, Dalwhinnie, a fifteen-year-auld malt whisky. An' then a ten-year-auld Laphroaig, which gets burnt under barley on a peat fire, and ye won't like it at all.'

He glares ferociously at me, but as he turns away I spot the slightest smile playing upon his lips, and I'm guessing he's an 'old dug' whose bark is worse than his bite. When he returns with the two whiskies, I regard them suspiciously, but the Dalwhinnie turns out to be a delight, with the flavour of heather, honey and vanilla, and as smooth as a sporran lined with elk suede. The Laphroaig, on the other hand, is nasty. Really nasty. It tastes like I've ingested the smoke off a slow-burning peat bog. Or burnt seaweed. Or melted bandaids. I can't decide which.

'That's horrid,' I splutter. 'People actually drink this?'

'It's a regional characteristic,' Roger sniffs. 'Some

people just love th' flavour ye know. People with a refined palate say it tastes like baked pears or toffee an' marshmallow. Perhaps Australians just have unsophisticated tastebuds.'

Well, I suppose I deserved that.

I can't think what food to match with Lorne, so I ask for his help. I know it's cheating, but he's got so many qualities I don't know where to start.

'Perhaps th' salmon,' he replies earnestly, 'tryin' tae find my direction in life.'

'And constantly battling upstream?' I ask, warming even more to this delightful young man, because despite his 'title', he's completely lacking in arrogance. And although he's at a bit of a crossroads, I reckon he knows exactly where he's going.

'Aye,' he answers, as if reading my mind. 'But when ah decide what ah want, ah really go for it.'

I'm feeling even cheekier now. I don't know what was in that liquidised peat bog, but it sure packs a punch.

'So, Lorne,' I say quietly so Roger can't hear. 'If you're a salmon, how would you like to be eaten?'

'Slowly,' he replies with a twinkle in his eye, 'and raw.'

I heave a sigh of relief. That's far more befitting of the sixth most eligible bachelor in Scotland than 'your eyes tell me everything'. There's hope for him yet.

We leave the restaurant at two minutes after midnight, and as we wait outside for a taxi, a thought suddenly pops into my head – like the first guest at Hogmanay, the Scottish New Year, turning up on your doorstep with armfuls of gifts. Lorne and I have got along famously all night, and now I'm thinking I wouldn't mind having a bit of a … well … Highland Fling with him. Why not? He's single, and I'm single. He's cute, and I'm lonely. And it wouldn't be like it had been with Ali, which was fuelled by alcohol and frustration, and left me feeling embarrassed and strangely empty. I really like Lorne – he makes me feel young and alive, and believing again that I too can realise my dreams if I put my mind to it. But then that infernal Miss-Goody-Two-Shoes taps me on the shoulder, and whispers that quick Highland Flings are either for Scots, or women who are comfortable with one-night stands. Meaning – not me. And I listen, because deep down I know that Lorne is never going to be The One. He still has countless uphill streams to navigate, and these days I'm heading more downstream, where I don't have to fight the current quite so hard. So what's the point of starting something I can't finish? I hold my tongue as Lorne hails me a taxi, and we kiss each other's frozen cheeks and say our goodbyes, and off I go. And that's that.

Well, not quite. The taxi has only travelled ten metres, when I have to jam my fist into my mouth to stop me from asking the driver to turn around so I can jump out and rugby-tackle Lorne to the ground.

'Did ye say sumat?' the driver asks as I make a gagging sound.

There's still a ten-second window of opportunity.

Lorne's adorable. And I do like a man who plays the bagpipes.

'No,' I say resignedly, 'Kirk Brae please.'

The next day I find the perfect match for Lorne at a

farmer's market. A stall is offering tastings of a range of whiskies blended with various fruit liqueurs, and I pick a bright red Brammle Scotch Whisky liqueur, which is bramble berries steeped in whisky. It's tantalisingly delicious – sweet and mellow, yet heartwarming all the way down my gullet, with a distinctive flavour of black-berries, honey, nutmeg and cloves – almost like a hot toddy. It gives my cheeks an instant glow, and I even feel like dancing a bit of a jig. Yes, it's Lorne to a T.

Damn. Maybe I should have hopped out of the taxi after all.

I leave Scotland feeling sad, even though I had another date after Lorne, making it three dates in total. Three 'dates', three misses. Which is a pity, as it would have been so romantic if one of them had worked out. To travel the world for forty-five years then return to live out my life in the country of my birth would have had a nice symmetry. And I could do with a bit of that in my life right now. Symmetry, order and a heart that doesn't keep losing bits.

Ah well – maybe tomorrow.

PORTUGAL
Sweet sorrow

I like adventurous men. Especially those with their eyes set on far horizons, the wind in their hair, and cheeks flushed with excitement as they head into the unknown.

From what I know about Portugal's rich history and its citizens' propensity for travelling to the farthest reaches of the earth, I'm hoping whoever I meet here will be equally as brave, curious, proud, passionate and perhaps even a little swashbuckling as Vasco de Gama was back in the sixteenth century.

There's only one problem. I have no dates organised in Lisbon, so I'm going to have to wing it. And having had a pretty easy run so far, I'm nervous about finally having to resort to chatting up men in bars, or down at the docks doing their swashbuckling stuff. Thank goodness my friend Lou has come all the way from Australia to hold my hand for the next week.

But first, we're starving, so we make our way to the centre of the city through a rabbit warren of medieval streets, and buildings so exuberantly clad in finely detailed tiles that I feel like I've fallen into a giant kaleidoscope of ceramic blues and greens and mustard-yellows. We've been told that to experience authentic Portuguese food we should try Uma, a cheap little eatery with faux stone arches and ugly brown-and-clotted-cream wall tiles, and a grumpy waiter who looks like he's only just woken up from a three-month nap. But the food looks a little more promising, with Senhor Rip Van Winkle pointing out an item on the menu highlighted in pink. 'Seafood Rice – Prize Winner in Contest', it reads, and I blithely order it without even contemplating what the contest was for. It may have been the Lisboa Annual Squid-Penis Cook-off for all I know. We order a bottle of Dão Meia Encosta *vinho tinto*, just in case we need something to wash down anything too alarming, and although it's a bit rough to start with – like a spicy shiraz before it's matured – it seems to get smoother with every sip. Which reminds me of some of the dates I've been on recently, where the men have also greatly improved after having had the chance to … well … breathe a little.

Indeed, after fifty-six dates, it's been constantly confirmed that even the initially unpalatable have the potential to turn from vinegar into wine, as long as they're given enough TLC. And to be fair, perhaps it was my own cultural narrow-mindedness that soured my initial judgement, and they'd been, in fact, perfectly drinkable all along. But the last two months have taught me how to carefully and open-heartedly savour and appreciate the subtle nuances of every dish – whether it be a man or a meal – so that pretty much everything tastes great. Which is a wonderful discovery, because I'll never go hungry again.

The seafood rice arrives, unceremoniously presented in a battered metal saucepan right off the stove, with twists of paper napkin around its handles to pretty it up. It looks like Spanish paella, with a rice and tomato base topped with prawns, scampi, mussels, tomato, onions, big chunks of crab, flame-grilled red capsicum and loads of coriander. It smells utterly divine – a heady fishy-steamy-seafood fragrance – and eating it is like taking part in a lucky dip, where you're not sure what you'll find next. Indeed, there's such a symphony of flavours – from sweet to spicy to savoury – that if flavour were a sound, then this would have to be Beethoven's *Fifth Symphony* played by Lisbon's Gulbenkian Foundation Orchestra.

We follow the meal with a tawny port, which I'm awfully glad is Portugal's national drink, because I'm getting sick of drinking stuff that tastes like petrol or cough syrup. But this is delicious – silky smooth, nicely viscous, and reminds me of Christmas with its complex flavours of raisins, brandy, fruitcake and marzipan. Just as I'm considering ordering a second, I get a text from Prince Pasquale back in Naples. I'd cheekily asked him during our date whether he knew anyone in Portugal for me, and bingo, he's set me up tomorrow with one Fernando Vendrell – a film director – and he wants to know if that's okay. Well, of course it is, because it gets me out of having to trawl Lisbon's bars for a date, so now I can relax. In which case I'll most definitely have that second port to celebrate.

The next day I'm regretting the third glass of port that somehow found its way to my lips, having clearly relaxed a little too much. My head feels like a codfish has defecated in it, which is not such a great thing when I'm having lunch with a famous film director. One who won an Oscar for Best Foreign Picture a few years back for *Belle Epoque*, and more recently a whole swag of awards at the Sundance Film Festival for *O Herói*. Still, after a strong coffee, Lou and I make our way to the 'white city' on top of one of the Seven Hills of Lisbon, and wait for Fernando in Accorda, a hole-in-the-wall eatery off a busy cobblestoned street, and down a small flight of stairs leading into a cosy cellar-restaurant. It's bustling with locals and is filled with wonderful cooking smells, and lining the back wall are ceiling-high shelves generously stacked with wine and – God help me – more port.

After waiting for nearly an hour for Fernando, and just as I'm beginning to suspect I really *have* been stood up this time – unlike Lorne who eventually turned up – Fernando arrives in a whirlwind of apologies. Despite having been about to chew my knuckles off with frustration, I take an instant liking to him. He's in his early forties and has very wild, curly, salt-and-pepper hair – a little less salt than pepper – and a neat beard that makes him look appropriately creative. He has thick long eyelashes framing intense green eyes like an alley cat, and although not particularly tall, has a certain stature about him. But most importantly, he's charming, engaging and has a nice easy warmth to him, so I'm quietly confident that we're going to get along splendidly.

Although, he doesn't know why he's here.

'Pasquale deedn't tell me anything,' he says, his brow deeply furrowed. 'He just tells me he 'as a friend coming, and can I look after 'er?'

This is the first time I've found myself on the back foot, and I'm worried that with Fernando being put under the spotlight without warning, the date will be over before it's begun. But it's just as well he's 'arty', for when I explain my mission in terms of it being a 'cultural exploration of the senses', he nods cautiously, and beckons the waiter over. Although I still don't think he quite knows why he's here.

Fernando orders the meal, and we tuck into tasty

codfish cakes, and *bacalhau grelhado de coentrada* – cod grilled with coriander. That's a lot of cod in one hit, but with a fish that can grow to two metres long, and is cooked in this country in more than one hundred and sixty ways, it's only the tip of the iceberg.

Fernando talks passionately about Portuguese food. In fact, I'm barely getting a word in. Which is great. That's exactly why I'm here. He explains that much of Portuguese food is 'the exquisite cuisine of poverty'. That the poor had to think of creative ways to turn cheap ingredients such as cod, beans, rice and chicken, into something very tasty. 'Because,' Fernando says, 'eet was important for them not just to survive, but to delight the tastebuds too. Even the poor need some dignity. Especially the poor.'

He says this with such sincerity that already I'm seeing in Fernando a deep and philosophical thinker with a keen sense of social justice, who seems to care as much for a beggar on the street, as a gaffer on a film set. And when it comes to Portuguese men in general, he has fairly strong opinions too.

'We do not push ourselves,' he says earnestly. 'If winning means beating someone else, we would rather not. But that does not mean we are weak,' he adds, 'eet just means we care for others. We do not want to be aggressive. We do not want to stand out. And I am 'appy enough weeth that.'

I like Fernando's attitude. I'm not fond of conflict either. In fact, in relation to my reworked checklist of the type of man I'd like to end up with, he's coming up trumps. Gentle? Tick. Generous of spirit? Tick. Considerate? Tick. Humble? Tick. But I have to admit that old habits die hard, and I still like adventurous men, so is he also the swashbuckling romantic stereotype?

'Well, we are not macho like we were een the days of old,' Fernando replies when I put it to him. 'But we 'ave something better now. We 'ave the Portuguese Suave, which means we are smooth and sensitive, and respond to inner beauty and intelligence, rather than just to a pretty face with no 'eart behind it.'

I'm even more convinced that I'm on to a good thing here. After all, I've got 'eart aplenty. But then Fernando goes and ruins it all by telling me he's happily married with three young children. Still, I'm intrigued by the way he looks at the world – not through rose-coloured glasses, but another hue altogether.

'Portuguese DNA ees pale blue,' Fernando says. 'Blue ees the Portuguese spirit. Blue ees 'ypnotic. Blue ees symbolic of the sadness at what 'as passed. The Portuguese people suffer from a profound sense of romantic melancholia. Ever since we 'ave lost our colonies, and along weeth them our power and relevance on the world stage, we feel we 'ave no real meaning een our lives.'

Fernando takes a good long swig of his red wine, and seems to have shrunk a few inches down into his chair.

'And you too?' I ask.

'Yes,' he replies. 'We call it *fado*, which means that my fate 'as already been decided, and I cannot change eet. I am cursed with feeling that something bad weel surely follow anything good I do.'

Fernando slumps back heavily in his chair, whereupon I'm tempted to give him a hug. It must be exhausting being so negative about life, especially when he's actually been very successful in his career. Although he explains that despite a revolution in '74, there's still a fascist structure in place in Portugal that undermines people's sense of initiative, and everyone wants to keep everyone down, in a classic case of Tall Poppy Syndrome. So he's never got quite the recognition that he feels he's earned.

'There ees a chronic emptiness of vision,' he says, and looks so dejected that we just sit there silently, mopping up the juice from the octopus with big chunks of bread. The air is so heavy with sadness and a palpable frustration, that I'm concerned if we keep going along this trajectory, Fernando might throw himself off the Castelo de São Jorge, an imposing Moorish castle overlooking the city. So I take a different tack.

'If you were an animal, what would you be?' I ask.

'Oh God,' he replies, looking doubly miserable. 'Per'aps a lion. But not een the sense of a powerful beast, but because a lion 'as to cope weeth solitude and loneliness.'

There's a slightly awkward pause as I ponder the wisdom of having asked such a question, and whether he'll choose the bell-tower or the parapet of the castle from which to leap. But he must see my discomfort, because he smiles at me warmly.

'Don't worry,' he says, 'I may be basically a pessimist, but I leeve as optimistically as possible. I'm an optimistic pessimist. I know things weel turn out wrong, but I try anyway.'

At that, the dessert arrives – a mouthwatering *sericaia* custard tart with cinnamon and prunes. Having decided that I've done quite enough damage for the day, I spend the next hour focusing more on Fernando's family, and his love for the historical culture of Portugal, which he 'relishes'. And – surprise surprise – he declares he doesn't see himself as particularly typical, because of his 'sense of revolt, and een wanting to change the system others are too lacking een confidence to tackle'.

As lunch draws to an end – thank God there was no cod ice-cream – I realise that the more I learn about Fernando, the more I'm seeing other colours apart from that depressing blue. Red for passion, orange for ambition, yellow for wisdom, green for vitality, purple for spirituality. Indeed, he's a veritable rainbow hiding behind a dark cloud, and I feel privileged to have taken a little look inside the soul of a famous Portuguese film-director.

The day after our date, I nibble on a *pastel de nata* – a popular local snack, similar to a custard tart. It has a rather chewy base, but its centre is all heavy sweetness and creamy lusciousness, with deeply complex flavours. The more you eat, the richer and heavier it becomes, but you don't want to stop, because it's just so damned good. Which gets me to thinking that it's a perfect fit for Fernando. Thank goodness I don't have to eat any more cod in order to find him.

Lou and I spend the next four days getting around Portugal, from the medieval hill town of Sintra, to the historical fishing village of Cascais. Along the way I manage to cobble together another four dates – a randy maître d', two cousins of the pensione manager, and a delightful waiter called Fernando who was as sweet as Casal Garcia port – although sadly none turn out to be The One. Indeed, I'm beginning to despair that even after having travelled to the four corners of the earth, and now having dated sixty-one men, it hasn't produced anything more than a severe case of Italian heartburn. To make matters worse, Lou and I will be parting ways tomorrow, so I'll be on my own again.

Still, inspired by a popular Portuguese phrase, 'You never know what lies around the corner', we decide to give it a final shot, and walk around a good many corners to see what we can find. And bingo, we come across Café A Brasileira, one of the oldest and most famous cafes in the old quarter of Lisbon. It has a completely over-the-top green and gold Art Deco entrance, complete with sculpted heads and dramatic acanthus flourishes, beside which we sit and watch the world go by. And what a world it is, especially as dusk falls and the fire-twirlers come out, their flaming staffs twisting in the air creating long trails of sparks behind them like comets. They're followed by a fire-eater who nearly takes my eyebrows off – no doubt a clever ploy to extract money from me, in return for him not doing it again.

As Lou and I nibble on tasty little lupini beans called *tremoços*, a young man sitting beside us strikes up a conversation. He has smooth olive skin, dark features and thick glossy hair that is starting to recede. I'm instantly intrigued by him, as quite apart from wearing sunglasses – in the evening – he's also rather appall-ingly dressed in an expensive blue pinstriped jacket, a designer denim shirt, shiny rayon trousers, and such pointy shoes that his bare feet must look like icepicks. It's an ensemble he wears so confidently that he clearly has no idea that he looks like something that's fallen off the back of a St Vincent de Paul recycling truck. Indeed, when Lou cheerfully tells him that I'm in town to 'research' the local men, it takes him all of two seconds to pull up his chair and sit at our table, with a cocky, 'Ah, so what do you want to know? My name ees Carlos.'

Carlos is the owner of three nightclubs, although my sixth sense tells me that's not the full story, and that if there were a Portuguese mafia, Carlos would be right into it. I've got a nose for bad boys, and something about him smells even fishier than the cod hanging up to dry in the fish markets downtown. Carlos is clearly not going to be The One, but he's still going to be a great 'date', as I suspect he's the sort of guy who's so full of himself that he doesn't think to lie to make himself look good. Indeed, he appears to have absolutely no idea that his answers to some of my questions are more politically incorrect than farting in a crowded elevator. So when I ask him what he thinks of Portuguese women, he falls for it beautifully.

'Men like quantity,' he says in a voice as smooth and viscous as an oil slick. 'We swap women regularly. Even eef we 'ave a beautiful one to start with, we weel swap her after a year, because there weel be another more fresh one.'

'Fresh?' I say, as Lou's eyes widen in disbelief. 'And will she be beautiful too?' I add, trying not to sound like I'm being sarcastic. Which I am.

'Of course,' he smiles, shrugging his shoulders. 'That's why I travel. To Czechoslovakia, Russia and Latvia. They are full of beautiful women. And beautiful women are good for the ego. My life ees a theatre where I am the first character. Everybody ees looking at me, so my women need to look good too.'

'And what do you think they find attractive in *you*?' I ask sweetly, trying not to look at Lou or I'll get the giggles.

'To interest a beautiful woman, a man needs to be difficult and cool,' Carlos replies unabashedly. 'But I weel always be kind, and I weel always be a gentleman,' he continues, which only serves to confuse me, because I didn't think you could mix oil with water.

'And how would you impress a woman once you've singled her out as being worthy of your attention?' I ask, taking another look at his shiny trousers, and wondering how on earth he could even think to wear them out in public.

'Eet's like driving a car,' Carlos replies. 'You don't go right een to fifth gear, but you start eet at first, then slowly een to second eef you like her, then third, and then fourth.'

'And quickly into reverse if you change your mind?' I tease.

'I don't often change my mind,' Carlos replies confidently. 'When I want something, I usually get eet.'

I'm just loving this. Carlos is as cocky as the black Roosters of Barcelos that can be found in every tourist shop in Portugal. He's positively crowing with self-importance, and I'm betting he chases all the chicky babes around in circles too.

'What car do you think I drive?' Carlos suddenly asks. 'It cost me a lot of money.'

I'm so taken aback I don't know what to say.

'A Mercedes,' Lou jumps in.

'A Ferrari,' I finally suggest.

'I have a Porsche, a Boxter,' Carlos replies proudly, his chest puffing up beneath his denim shirt, which I suddenly notice has one too many buttons undone. 'It's black. But I can't drive it at the moment because I lost my licence for doing 208 kilometres per hour.'

'And does it impress the girls?' I ask, chewing my bottom lip to stop from giggling.

'Well, I had a red Mazda once, the top model,' Carlos replies, 'but no-one ever looked at me. Now I have this car and I wear my dark glasses, and I sit at the traffic lights and everyone looks at me. And when a car revs beside me, I let it take off fast at the lights, then vroom, I'm already to 120 and I leave them behind.'

I can picture this so clearly that I nearly get whiplash. Indeed, the whole encounter has left my head spinning, and I think it's time to go.

My food match for Carlos? *Sardinha assada* – grilled sardines – because they're oily, rich and decidedly fishy. And you have to be very careful not to choke on the little bones.

'Come to my nightclub,' Carlos purrs when Lou and I say we're heading home. 'I will introduce you. I have friends who are forty and single, and are complete maniacs for women.'

'That sounds great,' Lou and I gush, lying dreadfully. Not because going to a mafia-owned nightclub mightn't be enormously entertaining, but I'm scared the friction from those shiny rayon pants might send off sparks and burn the whole place down.

WALES
A rarebit of insight

I have a rather fanciful idea of the men who live in Wales. A dash of the fiery Scots, a dollop of the cheeky Irish, and a pinch of cool English reserve. Plus a nip of randy, if Tom Jones and Richard Burton are anything to go by. And as there's a town in the northwest named Llanfairpwllgwyngyllgogery-chwyrndrobwllllantysiliogogogoch – that can only be pronounced with a throat full of phlegm – they clearly have a sense of humour too. But when I ask a woman on the train what they're like, she laughs.

'Not very romantic, and quiet,' she says, almost apologetically.

'That's it?' I ask.

'Yes, nothing special really,' she replies.

Great.

As the train trundles past black-faced sheep stand-ing stoically with their backs to the wind, bracing themselves for the huge steel-grey clouds to dump their loads pitilessly onto their wooly little heads, I know just how they feel. There's a dark cloud hanging over me too. In fact, with such a diverse range of experiences these last nine weeks, I feel a little like a windswept Welsh moor – bathed in sunshine one day, being rained upon the next. Still, it takes all four seasons to make a year, and if you never get to experience the bitterness of winter, then you'll never fully appreciate the warmth of summer. So I sit up straight as the train pulls into the station, and I vow to put a sunny smile on my face, come what may. Although I almost miss my stop, because the conductor phlegmatically announces we've arrived at 'Chhhhhhllandidnow Junction', but the sign reads Llandudno, which I learn – almost too late – are miraculously one and the same place. No wonder the Welsh are so quiet, if their own language defies all logic.

For the next few days I'll be staying in Portmeirion, a unique seaside resort owned by my British cousins. My father spent time here eighty years ago in Castell Deudraeth, an imposing bluestone Gothic-style castle now used as a luxury hotel. As I arrive, it is all lit up with fairylights, and there's a warm orange glow coming from the windows like a baker's oven. My cousin Robin meets me at reception, and after not having seen him for thirty-eight years when we were both aged nine, we greet each other like ... well ... long-lost cousins. He'll be my first Welsh 'date', and although he's not going to be The One – being both married, and closely related to me, neither of which I care to mess with – he's still a man, and he's Welsh, so he's a perfect candidate for exploring romantic Welsh stereotypes. Especially as we're soon sitting beside a toasty fire in the castle, set in an enormous carved stone fireplace that could be right out of the Middle Ages, and we're drinking champagne.

'Iechyd da,' Robin toasts me, and I think back to the last time I saw him, when he was a long-haired boy playing with his pet rats in the courtyard of the family home. There are no rats now, but his white-blond hair is still shoulder-length, and he still has that slightly faraway look like he did as a child. He's pale skinned, solidly built and somewhat dishevelled, with the sort of honest, homely features you'd find in the director of the Welsh Choir, or other such worthy institutions. He seems pleasant, although somewhat uneasy, as if he's either very shy, or not quite sure what to do with a long-lost cousin who's fronted up asking for a date with a Welshman. However, by the time we finish our second drink and have moved to the dining room, he's more relaxed, and I'm discovering that Cousin Robin is charming, and funny too. Not with a grey-not-quite-black humour like the Scots, which I find a little cynical, or a blue humour like the Australians, which I find a little crass, but one that is delightfully self-deprecating, and a bit off-the-wall. When I ask him what Welshmen are like in general, he fixes me with eyes the colour of faded hyacinths.

'Well, according to the English,' he says wryly, 'we are leek-eating, hymn-singing, rugby-playing coalminers, and probably shagging sheep at the same time.'

'So you don't sing hymns then?' I ask pointedly.

'Yes, we do actually sing hymns,' he replies without batting an eyelid, 'and we do eat leeks, and play rugby. And the sheep ... well, you'd have to ask them.'

Robin explains that singing and poetry are very strong in Welsh culture, and that he writes a lot of poetry himself. In fact he's a modern-day bard, regularly performing in the National Eisteddfod of Wales, a traditional festival of literature, music and performance.

'Culture isn't a dirty word to the Welsh,' he says earnestly. 'It's not an elitist concept. Even farmers write poetry, and coalminers. And living just up the road is one of the most famous opera singers in the world,' he continues, referring to Bryn Terfel.

'So does that mean the Welsh are generally romantic?' I ask, hoping such a trait applies to whoever he's arranged for me to meet tomorrow, for my 'real' Welsh date.

'Yes. Well, I certainly am,' Robin replies unselfconsciously.

'So if you were single now, how would you impress a woman?'

'Oh, I'd take her to a nice place for a meal,' he says, gesturing to the dining room's elegant furnishings, and the splendid oak staircase just beyond the door. 'A castle perhaps,' he smiles warmly.

'Which is even more impressive if you own it!' I chortle.

'I don't know,' he continues in his gentle, softly spoken, almost hesitant manner, which suggests that he's not someone to blow his own trumpet. 'Maybe washing the dishes with her after dinner would be even more special.'

Whilst the waiter hovers, Robin places our order in effortless Welsh, which impresses me no end, as only 19 per cent of the population can speak it fluently. Which is a shame, as it's a truly beautiful, melodious language, and the closest thing I've ever heard to singing. If someone was to woo me in Welsh, I don't think I could resist them. The food, however, isn't potentially quite as mouthwatering, with only a handful of Welsh dishes such as vegetarian Glamorgan sausages, and – excuse me – *faggots*, which are Welsh meatballs. And most disappointingly, there are no leeks anywhere to be seen.

'But aren't leeks the national emblem of Wales?' I ask.

'Well, yes,' Robin replies with an amused expression. 'They are, but so is the daffodil, and you wouldn't eat them would you?'

For dinner I order the Castell Deudraeth crab bisque, not only because the crabs are caught locally, but because my father's third given name is Deudraeth. The bisque is served in such a big white bowl that I'm hoping there's a life-ring nearby in case I topple in. It's a deep warm-orange colour, with a dollop of *rouille* atop a chunky crouton bobbing about like a little schooner – appropriate given that Portmeirion is set on an estuary. It's delicious – luxuriously smooth and wickedly creamy, with generous shreds of crabmeat playing hide-and-seek with my spoon. It's deep and rich and filling and fabulous, and if food had a sound, this would be anything sung by the Welsh Treorchy Male Choir.

As I contentedly mop up every last smudge of bisque with a fennel-and-caraway breadroll fresh from the oven, I ask Robin what he personally thinks of Welsh men. He smiles, as if pleased to have the chance to give both himself and his fellow countrymen a good rap, given the 'not very romantic, and quiet' description I shared with him earlier failed to impress.

'We are friendly and inquisitive,' he says, his eyes bright. 'We have a strong sense of cultural identity, as well as a strong sense of place. We are very connected to the land – the rivers, the moors, the mountains. It all has a deep resonance for us.'

Before he can burst into song with the emotion of it all – like *The Sound of Music*'s Maria singing 'The hills are alive …' – the main meal arrives. It's rack of Welsh lamb, and it's extraordinarily rich and sweet, pretty much melting in my mouth before I even have a chance to chew. It's very fatty, but I suppose that's to be expected in a place where temperatures can drop to minus fifteen degrees Celsius in winter, when frankly I, too, would need more than a sheepskin coat to keep me warm.

Robin tells me he loves cooking, and often goes cockle picking at low tide down in the estuary, then steams the cockles in cider to feed his family. There's something madly romantic about a man going cockle picking, and then bothering to do something about it, rather than just plonking them on the table for his wife to sort out. It reveals Robin's earthy, softer, humble side, which is a refreshing change to some of the more macho personalities I've come across this last couple of months, who've been more the hunter-gatherer-bash-it-on-the-head-until-it-stops-kicking types.

Which makes me curious as to what sort of animal Robin sees himself as. If he's so nationalistic, it might be the Red Dragon of the Welsh flag. Albeit a gentle dragon, because I doubt he breathes fire.

Robin answers without a second's hesitation. 'A red squirrel. Did you know they're an endangered species?'

'You're endangered?' I ask, somewhat confused.

'Well – no – but we used to have red squirrels when I was a kid,' he replies. 'And … um … they horde nuts.'

'And you horde nuts?'

'Well, I hide things and then can't remember where I've put them,' he says cheerfully. 'I suspect I'm a bit vague.'

I suspect he's right. But delightfully so.

After dinner, Robin walks me down the hill to the main resort, in which he's kindly put me up in an apartment. And when I give him a warm hug goodnight, and he responds in kind, I marvel how very wrong one can be about outward appearances. Robin might have initially looked a little dishevelled and perhaps even bordering on the bland, but after peeling off a few layers I discovered an immensely rich and deeply interesting man – modern-day bard, award-winning author, businessman, community delegate, sustainable development advocate, wit, romantic and cockle-picker. Then again, I should have known after sixty-two dates – not to mention the rationale behind Queen Elizabeth's love for rather dumpy Welsh corgis – there's often far greater character in the more unprepossessing packages.

I spend the next day walking in a dreamlike state around the rambling grounds of Portmeirion. It was designed by Robin's grandfather – my great-grandfather's brother – Sir Clough William-Ellis, to replicate an Italian village, as well as whimsically incorporating architectural styles from a host of other cultures and eras, so that you're not sure if you're in Italy or China, Ancient Greece or Mexico, or even Burma. The objets d'art scattered about the twenty-eight hectares of grounds are equally as eccentric. There are marble mermaids sooty with time, medieval bulbous-eyed fish, golden Buddhas, little spiral staircases leading nowhere, murals of naked men on prancing horses, gill-eared sea nymphs, and a huge bronze statue of Atlas with the world on his back. It's all deliciously over-the-top and oddly indulgent, a heaving smorgasbord of colour and texture and sometimes questionable taste, but still fabulous, like a huge bacchanalian feast. And although it's nothing close to a true representation of Welsh culture – and it's not meant to be – it's a great 'folly' set against a dramatic backdrop of the vast estuary of the River Dwyryd, beyond which tumble hills in rich hues of cinnamon, nutmeg and juniper, like old Mam Gwendydd's patchwork knee rug. And as the seaweed-tinged air burns my lungs, and the wind stings my cheeks, I can quite understand why the Welsh are so poetic and attuned to nature, when just to step outside must remind them that they're so utterly, gloriously, alive.

Robin has organised a date for me tonight with his friend Rhys, who meets me in the Castle bar for a pre-dinner drink. He's a slightly portly man in his early fifties, with a bright cheery smile and outgoing personality – perhaps even a little hyperactive, for no sooner than our drinks arrive, he tells the waiter to 'hold the champagne', and then whisks me off to a tiny pub in the picturesque harbour village of Porthmadog, where he parks the car illegally right out front, leaves its headlights on, and grabs my elbow to dash inside for a quick ale. A very quick ale, as before I've even finished it, Rhys is bundling me out the door again, and we head back to the castle, where the waiter – clearly used to such capricious behaviour – has indeed kept our champagne on ice for our return.

Rhys is loads of fun – upbeat, sweet, generous, with a larger-than-life personality, and a humour as warm and dry as a slice of oatmeal toast. Half the time I don't know whether he's pulling my leg, as demonstrated when I ask him what he'd do to impress a girl, and he replies – with a deadpan face – 'I'd take a bath.'

Still, he's great company, and the only reason I'm not elaborating on our date is because I'm not sure his wife of thirty years would like to hear about his increasingly suggestive comments over dinner. Indeed, by dessert the air is so thick with sexual innuendo you could cut it into slices and butter it. I'm not sure if Rhys is seriously trying to hit on me, or just venting his frustrations at the 'lack of action between the marital sheets', but either way I feel extremely uncomfortable, so after dinner I start wrapping things up. I think very carefully about my final question, avoiding asking Rhys what animal he is, as that's only asking for trouble, and I don't want to be fending off a roaming 'rhinoceros', or a pushy 'python', later tonight. But when I take the safer option of asking what food he'd be, he still says something so rude, I gasp. Let's just say it has something to do with spotted dick, but he's not talking about the British pudding of the same name.

'You are so naughty,' I squeak, my face turning beetroot.

'Well, eff I'm naughty,' he replies, 'then I should be spanked.'

It's definitely time to go.

With my two Welsh dates over, and a flurry of meals to find their best match, I allocate to Robin a dish of *cennin hufennog,* or creamed leek, which – despite his earlier misgivings – I eventually track down. A leek has multiple layers, which on first impression are pale, bland and unexciting. But with every layer you peel back and nibble on, the sweeter they become. And when baked with a cream, cheese and white wine sauce, the flavour intensifies to something far above 'nothing special' as suggested by the woman in the train. In fact, *cennin hufennog* is so rich and elegant I'm reminded of a Welsh expression, 'Don't be goin' judgin' a pastie by its crust.'

Or something like that.

Rhys is more of a challenge. He's too red-blooded to be rack of lamb, and too sophisticated to be shepherd's pie. But perhaps grass-fed Welsh beef is the right fit, as it's rich and rare and full of flavour. It was a little chewy though, so I suspect it came from a frustrated old bull who spent his last days looking longingly at the cows in the next paddock.

ENGLAND
Hot English mustard

Even though I'm fast running out of countries in which to find The One, I'm still hopeful that now I'm in London, the tide will turn. I like Poms. I like their stiff upper lips, impeccable manners, self-deprecating humour, and fondness for expressions such as 'splendid Old Boy', and 'pip-pip cheerio'. I'm not so sure they're overly romantic – having once had an English boyfriend who hated having his hair messed up in the throes of passion, and was scared of saliva – but I reckon Poms have potential. And even better, I have five dates lined up here.

For my first I head for a famous London landmark – The Wolseley, a café-restaurant in the grand European tradition of going completely over-the-top. It has vaulted white ceilings, huge black-ribbed columns, black-lacquered window-frames, and more gold trim than Queen Elizabeth's coronation cape. It's popular with celebrities, film stars, directors and politicians – which might explain the scruffy reporter hanging around out front with a camera as big as the London Eye. I'm early, so I tuck myself into a corner table where I can get a good view of the patrons – not being averse to stargazing every now and again – and I wait for my date to arrive. Well, Sebastian's not a real date. Apart from being a very old friend – which is a dynamic I don't like to mess with in case I end up with no friend – he's married. Still, I wanted to have lunch with him for the purpose of my cultural research, as Poms don't get much pommier than Sebastian.

He arrives dead on time in a flurry of brollies and cashmere, and even though I've not seen him for twenty years, he hasn't changed a bit – still very tall and solidly handsome, with a rather foppish fringe sweeping over twinkling blue eyes. In fact, he looks a little like Stephen Fry of English TV and film fame, so in a way I have my celebrity after all. We hug warmly, and are soon sipping a crisp chablis, and nibbling on miniature parmesan breadsticks to whet our appetites. Sebastian has chosen The Wolesley in which to dine because he thought it would be educational for me with its 'modern take on traditional cuisine', although I'm afraid I can't resist ordering a meal as quintessentially English as a bowler hat. It's spit roast suckling pig with Bramley apple sauce, with a side serve of sprout tops and chestnuts, and creamed mash. I have a twinge of guilt not trying a more modern dish as he'd intended, but at the end of the day you really can't beat the taste of a good, simple English roast.

And the men? Well, I'll just have to wait and see.

Sebastian is a banker, although not any old banker. Indeed, he's so unassuming that I practically have to squeeze out the full story like a garlic press, with him finally admitting that he actually runs one of the largest banks in England.

'Although,' he says, in his beautifully plum-in-the-mouth English accent, 'it's not really all that exciting.'

I love the Poms. They have the most marvellous talent for understatement, and Sebastian is clearly no exception. However, I suspect that deep beneath the polite restraint, and the off-the-cuff comments – neatly turned Thomas Pink double cuffs at that – he probably feels rather happy with his lot in life. Possibly even a teensy bit smug – not that he'd ever show it. That would be far too vulgar. I find this both amusing and endearing, especially after some of the men I've met recently, where they've laid their huge ego clearly out on the table where I couldn't miss it even if I was wearing a blindfold.

Over an entree of pea and lettuce soup, and as we're discussing romance and relationships in England, Sebastian asks if I'd like to hear his 'Great Theory on

Life'.

'Of course,' I reply. After all, that's partly why I'm here.

'Why do people divorce?' he asks, and then answers himself before I can reply. 'When kids arrive, the men are often shoved to one side, and the kids get all the attention. So he spits the dummy and marries a younger woman to make himself feel better. And guess what?' Sebastian asks with a chuckle that reverberates around the room. 'The younger woman wants to have a family, and the whole cycle starts again. Maybe even for a third time. Waste of time really, and expensive. My advice is to stay married.'

I reckon there'd be as much chance of Sebastian leaving his wife, or even having an affair, as Paddington Bear becoming a male escort, as he clearly adores his wife, with whom he has two kids. But as he gestures to the roomful of men wearing expensive pinstriped suits, and shirts with thick mother-of-pearl buttons, I'm guessing he has a few colleagues who don't feel quite the same way. Which probably explains England's whopping 45 per cent divorce rate. And it suddenly occurs to me this could work in my favour. After all, a sixty-year-old might regard me as a younger woman, so if I was to be his second wife, and I was too old to have those interfering kids, then I'd have a reasonable chance of ending up with a nice Pom after all. In which case I might hang around.

The meal arrives, and after just a few mouthfuls of the thickly sliced pork fillet, a generous wad of stuffing, and perfectly crisped crackling, I'm getting an idea 'who' it might be. It's sweet, it's rich, and it's delicious.

Even the potato mash – normally a humble dish – is so creamy and elegant that it's like eating a poem by William Wordsworth – 'And then my heart with pleasure fills, And dances with the Daffodils.'

'Sebastian,' I say excitedly, rather rudely waving my fork around, upon which the lady at the next table, with the coiffed hair and Burberry jacket, looks at me as if I'm a mutt that's snuck into a Cavalier King Charles Spaniel dog show. 'Sebastian, I think this might be you!'

'I don't want to be stuffed pork thank you very much!' he replies, looking insulted. 'Can't I be this nice white wine?'

'But it's perfect,' I insist. 'Both of you are heart-warming, rich, nicely textured, and uniquely savoury and sweet at the same time. And besides,' I add, 'pigs are very smart.'

'Delightful,' he says raising his eyebrows like the opening of the Tower Bridge, 'do please tell me if I am ever elevated to anything more refined.'

I'd always thought Sebastian was the quintessential English gent, but then he goes and puts a spoke in my wheel, by admitting that he's not so good at doing the Stiff Upper Lip thing.

'I'm too sensitive, emotional, argumentative, and I piss a lot of people off,' he tells me, as the lady with the Burberry jacket tries not to make it obvious she's eavesdropping. 'I'd rather do the right thing and not be popular, than do the wrong thing just to be popular. So I upset a lot of people.'

Sebastian is clearly a man of principle, and I'm even more curious as to what animal he thinks he is. But if he says lion – which will make it the twelfth for the trip – I'll cry.

'Oh God, the animal question,' he says, in mock horror. 'Okay, a monkey, because I'm always causing trouble. And I'm cheerful, energetic and reasonably smart. Oh yes, and frightfully witty!'

And he is too. As well as charming, and enthusiastic. And best of all, he doesn't take himself too seriously. I also suspect he's more romantic than he's letting on, but in true English style he plays his cards close to his chest. And he's the perfect gentleman, fetching my coat and settling the bill even though I try to thrust money into his hand to cover it.

'Absolutely not,' he insists, then calls me a big black London cab before disappearing into the crowd with his brolly clenched tightly under his arm.

Although I have four more dates over the next two days, it's date #68 in whom I'm most interested. My English cousin Eva has set me up with Ben – her ex-boyfriend – having written that he's 'dashing and dangerous, very good-looking, and if you sleep with him I will never talk to you again'.

I'm not too fussed about her threat to never talk to me again, because she owes me one, having gone out with my Swedish boyfriend Sten after we'd split. But I'm still a little apprehensive, given my theory that 'very good-looking men' would rather date very good-looking women, and preferably ones with breasts that haven't yet discovered the concept of gravity. Eva is my age, but is very attractive – almost regal – with a beautiful peaches-and-cream complexion, and a neck like a white swan. I'm worried that if Ben is expecting the same of me, he'll be disappointed. Which frustrates me no end, as after sixty-seven dates I know better than most that beauty is only skin-deep. Still, it's on with the show, although as I sit on a huge mulberry sofa in the apartment of my friend Maree, with whom I am staying, with a glass of white wine to give me extra courage before Ben arrives, I wonder why I'm putting myself out there and making myself so vulnerable, only to risk rejection. Again.

'Because,' says Maree, who knows a thing or two about life, 'you have to mix the pot. You can't sit in the same stew forever.'

I look at myself in the living-room mirror, and give myself a very strict talking-to. After all, this might be my last chance to find The One, and I don't want to blow it by being a whimpering has-been. Besides, I'm not really all that bad. I have long legs, white teeth, shiny hair and good skin – albeit more *beurré bosc* pear than peaches-and-cream. But most importantly I'm reasonably smart, occasionally amusing, am kind to small furry animals, and have a heart the size of Trafalgar Square. So when the doorbell rings, I take a deep breath, plump up my breasts, put on a big smile, and open the door to see what fate has in store for me.

And it bodes well. Ben is very tall and slim, with dark curly hair, and such angular features you could slice paper with his cheekbones. He's wearing funky black-rimmed spectacles, and a black scarf wrapped tightly around his neck – both of which give him a slightly intellectual and bohemian air. He's very much

'my type', but thankfully not as devastatingly handsome as I'd been imagining after Eva's description,
which gives me hope that he won't be over-critical of
me.

Sadly, that hope is as shortlived as a spare seat on
the 5.30 p.m. train out of Waterloo Station. From pretty
much the moment he sees me, Ben's manner switches
from being reasonably friendly, to a little brusque, as
if he suddenly doesn't really want to be here. I don't
know if it's my Australian accent, my convict hairdo,
or my clothes – which, after being shoved in and out
of suitcases countless times, are beginning to resemble
a retro shop dummy in Carnaby Street. Whatever the
reason, I can tell Ben isn't all that impressed with me,
and my chest tightens in familiar apprehension. But
I've learned these last two months not to let my own
feelings show, so I simply take an even deeper breath,
and smile an even smilier smile, and remind myself that
with just a few more countries to go, I can soon quit
putting myself through such torture.

Ben takes me to the Notting Hill Brasserie, a contemporary restaurant in a Victorian terrace house, with
a decidedly exclusive feel to it, like it's a secret dinner
club where you have to be frightfully posh, or exceptionally rich, to join. I'm neither posh nor rich, but I take
my seat at a cosy corner table and vow to enjoy myself,
no matter what happens. Although I do rather wonder
when Ben is going to thaw out, and make it a bit easier
for me. So I'm startled when he suddenly smiles.

'I was told this is the place to come for a romantic
dinner,' he says in a slightly mesmerising voice remi-
niscent of Heathcliff in *Wuthering Heights*, and which

leaves me wondering what his expectations of me are, despite Eva having already set the ground rules of 'hands off'. But has she told him the same?

Over an olive martini that I hope doesn't reflect how the night is going to end up – shaken, not stirred – I try to discover what's behind Ben's still somewhat guarded façade. Instead I find myself on the receiving end of *his* questions about my trip thus far, which he poses with the aplomb of a psychoanalyst. Indeed, I even find myself admitting how disappointed I'd been that things didn't work out with Stefano. Or Eduard. Or Albert. Prince Albert that is.

'Darling, you can tell in the first sixty seconds if you're interested in someone,' Ben says bluntly. 'They probably knew straight away it wasn't going to work out with you.'

Although I already know this is often true, I still wince. It brings up all those insecurities with which I've been battling pretty much my whole life, and certainly the last ten weeks. Plus it's a clear implication as to where he stands. But I'm not going down without a fight.

'But you can be wrong,' I say as cheerfully as possible. 'You need to give people a chance, as sometimes first impressions can be very misleading.'

'Sometimes,' Ben answers smugly, 'but usually not.'

The waiter arrives to take our orders, which gives me the opportunity to pull myself together. I can't help thinking that Ben has already prodded, weighed, held me up to the light, and put me back on the shelf without giving me a chance to show my true flavour. Which is ironic, given that's what I'd been a smidge guilty of two months ago with a couple of dates I'd evaluated over quickly – Christian, Martin, Claus and, more recently, Robin.

'So what do you need to know then?' Ben asks, perking up a little, as if pleased I've stuck up for myself. 'Although I don't think you can get to know anyone at all well without going to bed with them. It's the only way to really get intimate.'

I experience an unnerving sense of deja vu, and must look startled, because Ben leans back in his chair and smiles.

'Don't worry darling,' he says, 'I'm not talking about us. I've already made my mind up that scenario won't be happening tonight. Or ever. Definitely not.'

There's a strange thing that happens in a girl's head when she's told she can't have something. Even if she hadn't wanted it before – when she's told she can't have it, she suddenly wants it. Or if she still doesn't want it, then she feels insulted she's been told she can't have it. I'm experiencing the latter. I suppose because we all want to be attractive to the opposite sex – or whatever one's fancy may be – and when we're overlooked we feel diminished. Rejected. But it's not the first time it's happened to me, so I shrug my shoulders and tell myself that I don't fancy him either.

'Good,' I say. 'Well, that's cleared that up; now perhaps we can both relax and enjoy the night.'

Things improve somewhat once I've let Ben off the hook, and he opens up to me a little more. Although it's a two-edged sword, for as I get a clearer picture of 'who' he is, I feel increasingly inferior. He's very smart, extremely articulate, reads voraciously, loves culture, art, literature and music, and has a high-profile job as a European hedge fund manager.

'Is that in banking?' I ask, unsure exactly what a hedge fund is, but wanting to sound vaguely knowledgeable. At least I know it's not anything to do with horticulture.

Ben looks at me as if I'm closely related to a marine mollusc. 'You obviously don't know much about banking do you?' he sniffs.

'Okay … um … so do you think you're a typical Englishman?' I blunder on, trying to save face by getting back to stuff I do know a bit about. 'You know, wearing bowler hats and drinking copious amounts of Earl Grey tea?'

'Don't be absurd,' Ben snaps, 'no-one wears bowler hats.'

'I saw someone wearing one today in Fortnum and Mason,' I reply, wondering if there's an operation one can have that stops one sounding like a total imbecile.

'That's a ridiculous clichéd image of England,' he huffs. 'Bowler hats, and gin and tonics. Just ridiculous.'

'I'm just trying to be funny,' I say limply.

'Well, you're not,' he says.

Ouch.

As judgemental as Ben is, I get the impression throughout our conversation that he's quite evolved when it comes to relationships. My theory seems to be supported when he reveals he's dating a woman with whom he's very much in love.

'There's total honesty between us,' he says, his voice gentle now. 'It's essential to be really naked, that they see you as you are – physically, and emotionally, on your good days and your bad days – and that they still accept and love you no matter what.'

As Ben bares his soul bit-by-bit, and even starts to get quite emotional, I'm inclined to think that behind the brusque and critical exterior, there's a man who just wants love and validation. But I'm still curious as to how deep it goes. After all, there's naked, and there's naked.

'Is your girlfriend beautiful?' I ask.

'Yes,' he replies. 'She's 48 with a body 38-year-olds would envy. But what's most important to me is intellect, and she's got that in spades. So we constantly challenge each other, and have the most amazing conversations.'

'You sound like soulmates,' I say, impressed he's not as superficial as some very smart and successful men I've met, more interested in 'tit than wit'. 'Do you believe in forever?'

'Forever is a silly prescription from a *Cosmopolitan* magazine,' Ben snorts. 'Of course I don't know what's going to happen in the future. Or even tomorrow.'

Over the course of dinner Ben continues to correct me for the slightest gaffes or inconsistencies, and flippant remarks that are supposed to be fun go down with him like a lead weight being hurled off Big Ben. It's clear he thinks I'm just not in his league – so much so that I decide I have nothing to lose, and may as well go for broke.

'And what about the reputation of the English male being rather lame in bed?' I ask, secretly delighted that I'm hitting below the belt. Literally.

'Well, that's just coming from an Australian culture where the men are all macho and overly loud,' Ben replies, leaning back in his chair, and now eyeing me as if I'm something that's gone off in the fridge. But to his credit, he spends the next ten minutes defending the honour of English men, and not the least himself, implying how far from lame his own sex life is. Indeed, it sounds like it's positively doing somersaults. But even so, he's not all chest-beating and Neanderthal about it, focusing more on the importance of a man to be 'generous', and to care as much about the woman's pleasure as his own.

Hmm ... if the same applies to most Englishmen, I'm moving to England next week.

'So how many men have you slept with on this adventure?' Ben suddenly asks, his kestrel-bright eyes boring into mine.

This question is quite fair enough, although I find myself completely lost for words. It's one thing for me to invade someone else's privacy, and quite another to have my own intimate secrets laid bare. Besides, I don't want to look like a Scarlet Woman. Perhaps just a nice Pale Pink.

'Well, darling,' Ben says when I don't answer straight away, 'I certainly hope you've slept with at least one.' Then he grins crookedly, as if challenging me to a duel.

'At least one,' I reply, smiling right back.

Ben calls for the bill – so abruptly it's like his Tolerance for Imbeciles Meter has just run out, and he can't stay clocked in for a second longer. We've eaten appropriately English fare of jerusalem artichoke soup, and roast quail with wild mushrooms, but I can hardly remember what they tasted like, given I was more focused on not putting my foot in my mouth, than putting the fork in.

It was a frightfully expensive dinner, and although I was originally planning to pay for Ben too, I end up just thrusting into his hand enough to cover my half and the tip. After all, the posh restaurant was his choice, as were the martinis at £8.75 a swizzle stick. And besides, I'm no longer quite so inclined to be as generous, given that over the course of the meal he'd implied that I was stupid at least thirty-seven times. And yes – I kept count.

As we wait for our credit cards to be returned, I sneak in one last question, and given Ben's intellectual arrogance, I'm curious as to what his response will be.

'You'll really hate this,' I say, at which he raises one black eyebrow at me like it's a raven from the Tower of London about to take flight. 'But if your personality was an animal, what would you be?'

'Pass,' Ben replies curtly.

'Pass?'

Ben sighs impatiently. 'Darling, animals don't have personalities, they have genetic imprints that create behavioural patterns.'

'It's not science,' I say, feeling my own patience stretching a bit thin. 'It's fun. For example a confident person might say he was a lion, and a shy person a mouse.'

'I'm not an animal,' Ben snorts. 'This is a totally ridiculous question more befitting of a mindless women's magazine, and I refuse to answer. It's absolute bullshit.'

Ben is sitting way back in his chair now, a metre from the table with his arms locked behind his neck, regarding me as if that thing in the fridge has just crawled out and is morris dancing on top of the table. Still, the defiant optimist in me believes that there's a little boy vulnerability somewhere underneath all Ben's caustic remarks, and a need to be loved and validated.

Then again, maybe I've got it all wrong, and he really *is* just a self-opinionated tosser.

The next morning, still feeling like I've been strapped to the stocks and pelted with tomatoes, I receive an email from Ben.

```
Bambi. Thanks for last night. Great fun.
If you are around in the UK over Xmas New
Year & in need of company let me know.
You would be welcome in the Cotswolds. I
even have wellies to spare.
Ben x
```

I'm confused. I thought he'd had a dreadful night. I certainly did. But maybe an acerbic wit and a critical tongue is simply his default personality. And it's even conceivable he enjoyed the banter because it gave him something to chew on. Which makes me think of a perfect food match for him – the hot English mustard I had with the pork roast at The Wolesley. It's sharp, complex and flavoursome, but so blistering it can blow your head off. Best consumed in small doses. Or quite frankly, if you value your sense of self-preservation, not at all.

As I fly out of London, I feel very low. I'm so sad I didn't find The One here, as I really like Englishmen – even without their bowler hats. And I'm only too conscious of the fact I'm fast running out of time, with only three countries to go on this odyssey.

But as my dear friend Maree so wisely said, I have to keep mixing the pot. And I'm hoping, like a good soup or casserole which improves over time, when I eventually find The One, he'll be so well infused with hearty flavours, that with me as the bread to soak him all up, life will be a feast for years to come.

UNITED ARAB EMIRATES
The art of peeling onions

As I fly into Dubai I'm reminded of the desert tribal scenes in *Lawrence of Arabia* – of handsome men with smooth olive complexions and noses the size of yacht keels, staring intensely into the distance, with hooded falcons perched upon their broad shoulders. And yacht keels for noses don't bother me at all; in fact, I find them quite noble, as if they're descended from Egyptian pharaohs. Indeed, it's all very exotic and oddly thrilling, and I'm finding myself quite open to the idea of being swept off my feet and thrown over the rump of an Arabian stallion, to spend the rest of my life swanning about verdant oases and eating vast quantities of figs.

Then again, I may be ninety-odd years out of date, and the oases could well have been replaced by Oberoi luxury hotels. Still, I'm curious to see if either of my two dates in Dubai fit with more contemporary descriptions of the Emiratis – on one hand proud, brave, friendly, generous and loyal, and on the other volatile, zealous, unsophisticated, hot-headed and chauvinistic. Either way, it's going to be an interesting week.

I'm staying in Dubai with Richard, an old English boyfriend – no, not the one who was scared of saliva. He lives thirty-six floors up in a vast and luxurious apartment overlooking one of the world's most expensive, and newest, cities, and across to the hazy desert beyond. The city skyline is filled with dramatic new office blocks with reflective glass and shiny gold panels, including the tallest skyscraper in the world, Burj Khalifa. Known as Burj Dubai prior to its inauguration, it measures 829.8 metres, well over twice the height of the Empire State Building. And there are even more skyscrapers to come, with nearly as many construction cranes as there are telegraph poles, skewering the city like giant shish kebabs.

But it's the old Dubai I want – at least today – so I catch a taxi to the Gold Souk, passing by delicate pink minarets poking shyly above the date palms, and mud-brick apartment blocks festooned with laundry flapping on balconies. The underwear here is much more modest than what I saw strung up in Naples. It's mostly white cotton briefs or oversized bloomers that whisper 'devout wife and mother, or daughter', in polite contrast to Italy's far more brazen pink satin G-strings shouting out 'spank me'.

At the entrance to the souk I buy freshly squeezed

orange juice from a barefoot ten-year-old boy pushing a rickety wooden cart, and drink it as I watch the local women bustling to and fro about the market. Most are covered from top to toe in their all-enveloping black *abayas* – robe-like dresses, and *niqabs* – veils with just a letterbox slit through which their dark kohl-lined eyes are revealed. They look like giant black mussel shells opened up just enough for their residents to peer out at the world beyond. One woman is wearing a full veil over her face, so I can't see anything of her at all. At first I feel oddly insulted that she's being so antisocial. As if she's too arrogant to share herself with the world. And then I feel sorry for her, being so subjugated by an oppressive religion that hides women away like laundry in a linen press. But then when I get the sense that she is calmly watching me watching her, I think perhaps there might be an advantage in her being able to watch the whole world go by, with no-one knowing what's going on underneath her camouflage, and the anonymity that comes with that.

Which gets me to wondering about my two dates, and whether they prefer deeply conservative and chiffon-shrouded women like these, or slightly more liberal ones, like the woman striding confidently past wearing the usual black *abaya*, but with a bright pink cotton headwrap, and even brighter pink lipstick. I also wonder if either of the men I'm to meet has ever dated a Westerner. I wonder what they'll think of me with my cotton trousers that clearly indicate I have two legs, and ears exposed for all the world to see. I wonder if they'll think me a promiscuous hussy who has no shame.

I wonder what on earth I'm letting myself in for.

As I head deeper into the bowels of the souk, the older vendors look like something straight from *Ali Baba and the Forty Thieves*. Their intense black eyes and wildly hooked noses are set upon fabulously weathered faces as wizened as raisins, and they have great bushy grey beards, with who knows how many larks nestled within. Their black-and-white *keffiyehs* are neatly draped upon their heads, which makes them appear quite dignified, although they have an unnerving habit of spitting loudly into the gutters as I pass. After half an hour of negotiating my way past a hundred such vendors trying to sell me stuff I'm pretty sure I don't need, from gold-threaded bedspreads to belly-dancing outfits – I mean, I've got a belly, but after ten weeks eating my way around the world it's best left tucked out of sight – I eventually get to the Spice Souk. It's heaven, with tiny shops crammed side-by-side offering delights straight from the storybooks of my childhood, including wooden boxes of frankincense and myrrh, which makes me think of the Three Wise Men. Hessian sacks overflow with vanilla pods, aniseed, cardamom, star anise, turmeric, cloves and whole dried lemons to cook with chicken or fish. There are rose and hibiscus petals for aromatic teas, clutches of cinnamon sticks like tiny bundles of firewood tied up with purple string, and huge sacks of dried prawns and shrimps. Their combined scent hangs so thickly in the air it clogs my nostrils, and I feel strangely alive, as each and every sense is challenged. Stefano would be proud of me.

One shop has an Aladdin's lamp displayed on a dusty shelf. It looks authentic, although I suspect there are another dozen just like it stacked up in a box behind the gap-toothed vendor who's trying to catch my eye. Nonetheless, I find myself imagining how many wishes I'd get for fifty dirham. And what would I wish for? And then I realise I mustn't be too greedy, and should ask for just the one wish. The same one I've had most of my life: To find The One. It's just that up until now I've never had a genie to grant it. But I leave the lamp with the vendor, who's now studiously picking his cavernous nose. I'll put my faith instead in the power of the universe – with which I'm more familiar. I just hope it will listen this time around, because time is running out for me as fast as Saharan sand through an hourglass.

My first date is with Nasser Al-Aqil – not his real name, but Richard has explained that because he's the nephew of a prominent politician, I must use a pseudonym 'to throw people off the scent, and not disgrace his family name'. So 'Nasser' has requested that I use the moniker of the hero in a book he's writing. It means 'victory' or 'triumphant'. He already sounds interesting.

'He's a bit wild, and not at all typical,' Richard warns me with an unsettling laugh as we await Nasser's arrival at the apartment, where Richard has poured me a generous glass of wine to help soothe my nerves. 'And I forgot to mention it before,' he continues, 'but when I told him that you'd like him to wear traditional dress, he insisted that you'll have to as well. So he's bringing his mother's *abaya* for you to wear.'

I'm dumbfounded. Me in an *abaya*? I don't think so. First of all, I don't look good in voluminous black.

I'm too tall and too thin, and will end up looking like one of the Evil Horseman in *Lord of the Rings*. Secondly, I'm guessing Nasser's mother is much shorter than me, so my skinny white ankles will stick out ridiculously from the bottom of the robe, and be a dead giveaway that I'm a fraud. Indeed, I'm worried about what the punishment is for a Christian masquerading as a Muslim. You can get one hundred and fifty lashes in the UAE for adultery, and although fraud is surely a lesser evil, things could still get nasty.

Nasser arrives right on time. He's quite handsome, in a dark, brooding and attractively villainous way. He's neatly bearded and olive-skinned with a slightly humped nose, and long camel eyelashes framing heavily hooded eyes. He's in his late twenties and wearing the full white *dishdasha*, and a colourful red-and-white *ghutra* headdress tied with a black rope, or *agal*. He's instantly charming and friendly, and the twinkle in his eye is more than just the reflection of his rimless spectacles. Thank goodness, for it suggests I've passed the 'first impressions' hurdle. Which makes it just a hundred or so hurdles to go, given that coming from completely different cultures, we'll probably have as much in common as a camel burger and a strawberry milkshake.

Nasser firmly hands me his mother's black *abaya*, and a *sheyla* – chiffon headscarf – so I have no option but to slink off to the bathroom and put them on. Thankfully the robe reaches right to the floor so I won't look too conspicuous, and even better, it looks rather fetching, with finely decorated black jet beads along the sleeves, around the cuffs, and all the way down the front. Still, as I stand in front of the mirror, breathing in the rich perfume that's infused into the material – a heady mix of creamy tobacco, leather and smoky wood – I can't help feeling like an impostor, and more than ever wondering if I've taken this whole dating idea too far. It's one thing to want to meet a fabulous smorgasbord of men from which I hope to find The One, but now I'm in an Islamic country far from home, wearing a stranger's mother's clothing, and have no idea what to expect of my date. Nasser could turn out to be a slave trader for all I know. But as I continue inhaling the perfume that I now recognise as *oud*, the local scent favoured by Emiratis, my mind starts to conjure up exotic images of sumptuously decorated tents and being hand-fed figs by handsome eunuchs. So I take a deep breath, and decide to get on with the show.

Nasser looks at me approvingly when I reappear, and wraps the delicate chiffon scarf around my head, showing me how to hold the tail end of it in front of my face, for when we go out in public. I look very odd with my convict-cropped brown hair sticking out the edges of the *sheyla* – like a black mussel that hasn't been debearded. My blue-green eyes and pale skin are also a dead giveaway that I'm not a local, although Nasser seems happy enough, and announces that my name will be Noori for the rest of the evening. I can't help but wonder what role Noori plays in the book he's writing. I do hope she's not the village idiot. Or a hooker.

Nasser smiles conspiratorially with a sideways glance to Richard. 'I am taking you someplace where a single woman must cover herself. It is where unmarried couples go to be discreet.'

Brilliant. Fancy-dress parties have always been my thing because I could become someone else and lose myself in an outlandish fantasy. So tonight I'll be Noori stepping out as a shameless wench.

Nasser has no hesitation in joining Richard in a pre-dinner drink, despite it being illegal for Emirati Muslims to drink alcohol – punishable by flogging or a stint in jail. Indeed, apart from his crisp white *dishdasha* and *ghutra*, Nasser acts and speaks like a perfect Westerner, so I suspect he's had a healthy stint in overseas' boarding schools or universities.

After Nasser's tossed down his drink – and another – we head off to a local restaurant. I'd been hoping for a night in a carpeted Bedouin tent in the desert, reclining on tasselled cushions and eating stuffed pigeon, but our destination turns out to be Abu Ali, a large two-storey eatery, its front windows festooned with gaudy Christmas decorations. I can't help being disappointed – it's about as Middle Eastern as a Hungry Jacks – and I'm guessing I'll be missing out on the pigeon tonight, and ending up with fried chook. Before we enter, Nasser readjusts my headdress, looping and tightening the scarf around my ears, so I feel like I've just had brain surgery. The doorman looks rather surprised by my awkward shuffle, and the fact I'm hanging on to Nasser's arm for dear life, as I now have no peripheral vision whatsoever, and very little sense of hearing. As instructed, I hold up the scarf to hide my face, so I have to peer through the chiffon to vaguely figure out where I'm going. I feel quite disembodied – like I'm walking through a black fog – and it's not a pleasant sensation at all. Stefano can keep this one.

Navigating the stairs up to the second floor is a nightmare. I keep stepping on my hem as I mount each step. Step, trip. Step, trip. Step, trip. Which makes me appreciate why Bedouins live in tents. We finally make it up to the restaurant, and Nasser asks for his private cabin, in which he tells me 'inappropriate behaviour' between local unmarried couples can be carried out without detection, because 'it's shameful to be a single woman out with a man. So if you want to go on a date you must be discreet.'

I certainly hope Nasser isn't thinking of trying on anything inappropriate himself tonight. I mean – I love Arab noses, but I don't need them getting into my private business. As it is, there's been a mix-up with his booking, and all six cabins are taken, so thankfully I'll never find out if Nasser had any mischief up the voluminous sleeve of his *dishdasha*. We're shown to a table in a discreet, shadowy corner, where Nasser informs me that I can finally loosen the infuriating scarf, so that it's draped lightly over my head, thus making it less of an instrument of torture, and more of a Mona Lisa veil. A waiter materialises by Nasser's side and takes the order, and I'm enthralled how he's able to ignore my very existence. Indeed, I get the distinct impression that he simply regards me as a large piece of black fabric arranged cleverly on the chair. Nasser, however, is far more engaged with me, and only too happy to answer my questions about meeting women in a country with such repressive social codes of conduct.

'So how do you meet girls here?' I ask. 'At parties?'

'No. Most parties I attend are only with men,' Nasser replies. 'We don't have parties with men and women in the same room.'

'What? So how do you get to meet women then?'

'We don't – it's nearly impossible to meet women in Dubai,'

Nasser says, shrugging his shoulders. 'Well, at least local women. The only way to meet them is through arranged marriages or introductions, and even then the first date is in front of her whole family.'

I'm shocked. It would be ghastly having my whole family watching on whilst I'm trying to make polite conversation with some bloke my father picked out for me at the local camel races. But I'm also intrigued.

'Okay,' I press on. 'So once you get introduced to someone you like, what happens then, where do you hang out?'

'We don't hang out. There is no courting period,' Nasser replies. 'You have to decide by the second date if you want to marry her, and then you make a commitment and get engaged.'

'By the second date?' I squeak. 'But you can't possibly know anyone well enough to marry them after only two dates.'

Nasser sighs patiently. 'It doesn't really matter if you don't know her well. You only get married if you want children and a wife to raise them.'

'What about love?' I ask weakly, feeling a knot tightening in my stomach at the romantic wasteland of this approach, although perhaps it's got something to do with living in the desert. Empty spaces – empty hearts.

'Marriage isn't about love,' Nasser replies bluntly. 'And anyway, I'm just an intellectual primate, so genuine romance doesn't figure in my thought processes.

I'll write poetry for the girl because they like that sort of thing. But I don't actually feel any of the emotions associated with it at all. I just know how to woo with words to get what I want.'

As my image of romantic Arabs on horseback vanishes – just like a mirage does as you're about to reach out and touch it – Nasser's phone beeps. He reads the message on it cradled out of sight on his lap, before quickly texting back. I figure something's up, so I ask him if he has a girlfriend – perhaps a foreign one he's snuck past his parents.

'Let me tell you something,' he says huskily, leaning towards me. 'At the moment I have five girlfriends. One is a 28-year-old local girl. Then there is a 28-year-old in Lebanon, a 40-year-old American living in London, a 21-year-old Iraqi-Canadian, and a 24-year-old Moroccan living in Bahrain.'

'And they all think they're your girlfriend?' I ask, slightly appalled, given I'm no great fan of polyamory.

'No,' Nasser shrugs. 'I have told them all about the other girls, and they don't mind. They know the deal.'

'Do you think being with so many girls at the same time is a leftover from the days of the harem?' I ask.

I'm not being rude. I'm genuinely interested in the whole idea of such an institution, especially back during the Ottoman Empire, when it all sounded frightfully glamorous. After all, where else would you find beautiful women lounging semi-clad or naked on exotic day beds, fiddling idly with flowers or fans, or soaking in jasmine-scented Turkish baths? And I'm not talking Spearmint Rhino or the Bunny Ranch type venues. Although I suppose at the end of the day they're pretty much the same thing.

'Is it because of the romance associated with harems?' I continue, hoping there's a soft side to Nasser.

'No, I am simply incapable of fidelity,' he smiles. A bit creepily. It's the sort of smile a sultan might make before picking who's going to have the honour of sharing his bed next. 'But when I am with them they are the only ones in my life,' he continues. 'They are all different, all special.'

The phone beeps again, but this time Nasser ignores it, and I can't help but wonder how special these girls really are to him. But then – like finding water in the desert by digging deep enough – I discover that Nasser hasn't always been as superficial as he's just made out. Indeed, he admits he's still nursing a broken heart from when he was a young man.

'It was so bad that from then on I decided just to have fun,' he says, but from his pained expression I'm not so sure whether he's trying to convince me, or himself. 'So it's not fair for me to marry anyone whilst I'm in this frame of mind. And also I have a low boredom threshold. I'm fascinated by new people, new experiences, and discovering new positions to have sex.'

I'm not sure how to respond to this – so I don't – and am thankful when our food arrives, allowing me to have a break from the conversation. It's exhausting trying to negotiate a path between being judgemental or accepting of Nasser's behaviour. He's certainly proving the chauvinistic stereotype I had of Middle Eastern men. But then in other ways he's far more sophisticated than I expected – cultured, educated, well-travelled, and interested in literature and philosophy. In fact, although very religious as a younger man, he now sees himself as agnostic, and questions everything, including much of his family's traditional take on how a young Emirati should behave.

'They'd be horrified if they knew what I got up to,' he laughs, replying to yet another text under the table.

'*Bismillah*. In the name of God,' Nasser says, tucking his *ghutra* out of the way, and encouraging me to sample all the food, even though it appears to be mostly Lebanese. Nasser explains this is because uniquely Emirati food has never really been commercialised, so the majority of restaurants serve broader Arab, European and South Asian food. Still, I'll work with what I've got, as I'm curious as to whether Nasser will match any of the dishes on offer. A plate of bright-pink pickled radish shows promise, as he's certainly a colourful character, but upon tasting is too sweet for him. Grilled red capsicums are close, but again too sweet. Hummus served with pita bread is too bland. Lebanese-style baby sausages are too – well – Lebanese. *Shish taouk*, marinated chicken kebabs, doesn't quite sum him up. There's also a dish of spiced raw meat patties called *kibbeh nayyah*, which looks alarmingly like the aftermath of a woodchipper murder. But the flavour could be right, so I shut my eyes and try just half a forkful in case I regret it. Nasser's hoeing into it with great enthusiasm, so it can't be all bad.

Or can it? Many times during this trip I've wondered how certain dishes ever got to be invented, let alone embraced as a popular cuisine, and this is one of those moments. The raw meat is slimy and the texture is like pâté, and it tastes of – well, slimy raw meat. I can't help thinking what icky little bugs might be living in it, who are now shrieking with delight at the prospect of giving me food poisoning. Still, I nibble away at it politely, and just hope my travel insurance covers botulism.

Over a seven-course meal, I discover much about Nasser, and am as confused as ever. He writes poetry, but isn't actually romantic. He likes women who know what they want, but he wants to be in charge. He likes women who are refined and feminine, but who enjoy red meat, as 'women who only eat salads are a turn-off'. He's a bit all over the place.

'And besides,' he suddenly declares, 'I've discovered something about women.'

'Hmm?' I say, only half listening now, tiring of his narcissism.

'Most girls want crazy sex,' he continues unselfconsciously. 'Something intense and kinky. They like the streak of the bad boy in me, the sense of danger that comes with it. They want me to be the man, so they can be the woman. They want to play too.'

As if on cue, Nasser's mobile phone rings. It's a voice call, and I suspect it's the girl who's been texting all night. Poor love, she's probably half crazed with jealousy thinking Nasser's out with someone else. Indeed, I'm guessing that 'they don't mind' is just a convenient figment of Nasser's imagination.

Nasser hurriedly excuses himself from the table, and heads to the lobby to do some damage control. He's away for ages, but I'm rather enjoying just sitting here – smelling delicious and feeling mysterious. And strangely enough I'm beginning to enjoy the anonymity of wearing the *abaya*. For all anyone else knows, I could be sitting here wearing nothing more underneath than frilly black knickers and a peek-a-boo bra. I feel feminine and sexy, and oddly powerful. Not that I'd want to have such sensory deprivation thrust upon me day after day, which I find deeply sexist and oppressive. But being Noori for just one night, suits me fine.

Nasser returns looking harried. He's clearly in need of something to calm him down, so he orders a shisha, or water pipe, which he also offers to me. I've never smoked in my life, apart from a puff on a joint when I was twenty. But if I'm here to get a proper sense of the Emirati culture, then I better go all the way. There's a choice of mint, grape, rose or apple, of which mint sounds the most refreshing. In minutes we both have a shisha sitting beside us on the floor, the rubber hosepipes snaking up to our lips. I carefully watch Nasser as he takes a suck of his, then blows out a little puff of white smoke. I mimic him, inhaling carefully to start with, wanting to avoid scorching my lungs. But I can't feel anything, so I hold my breath and suck in a little harder. I still can't feel anything going down, so I inhale again, using the last of the space in my lungs, and beginning to think it's all a waste of time. I open my mouth to say as much, whereupon I blow out a volcanic-worthy eruption of mint-scented white smoke. Nasser laughs warmly at my ineptitude, although I eventually get the hang of it, and puff away happily. But I soon call it quits, as I'm getting so light-headed that I feel like the spaced-out Caterpillar in *Alice in Wonderland*. No wonder he was green if he smoked these all day.

Before I risk passing out, I ask Nasser what animal he sees himself as, to which he snorts dismissively.

'No, ask me what musical instrument I would be. That's far more interesting,' he says.

I oblige, intrigued.

'A piano. A grand piano,' he replies triumphantly. 'It's majestic, and proud. Its music starts off very strongly and very aggressive, full of energy, then it mellows out. It eventually becomes nostalgic, philosophical and sweet ...'

Nasser certainly has a great many keys to press, but I'm not sure that this metaphor is a completely good fit for him, as he comes across to me as more of a heraldic trumpet.

'But being a piano is a problem for me,' he adds despondently. 'Some teachings say that Islam forbids all forms of music, as it may lead to dancing which may lead to sex. Islam says music was invented by Satan, and has a toxic effect on the human mind.'

I suddenly feel sorry for Nasser. He's a man of great intellect and passion for exploring his 'senses', but his country's strict devotion to Islamic tradition obviously restricts him to just skirting around the edges of his desires – in public at least.

'But I think what the fuck,' he continues defiantly. 'I want to play my music and to dance and to have women, so I'll just go to hell.'

Right.

Nasser's phone rings yet again, whereupon I suggest we call it a night so he can put his girlfriend out of her misery. Which he's clearly keen to do, as after driving me home, he stops outside the apartment block, keeps the engine running as I say my goodbyes, nearly drives off before I've fully disembarked, then skids off into the night, leaving me and my *abaya* covered in a cloud of fine Arabian Desert sand.

Sliding silently back up thirty-six floors in a glass elevator – through which I can see the stars above blazing like diamonds on a sultan's velvet bedspread – I consider what food best suits Nasser. And I can't go past a *kibbeh nayyah*. The raw beef patty represents his red-bloodedness, the onion his many layers, the paprika his spiciness, and the mint his colourful personality. Even so, for all this richness of flavour, Nasser was never going to be The One. Raw and slimy just doesn't do it for me – either in food or a man.

Besides, he's already got five girlfriends, and I don't like to share my men. Well, apart from in Switzerland, but that was … um … different.

OMAN
The sweetest date

My friend Richard is taking his wife and two young children to Muscat for the weekend, so I hitch a ride with him to get to my date in Oman. It's a gruelling 400-kilometre drive, but I'm loving it. It's the first time in eleven weeks I've not been in busy airports, smelly train stations, noisy cafés, smoky restaurants and all the other manic accoutrements of civilisation. Indeed, I can finally relax and allow the emptiness of the desert to become one with my soul. Which is what it's craving, just as a falcon craves open skies in which to soar. And who knows, maybe at the other end I'll meet someone. Someone special with whom I can share the peace and

tranquility of a place that seems to be lost in time, exist-
ing just like it had several hundred years ago, before the
rest of the world got completely crazy.

I don't actually hold out that much hope for such a
scenario though. Oman has a primarily Arab culture,
which means I most likely won't have a whole lot in
common with the local men, being more of a burlesque
than a burqa kind of gal. But it's still worth going ahead
with my date, as I'm enjoying the challenge of meeting
men in this part of the world, who must think that I'm
a creature from Mars, given my wildly liberal ways,
which most women from Islamic backgrounds could
only ever dream of. The knowledge of which is quietly
giving me confidence that I'm an extraordinarily lucky
woman, leading a very privileged and unshackled life.
And that even if I never find The One – well – I'm still
way better off than most. Which is perhaps a lesson I
needed to learn.

Halfway to Muscat, the dramatic Al Hajar Mountains
loom into view like giant loaves of black pumpernickel
bread nibbled at their peaks by hordes of marauding
mice, and signs of habitation are beginning to appear.
A man leads his camel along the side of the road, its
huge knobbly knees almost in caricature, and its long
neck elegantly curved like the spout on an Arabian tea-
pot. Ancient tan-on-tan mud forts dot the landscape,
looking exactly like the sandcastles I used to make as a
child using those plastic buckets with crenellated par-
apets on the base. They've even got little poke-through
windows, and although they seem to be deserted, I'm
half expecting ghostly sandcastle people to morph up
out of the dunes and head back inside for a nice cup of

chai haleeb.

After a bottom-numbing seven-hour trip – made a great deal more uncomfortable by a two-year-old boy who has the very-well-deserved nickname of Pooh – we reach the centre of Muscat, where I'm struck by the inordinate amount of men walking around holding hands. I've been to several Middle Eastern countries in my time, so I know it's a sign of affection and respect, rather than anything to do with a particular sexual orientation, but it still always startles me. Never in a million years would straight Aussie men wander around holding hands with their 'mates'. Indeed, they'd much rather smack them cheerfully over the back of the head, and then buy them a cold beer.

We're staying in the Radisson Blu Hotel, and needing a circuit breaker after the long trip, Richard and I head straight for the Coral Bar. Drinking alcohol is forbidden in Oman, unless it's in registered hotels or you have a licence to drink it at home, so the locals look somewhat furtive – hunched over and staring intently into their imported ales, trying to look inconspicuous. They're wearing ankle-length white *dishdashas* and either embroidered pillbox-style hats called *kumas*, or flat-topped turbans called *muzzars*. Both styles look very dapper, and the men themselves are rather handsome, with dark features and either smooth olive skin, or ten-o'clock shadows. They have an air of mystery – even danger – about them, like they're drug runners plotting their next haul of hashish across the Oman–Ras Al Khaimah border.

Richard's family and I head to dinner just as the persimmon-hued sun is settling in for the night, slowly disappearing behind the jagged hills that form the back-drop to Muscat, and that look so much like big slabs of tasty halva, I want to break a bit off and nibble on its gritty sweetness. The hauntingly beautiful Islamic call to prayer rises up from the city all around me and then bounces back from the nearby mountains, so I feel cocooned in its almost seductive melancholy. The spires and minarets of a hundred mosques are brightly uplit, like glowing cyber torches from Darth Vader's arsenal. I feel like I'm in quite another world, where the ancient call of the wild meets the equally ancient call of a culture well over eight thousand years old. I'm truly at peace for the first time in months.

The restaurant we've been recommended by the concierge for its 'typical Oman food in typical Oman restaurant, and very good indeed', is in a drab two-storey building with two dead potted palms out front, and sandwiched between a tailor and a rather dodgy-looking café named Off Air Public Food. Still, I've learned not to judge a book by its cover – or a restaurant by its peeling paint – and I enter excitedly, hoping to find an Aladdin's kitchen full of reclining Omanese eating peeled grapes and deep-fried song-birds, with exotic belly dancers wafting around pouring peppermint tea into little porcelain cups. But there's just a long, dimly lit corridor with five doors leading off it to the right, and we're led to the end room and ushered in unceremoniously. Our 'private dining room' is a little, square, wood-panelled box with arched windows, and small Persian carpets arranged around a large plastic sheet on the ground. Yes – a plastic sheet, which I find somewhat insulting, given I'm no toddler who throws my food around. But then I realise perhaps it's for the locals, who traditionally dip the first three fingers of their right hand into the food bowl to scoop out the contents, so some of it's bound to end up on the floor. There are no tables or chairs, but plenty of chunky red-and-black Berber cushions, upon which I cheerfully throw myself – to get into the mood – only to discover that they're not softly stuffed with hand-plucked ostrich feathers, but sandbags, upon which I nearly break my hip.

The night is rapidly going downhill.

Fortunately the menu is in both Arabic and English so we won't be ordering blindly, and can avoid dishes such as 'boiled stomach', 'salted wet fish' or 'bull's eye', and stick to the things that – in most cases – sound quite edible. Even good. I order a number of meals to share, including *foul medammos* – a broad bean and garlic dish – at which Richard comments that he's glad it's me sitting next to Pooh on the way home tomorrow.

The meal is essentially a disaster. Cheap blue-and-white melamine bowls are piled high with mounds of yellow rice stirred through with a few bits of grey meat. It's quite impossible to tell which is chicken, or lobster, or prawn. Or camel roadkill. And everything is cold. Not the sort of cold like a cold salad is supposed to be, but cold like it's been shoved in the oven for a minute to reheat, and is still semi-frozen in the middle.

'What's that weird smell?' I ask, sniffing the air suspiciously.

'They cook with ghee,' Richard replies glumly, clearly wishing he'd stayed at the hotel and got room service. For pizza.

'Oh,' I shrug. 'Well, let's give it the benefit of the doubt. It may taste absolutely fabulous.'

'Ever the optimist,' mutters Richard with a pained smile.

I cautiously pick my way through the meal, and although some dishes like the *qabooli laham* – chickpea rice with 'freshly boiled meat cow', and the *marakh dijaj* – chicken curry, are quite tasty, the rest of it is pretty much inedible. The prawns taste like they've hauled themselves overland from the Dead Sea. The lobster – which is clearly not lobster but some previously unidentified sea creature – tastes like wet socks. And the *foul medammos* – even though I think it's a typo – is called 'foul' for good reason. It's mashed broad beans served as a thick greyish paste, and appears to have been made back when Sinbad was a boy.

'This looks like cat sick,' Richard's Vietnamese wife Ahn says solemnly. 'You know, when they sick up in the middle of the carpet after they've eaten a little sparrow.'

But it's not all bad. A huge bowl of dates are quite the best I've ever eaten. They're rich, dark, super sweet and deliciously fudgy, and I can't help but think that if I had a date – as in a man date – like these, I'd be in heaven. Which makes me wonder what my Omani connection – Hilal – will be like. I'm still open to falling in love with a local. I rather fancy the idea of living in a country that has more sand than you can point a water-divining rod at – just for the simplicity and solitude of it all. But it wouldn't be easy, as even though Oman's Sultan Qaboos is a pioneer when it comes to women's rights, I'm still not sure I could cope with never wearing a miniskirt again in public. Nor to have to ask permission to travel abroad. Nor be happy with the prospect of waking up one morning to find my husband has taken on an additional wife. Still, who knows, Hilal might turn out to be as much of a surprise as our dessert. It's *lokhemat*, which looks like uninspiring little balls of deep-fried dough, but which I discover have been flavoured with sweet lime and cardamom syrup, and are so totally, wickedly delicious, that all thoughts of cat sick disappear completely.

The next morning I'm looking forward to my meeting with Hilal, which has taken three months and four go-betweens to set up. But twenty minutes before I'm due to meet him in the hotel lobby for lunch, I receive a text.

Sorry, too much work to do, will have to pass on meeting. H

I'm horrified. I've come all the way to Oman especially to meet him, and I don't have a back-up plan whatsoever. And given Richard needs to start heading back to Dubai in a couple of hours, I'll need a miracle to find anyone else at such late notice. It seems my goose is well and truly cooked.

Or perhaps not. I may not be beautiful, or any good at maths, or able to get more than ten words out on a cryptic crossword, but I'm darned resourceful. So I take a deep breath, and brazenly front up at reception and explain my dilemma to the hotel manager. Now most people in such a position would be quite used to fielding requests from guests for bigger rooms, more towels, or even whether little Haakim can bring along his pet alligator. But asking for a date? I don't think so. Which makes it even more impressive when just ten minutes later, the manager of one of the smartest hotels in Oman has organised a date for me with Fahad – the Assistant Director of Sales and Marketing for the Radisson. And even better, he's meeting me in the lobby in five minutes. Now that's what I call Customer Service.

Fahad is in his late twenties, with warm nutmeg skin, soulful mud-brown eyes, and a cute little tuft of beard just below his lip that shows he has some personality, even though he initially comes across as quite conservative, and excessively polite. He's wearing a crisp white *dishdasha* and neat leather sandals, and a striking black, red and gold embroidered turban. Despite the rather unusual circumstances behind our introduction, Fahad is very open and friendly, with a ready smile, and seems quite comfortable sitting with me in the hotel's restaurant as I have exactly one hour to find out all there is to know about Omani men. Well, at least their love lives.

It turns out that Fahad has travelled a fair bit through his work, so has some reasonably liberal ideas on such matters. He's not interested in marrying a 'covered girl – a girl who wears an *abaya*', although he'll still be restricted to finding himself a local wife. Omani men aren't allowed to marry a foreigner unless 'she is very old – like over forty-five – or is handicapped', he tells me earnestly.

I nearly choke on my coffee. To think – at forty-seven I'm already regarded as old. Very old. I knew my use-by date was drawing ever closer, but in Oman it seems I would have been tossed onto the rubbish heap years ago. With my only chance of getting hitched being via a charitable concession. Good grief! Fahad must see the horror on my face, as he kindly explains this initiative is just to protect the local women.

'You see,' he says, in a voice as smooth and sweet as pomegranate syrup, 'Omani men had been taking Indian and Filipino wives so they didn't have to pay the large dowries, and even larger wedding expenses, that Omani women expected. And as a result Omani women were being left on the shelf.'

I know the feeling.

Intrigued, I press Fahad to continue, whereupon he speaks cheerfully of the whole dating ritual, which appears to have much the same restrictions as in the UAE.

'But we're lucky these days,' Fahad says with a smile. 'Twenty years ago you would marry without even having met your wife. You would have just seen her in a photo, and you would only meet her the day of the wedding. And sometimes it is quite a shock to see what you have married when you've gone from fully clothed to naked. These days it's not quite so strict, and at least you can try before you buy. Well, with foreign girls anyway.

A mischievous little twinkle in his eye suggests that Fahad isn't averse to the odd Foreign Affair or two, and he happily admits that he often dates Russian and Filipino women, who are 'a lot more fun' than the locals. Indeed, bit-by-bit I'm finding out that Fahad isn't quite the angel I'd first thought. He's full of fascinating cultural insights too, describing how his grandfather was allowed to have four wives, but limited it to two because otherwise it would have been too expensive, especially with up to six children apiece. How, when wanting to divorce, the men simply need to say, 'I divorce you' three times, and it's done. How a woman has to be a virgin on her wedding night, or she can be sent back home to her parents in disgrace.

'And sometimes her father may kill her for the shame of it,' Fahad says with a casual shrug, which gives me the impression that although not condoning such a brutal response, he certainly isn't railing in protest either. 'And these days,' Fahad adds, 'some girls who can't control themselves will get surgery to fix themselves back, so their husbands will never know what they have done.'

I bite my lip – hard – to stop myself commenting that perhaps it's also the men who 'can't control themselves'. Still, I mustn't be too critical, as such attitudes are clearly deeply ingrained in his culture, and underneath he's probably still a decent guy. As if reading my mind, Fahad suddenly leans forward and fixes me with his warm brown eyes. They're kind eyes, and compassionate, so perhaps his bark is worse than his bite.

'But for me love is still the primary objective,' he says, 'and I don't believe that love always follows marriage – arranged marriages I mean. I would prefer to do it the other way around.'

Fahad leans back in his wicker chair and smiles broadly, scratching at an itchy spot under his turban. His eyelashes are so long that a small army of desert mice could find ample shade beneath them. I'm pleasantly surprised how open and friendly he is, and although I don't agree with some of the more sexist attitudes of Omani culture, Fahad appears to be the perfect example of a modern-day Omani embracing the tradition and romance of the ancient days, and the practicality and freedom of modern times. He wears a *dishdasha* at work, but changes into jeans at home. He speaks Arabic most of the time, but switches to English – with a rather toffy accent – when need be. He fasts during Ramadan, but drinks beer twice a week at home with his friends.

He's eight thousand years old, and twenty-seven years young.

It's nearly time for me to go, but I've still got the animal question up my sleeve. Fahad leans forward with his elbows on the table, and carefully considers his response. His fingernails are beautifully manicured, and his wrists brown and slender. He smells nice too, of something spicy and soft and earthy, like he's been absorbing all the most beautiful scents from the shaded alleys of the Muttrah Souk – one of the oldest market places in the Arab world.

'A tiger,' he finally responds. 'My name in Arabic means "tiger", and I think maybe I am one too. A tiger is sharp, quick-tempered, and can attack, but what you see first is gentle and unassuming. You think I am safe to walk into the cage with, but I am not.'

With such a declaration, I'm not sure I've figured out Fahad after all. But it's time to go, and as I start the gruelling trek back to Dubai – with the windows wound right down to allow for any dramas from Pooh – I consider what Omani food would best suit Fahad's personality. And even though I've only had two meals here, I think I've found the perfect match.

Fahad is a big, round, delicious date. Very sweet, rich, dark and easy to digest. He also has a great texture – pliant and smooth but with just enough 'chew' in him to make him interesting. A delightful 'date' indeed.

I've bought Richard a present from the antique shop in the souk. It's a handsome brass compass from the early twentieth century – probably a leftover from the days when the British Army was helping defend the Omanis from attack by the Portuguese. It's meant to please him, but my heart feels heavy as I draft a note to go with it, sitting at the kitchen table surrounded by futuristic sky-scrapers all lit up like phosphorescent shoals of fish in an inky black ocean.

'In case you ever lose your direction in life, this will help you find your way again,' I write. Although to be honest I don't know whether the sentiment is more for him, or for me, because I don't really know where I'm headed anymore. My needle is constantly wavering between the North of my brain and the South of my heart. Between the gritty practicalities of everyday life, to the romantic notion that I still have a tiny window of opportunity to find myself a husband, and then maybe have one good egg left to cook up a kid.

So which way do I go? North or South? East or West? Time is fast running out.

JAPAN
Brain food

I've always been fascinated by Japanese men, most likely because as a child I watched TV programmes such as *The Samurai*, where the men were all oiled muscles, topknots and dragon tattoos. As I sit in a Tokyo coffee shop to observe the modern-day locals, and have to accept that not every Japanese man is going to be a ninja warrior, I still think they're very handsome – tall and slim with square jaws, and beautiful almond-shaped eyes on faces that look like they've been carved from soapstone. Which gets me to thinking what an adorable baby I'd have if I ended up with a Japanese man. There's one right here – a little porcelain doll of a thing with a perfectly round face and a little radish-top sprout of jet-black hair, the cutest-ever button nose and rosebud lips, and eyes as black as ink-wells. She's so delicious I could almost eat her. One of these would do me just fine.

But one step at a time – how will I get along with the local Japanese men? They have been variously described as 'gentle, thoughtful, private, proud, conservative, modest and incredibly polite'. And as for any negatives – well – it's probably best not to mention the war.

My first date isn't until this evening, so in the interim I'll be checking out the food. I can only speak a few Japanese words – *konnichiwa, arigatou* and sumo wrestler – which aren't going to get me far, although the latter *could* cater for any 'meaty' requirements, so I find a restaurant that has a menu with English captions under glossy photos of both Japanese and Western food. But once I'm seated, I realise I may have made a mistake. There's an odd mix of culturally confused dishes, including 'hamburg with harf done egg, loco-moco style', 'Indian chicken with Mexican pilaf', and rather dubious 'tomato ice-cream'. The Japanese offerings sound just as unappetising, with 'pig placenta jelly drink' taking first prize. I opt for a simple Chinese yam and seaweed salad, although when it arrives I think I've made my second mistake for the day. The bright-green seaweed initially looks promising, and at first taste is gelatinous and a little sweet – which I like. But the second bite results in a long string of gooey, transparent stuff, stretching half a metre from the fork to my mouth.

My God – what is it?

My first panicked thought is that a fish has been doing something very rude in amongst the seaweed with another fish. But as I look around wildly to see if any other diners are freaking out – they're not – I realise it's more likely to be raw egg white, in which I take some comfort. But still, I'm unable to finish the rest of the meal, and leave the restaurant hungry, hoping the three dates I have organised here won't be quite so ... well ... ooky. Indeed, I'm becoming increasingly depressed. After nearly three months on the hop I'm physically exhausted, emotionally drained, nearly broke, five kilos heavier, and worst of all, still The Oneless. Perhaps not so coincidentally, in the train I notice a boy reading a comic book – backwards – and I think how handy it would be to start life off like a Japanese novel, and read it from back to front, and thus somehow miraculously know stuff before it actually happens. Then maybe I wouldn't have screwed up my life so much. I'd have seen the queue of cads and bounders, the players and the heartbreakers, coming well before I'd even met them. Which means I probably wouldn't be sitting on a train in Japan wondering if I've just eaten fish semen.

Back at my *ryokan* I indulge in a traditional Japanese bath, hoping to relax before my date with Naoki tonight. The tub is made from pale Japanese cypress, with broad wooden slats on top, which, when removed, releases fragrant steam that billows up into my face like opening a lid on a pot of jasmine rice. Written instructions are taped to the wall: 'Please make sure you are clean before entry. Please make sure all soup has been clean for anybody.' I don't know where the soup comes into play, but I get the general idea, and perch myself on a tiny wooden stool to wash, using a ladle and a wooden bucket filled with hot water. This is by no means easy, as being close to six feet tall, my knees are up around my ears, and I nearly slide right off the stool, whilst the 'soup' goes skidding across the floor like a hockey puck. But I persist, and once I'm washed and rinsed, I remove the rest of the slats and lower myself into the tub. The water is a perfect temperature – hot enough to soak into every fibre of my being, but not enough to par-boil me. I immediately relax into its warm embrace, shutting my eyes and resting my head on a floating pillow. The world can wait a few minutes. After seventy-two dates over seventy-six days, I think I deserve some respite.

An hour and a half later, I wake up looking like a giant white prune – even my ear lobes haven't been spared. I'm appalled. Naoki has never met a Westerner before, and I don't want his first experience to leave him permanently scarred. If I ever find him that is, as his instructions to look out for a man with 'black hair and medium height and wearing a black jacket' may cause some issues in a city of twelve million Japanese. In the end I wait at the bustling Shinjuku Train Station for Naoki to come and find *me*. This way it will be much easier, given I'm so tall I'm standing out like a stork in a colony of penguins.

I was introduced to Naoki through two go-betweens – first through Elly, a colleague from work, and then through her friend Kym. Kym lives in Japan which is useful, but even so, she had a hard time finding someone suitable for me, because most Japanese men she knew were 'kind of stereotypical – cute but a bit geeky', which had me worried I'd end up with a little *Pokémon* character. Still, I was going to have to take whatever Kym could find me, especially as the Japanese Lifestyle Friends Alert website that had as good as blacklisted me because I was using 'insulting or offensive language' was never going to work.

Twenty minutes tick past, and just as I'm thinking that Naoki's going to be another no-show, one of the penguins peels away from the crowd and shyly introduces himself. It's Naoki. He's a fresh-faced man in his mid-twenties, with thick ebony hair sticking up like a shoe-brush, and elegant almond-shaped eyes, that although black as black, are friendly and warm.

Naoki's English is hesitant, but good, so we're able to chat easily enough as he leads me out of the subway and toward the restaurant district, where he's booked a table at Juraku Restaurant. We enter beneath a low-strung flag of a blazing rising sun, which requires us to bow as we enter. A pretty waitress in a traditional kimono bows back, and shows us to a cosy wooden gazebo-style seating area, separated from those either side by fine cane blinds.

'You rike Japanese food?' Naoki asks. 'Wirr I order for you?'

I nod enthusiastically, and Naoki swings into action, ordering everything in rapid-fire Japanese, starting with a small blue-and-white pitcher of hot sake – an alcoholic beverage brewed from fermented rice. Naoki grins broadly as he lifts the fine porcelain cup to his lips and looks me unwaveringly in the eyes.

'*Kanpai!*' he says, clearly enjoying himself.

I take a sip, and it's very light and a little sweet, gently warming my gullet on the way down. But before we've even finished the first pitcher, another arrives – a *shochu*, distilled from sweet potatoes. It's quite heavy, with a distinctively rich sweetness and underlying earthiness. It's good, but I'm a little concerned that given it has a 25 per cent alcohol content, I'll end the night on the floor of the restroom folded up like a piece of origami.

Naoki and I are soon chatting away happily, and although he's still somewhat shy, I pick up that behind the formality of an infantry officer in the Imperial Guard, there's a delightfully open and fun-loving young man. He's been married for a year, although he and his wife, Ikue, haven't had their honeymoon yet, as they've both been too busy with their careers. But he always tries to find the time to be romantic, with drives to the beach with Ikue, and 'just being togerrer', and writing her short love letters with the traditional *shodō* paintbrush. He also seems to have shaken off the customary male-dominant dynamics for which Japan is known, with he and Ikue both wearing the pants, although he laughs when he admits, 'But hers are a rittle ronger than mine.'

'There are four in my family,' Naoki tells me proudly when I ask him about his background. 'My father, mother, sister and me. It is a small family, what do you call it? A tight family unit?'

'We call it a nuclear family,' I reply. Without thinking.

'Exprain nucrear?' he asks politely.

'Nuclear, you know, like … um … nuclear. Oh.'

With my foot wedged so firmly in my mouth it would take a Suzuki on full throttle to extract it, I realise with horror that I'm explaining the word nuclear to someone who may have a very clear understanding indeed of what it means. And – God forbid – who may even have had relatives living in Hiroshima and Nagasaki.

'Nucrear?' he repeats, reaching for his electronic translator.

'Yes, nuclear. Um. A nucleus is the core of something, like the yolk of an egg,' I stumble desperately, forming my hands into a neat egg shape.

'Oh, nucrear, rike the bomb,' he says, reading off the screen.

'Um, yes, no, that's right,' I gabble, 'but in this case

it's like an egg with just a small yolk. The yolk is your family.'

'Aah. Yes, nucrear,' Naoki repeats, apparently oblivious to my distress, and the fact I've just downed the last of the *shochu* to hide my embarrassment.

Thankfully, the first dish arrives and I can depart the subject, not wanting to get into further debate about World War II. It's quite conceivable my father lobbed a few missiles Japan's way when he was serving in the navy as a Gunnery Control Officer, and I don't want to go there right now.

In a turquoise glazed bowl is a slab of bright-white tofu, which I slurp rather than chew, as it's as slippery as a *shubunkin* goldfish, and pretty much falls apart as I try to lift it – clumsily – with chopsticks. It's a good move though, as Naoki seems impressed that I'm even giving them a go, perhaps believing Westerners are only versed in knives and forks. I've eaten tofu plenty of times, but still, it's a curious dish, as the tofu has neither taste nor texture, and I feel like I'm eating not-quite-set soy jelly. But then Naoki gestures to a bowl of miso soup in which to dunk the tofu, along with some dried *bonito* flakes and grated ginger, and all of a sudden it goes from bland to grand, like a contestant in a Japanese geek-makeover show. Next is a large platter of sashimi artistically arranged on a bed of crushed ice and seaweed – neat slivers of raw salmon, octopus, bream, scallop and yellow-tailed tuna, and two whole shrimp. There's a fat dollop of wasabi on the side too. It's pretending very hard to look like innocent mashed avocado, but I know better than to fall for that old trick. No way. Wasabi and I have had run-ins before, and I don't need my eyes weeping like the Fukuroda Falls, and my nostrils burning as if I've just inhaled mustard gas. So I avoid it, and contemplate my shrimp. It's very big – more like a prawn – and its naked body looks suspiciously translucent.

'Is this raw too?' I ask Naoki, who's watching me carefully now, a cheeky smile playing across his face.

'Yes.'

I've never eaten raw crustacean before, but I figure it's much the same as eating raw fish, which I like. So I smile breezily at Naoki, and yank the shrimp's head off, putting it to one side. Then I hold the body aloft by the tip of its tail, hold my breath, and take a tentative bite. Then another – more boldly – because it's surprisingly good. I'd been expecting something all squishy and fishy, but this is creamy and smooth, almost like set mayonnaise.

'Hoaaaghhh,' says Naoki, just like they do in the movies, which impresses me no end, because I always thought that was parody. And perhaps a teeny bit racist. But it seems Japanese people really do say it.

'Hoaaaghhh. Now ret me show you how we eat shlimp in Japan.'

Naoki picks up his shrimp, pulls the head off, and stares knowingly at me as some long gloopy bits of yellowish guts slip out of the head and go 'plop' onto his plate. Then he puts the open end of the shrimp's head into his mouth, and sucks hard.

Oh God. He's just sucked its brains out. Raw brains. In his mouth. Sucked right out. Gross.

Naoki grins and wipes his lips, and looks at me with one eyebrow raised, as if daring me to do the same.

I hesitate a moment, but then – not wanting him to think Australians are wimps – pick up my discarded shrimp head, and wave it in the air.

'I can do that,' I say, shutting my eyes before shoving it in my mouth and sucking hard, before I can change my mind. Good grief, I can feel sloppy stuff cascading down my gullet like a bunch of kids on a water slide. It's at this point that I determine it's quite acceptable to wimp out just a little, so I follow it immediately with an emergency gulp of sake, from another pitcher that the waitress has clearly calculated I may need. This means I hardly have a chance to taste the brains, but still, I faintly register that they're quite sweet, and not all that bad. Naoki smiles, his already narrow eyes nearly disappearing into his head.

'Velly good,' he says. 'Now you are neary Japanese.'

The food keeps coming, with Naoki clearly keen to do his best to introduce me to the world of Japanese cuisine. There's *unagi* – eel – with a delicate earthy flavour, baby-pea-sized orbs of salmon roe that pop like saltwater-filled balloons when I squish them against the roof of my mouth, and seaweed salad – thankfully sans semen. Although I might have had a near-miss, as Naoki suddenly reaches for his translator. 'We also sometimes eat ... um ... *shirako*,' he says, waiting for it to show up on the screen. 'Yes, cod-fish sperm.'

'I beg your pardon?' I splutter.

'Hoaaaghhh, yes,' he replies with great enthusiasm. 'We call it a dainty here, a dericacy. It's velly good.'

Charming. Next time I'm offered anything that looks like raw egg white, I think I'll pass.

Our last course is *okonomiyaki* – Japanese pancake – a

mushy disc of fried-up mushrooms, red ginger, green onions and cabbage, with neat zigzags of mayonnaise that looks like phlegmy snails have been going through cadet drill.

Naoki nods at me encouragingly. 'The appearance is a rittle bit bad,' he smiles, 'but the fravour is good.'

I smile back, although with a sudden pang of sadness. I wish I too had been given the same opportunity to prove myself over the years. To show my flavour was superior to my presentation. Not that I'm saying I'm ugly – like this squooshy old pancake – but it seems that it's the pretty little pale-pink cupcakes that get all the attention. And the rings on their fingers. And the babies.

And let's face it, I'm just not cupcake material. And after this trip, perhaps just a big fruitcake …

Having adequately depressed myself, I'm hopeful that Naoki is ready for my animal question. It will be a good way to lighten things up, but I'm still worried that such an off-the-wall concept might be misunderstood, and possibly offensive, in such a formal and conservative culture. But he loves it.

'Hoaaaaghhh. Maybe a monkey.'

'Monkey? Why?'

'I rike gloops.'

'Gloops?'

'Yes, I rike gloops. Many people together. I don't rike being single. And a monkey is funny, and happy. Yes, I am a monkey. And being a monkey was good for sumo at Miritary School.'

'Sumo wrestling?' I ask, amazed. 'But you're not fat enough!'

It turns out that Naoki was a sumo wrestler in the

lightweight division, which gets me to wondering if he wore one of those white loincloths – which look like giant nappies – whereupon I have to stifle a giggle. But it's no laughing matter for Naoki.

'Yes of course, the *mawashi*,' he says, with nary a blink or a blush, which I admire, as an Australian male forced to wear such attire would most certainly die of self-consciousness. But Naoki speaks of it proudly. 'It is the uniform for sumo.'

'But weren't you embarrassed jumping around with your backside showing?' I ask, perhaps a bit tactlessly, but by now I can blame it on the sake.

'No, not rearry,' he replies cheerfully. 'We all looked the same. No probrem.'

At that I can't resist making my own toast to match the theme of the conversation. 'Bottoms up,' I say, draining the last of my sake, at which poor Naoki looks rather perplexed.

The bill arrives and Naoki absolutely won't let me pay, despite my repeated attempts to pick up the tab. It's a generous act that once again demonstrates how polite and gracious he is. There's a certain innocence about him too – a kind of wide-eyed wonder at how a white woman thinks, which I'm guessing is quite a few shades off a typical Japanese woman. Women here seem to put up with a lot from their husbands, who are known to regularly spend half the night out drinking with their mates, yet still expect their wives to have their slippers out upon their return. Whereas I'd be more likely to have the shotgun out. But despite the odd cultural difference, Naoki is clearly enjoying my company, and when it's time to depart, he insists on walking me to the train station. It's well out of his way, then a ten-minute wait, and when the train arrives I start to make my usual farewells.

'How many kisses in Japan?' I ask playfully, planning to give him a friendly little peck – or however many are the go here – on his cheek. However, when I sense his unease, I stop myself mid-pucker.

'In Japan, we do not kiss,' he explains, blushing sweetly.

'What about hugging?' I respond, not wanting to just walk away. I've become really rather fond of him, in a big sisterly way.

'No kisses or hugs,' he replies politely. 'We are uncomfortable with that. We just say *"sayonara"*.'

The train arrives and I jump on board, although it stays at the station for another five minutes. Naoki, being the perfect gentleman, waits on the platform for it to depart, standing almost to attention on the other side of the window. When the train finally moves off, I cheekily blow him a kiss anyway.

By the big smile on his face, I don't think he minds a bit.

The next day I have a lunch date with Vori – one of my most circuitous introductions. It started with my English cousin Harriot, then her Australian friend Andrew, then his Japanese girlfriend Rie, and finally her friend Vori, whom Rie described as a 'cheerful graduate student who is capable to talk in English'. Not that Vori looks like a student, with his smart navy-blue jacket and broad silver tie, and shoes that are so highly polished I can see in them the reflection of Mount Fuji. He's quite short and rotund, with such a close-cropped #2 haircut I can see his scalp between the hairs. For someone in his early twenties he's strangely baby-faced, with two enormous dimples in his cheeks so he looks a little like a Cupie doll. He greets me brightly, and then takes me on a wild-goose chase around Tokyo. Well, it's actually more of a wild rockhopper penguin chase. Vori walks briskly ahead of me with his head and upper body well forward, arms tight to his sides, and his stocky legs barely able to keep up with him. Indeed, I practically have to jog to keep apace. After breaking the record for a five-kilometre dash over a couple of blocks, catching two buses, and getting completely lost, we eventually reach our destination.

Saboriya restaurant is a 'fantasy *kissa*'. *Kissa* is short for *kissaten*, a comfy neighbourhood Japanese coffee shop, and fantasy *kissa* is a concept inspired by the hugely popular Japanese manga, or comic books, where diners are made to feel like they're inside a fantasy. Behind a window decorated in childish handpainted fairies and cartoon animals is a chaos of mismatched furniture, porcelain figurines, stuffed animals, cuckoo clocks set at different times, stacks of comic books, and pretty much whatever you'd find in a Disney collector's garage sale. It's truly, delightfully, bizarre.

The menu offerings are less imaginative, as if the food takes second place to the setting, so I end up ordering *tonkatsu*, a popular pork dish. Vori orders several other dishes for my 'education', pointing them out to me on the slapdash menu, handmade with a crazy collage of comic-book cutouts. I'm not quite sure what we'll end up eating, but it's looking like *tonkatsu* plus two gnomes and a daffodil fairy.

Vori speaks flawless English, and is a wealth of information on Japanese culture, anthropology, art, history and politics. He's clearly highly intelligent, and seems to know a little about a lot of things, although after a while I have a sneaking suspicion he's embellishing some things just to impress me. But he's quite a character, and not scared to defy traditional Japanese customs, and 'a very formal samurai mentality'. Indeed, he seems to enjoy being a bit of a rebel, telling me that he's living with his girlfriend even though her parents don't know.

'They would be very angry if they found out,' he tells me almost proudly, although concedes that if they were discovered he'd most likely marry her, because 'after living with her it would be very rude if I didn't'.

I'm impressed with his sense of honour, although it hurts a bit too. If Mark had thought to do the same – after six years of living with me – then maybe we'd still be together.

I'm keen to get a further understanding from Vori of how the Japanese view romance, given their cinematic offerings can be a little over-the-top, with samurai warriors and politely dishevelled women, and cherry blossoms in every second shot. But maybe Vori hasn't watched those films, because when I ask him how he'd impress a girl on his first date, he puffs up his chest and looks rather pleased with himself.

'I'd give her a cute nickname, whisper in her ear. Maybe sit together on a park bench, and ...'

'And make out?'

'No,' Vori replies, shaking his little hedgehog head vigorously. 'Hold hands. And maybe I would give her shoulders a hug if I like her. And kissing is okay if I really like her.'

Luckily our meal arrives so Vori can't see the smile on my face. It's all really rather sweet and innocent. Give her shoulders a hug? No wonder Casanova was Italian and not Japanese.

The meal has been unceremoniously plonked down in front of us on three melamine trays decorated with Snow White, Goofy and the Little Mermaid. And what with the Hello Kitty chopsticks, I feel like I'm back in kindergarten.

'*Itadakimasu*,' says Vori, hoeing into his meal without further ado. 'That means "good eating",' he adds, his mouth full.

My *tonkatsu* is a pork cutlet coated in breadcrumbs then deep-fried, and presented on a bed of limp lettuce. It looks pretty ordinary, but once again I'm reminded not to judge a book by its cover, as it turns out to be quite delicious. I just hope it's not Porky Pig, given the establishment we're in.

Which prompts me to ask the animal question.

Vori scratches his fuzzy scalp and looks thoughtful. 'Something simple but difficult,' he replies cryptically. 'An elephant perhaps. They look slow, but are actually fast and smart. They look kind, but are actually quite aggressive. They don't look like they're thinking anything at all most of the time, but they are.'

I laugh at this, although it gives me the impression Vori feels misunderstood, and that behind his somewhat bland façade there's a sumo wrestler trying to get out. Or else he's just trying to impress me again. Indeed, when I ask him what food he sees himself as, he replies, 'Hoaaaghhh, wasabi.' But I strongly suspect that he's more the avocado mash that just *wants* to be the wasabi when it grows up.

The next day, hoping to get some extra inspiration for what food to match with Naoki and Vori, I head for Tobu, a Japanese department store that has a 'ready to go' food section with enough prepackaged food on display – snack-sized, family-sized, party-sized, Emperor's banquet – to feed a 300-kilo sumo wrestler for a year. Or maybe a month if he's in training for a Grand Sumo tournament. There are mouthwatering variety boxes of sushi and sashimi. Platters of pork buns, bamboo-skewered prawn dumplings, gyozas and crescent-shaped wedges of tempura pumpkin. Ceramic bowls of teriyaki, *atsuyaki*, *ikayaki*, *monjayaki* – ironically none of which look 'yaki' at all. In fact they all look good, and I'm certainly spoilt for choice, but I decide on a handful of bright-green wontons filled with minced pork and water chestnuts, neatly gathered at the top like a miniature drawstring purse. I eat them right away. They're deliciously sweet with a wonderful crunchy texture, and are a perfect match for Naoki. The colour green is friendly and cheerful, just like Naoki, although he's a little shy at first so it takes time to unwrap and find the bolder flavours within. He's sweet and young and fresh, with many tasty elements to his personality. And if you have one, you certainly want more.

I also find Vori here, in the shape of a *nikuman* – a steamed pork bun. Vori too is round, plump, pale and a bit puffed up with himself. But once past all that fluffy stuff, there's a juicy little centre of slow-roasted pork, ginger and shiitake mushrooms, which is quite a treat. And if Vori really wants to be seen to pack a punch, well, he can always add a good dollop of sweet chilli sauce.

My final date for Japan – and indeed the whole trip – is with Shin, a Japanese diplomat who unfortunately turns out to be married, so my last chance of meeting The One has just melted away like tofu in miso soup. Still, he's impeccably charming and polite, and takes me out not only to a fabulous traditional restaurant for lunch, but also to a local fish market. It's here that I have a close encounter with an enormous dark brown sea cucumber, which, when I lightly prod it to see if it's alive, impudently oozes out a long string of yellow poo at me. I take this to be a sign that it's time to wrap things up before I get into any more shit. And frankly, after seventy-five dates in eighty-one days, that's fine by me.

The next day I head for the airport on the N'EX express train, which travels faster than a bad oyster on its way back up your gullet. In fifty-three minutes I'll be checking in, and checking out of this amazing odyssey. And I'm thrilled, because it means I can finally let myself go.

Just stop. Just be. No longer will I have to meet someone new every day, be polite through thick and thin, eat weird food, and drag my exhausted, foot-sore, bloated-belly carcass from one end of the globe to the other looking at men as if they're wontons, or beef pies, or *paprikás csirke*, or mushy peas, or parsley soup.

Or a *doppio espresso* – damn him.

Sure, I'm still single, but for the first time in ages, I don't really mind. I've well and truly had my fill of men the last twelve weeks, and I've discovered an extraordinary amount about them – and myself as well – that will surely serve me well as I turn the next page, and start the next chapter of my life. Or, to coin a little known Japanese proverb, 'As one restaurant closes, another one opens.'

Or something like that.

Dessert

*Desserts should bring a meal towards its close, never with
a coup de grâce to the stomach, but with the most satisfying
of good feelings that combine harmony and pleasure.*

– RENÉ GORDON, *THE COMPLETE AUSTRALIAN COOKBOOK*

Two weeks after returning home, I'm still exhausted.
I've traversed twenty-two countries across six
continents, travelled 52,794 kilometres by air, land
and sea, and eaten over 294 local dishes – some of
which were more challenging to eat than they were
to pronounce. And with dishes such as *sfogliotelle* and
capucijner, that's impressive.

And of course there's the men – all seventy-five of
them. Some of whom were quite delicious, and several
… well … nothing a good dose of Alka-Seltzer wouldn't
fix. Which is one of the reasons why I didn't include
Ireland in this tome even though I had no less than eight
dates there. Most of my Irish dates were just lovely –
witty, boisterous, intelligent, and very, very cheeky, but
no-one was remotely suitable as The One. And more-
over, one date was so completely hideous and cynical
that he temporarily quite spoiled my appetite for all
men. And he also made it quite clear that he wouldn't
give me permission to write about him 'in any form'
without vetting it first. What a spoilsport. If it looks
like a creep, talks like a creep, and behaves like a creep

– it usually is a creep. In fact, the food match I designated to him was one of those green potatoes that have turned poisonous.

Still, just about every one of my other dates taught me that what you put in, you generally get back, like with a dodgy recipe that comes good with enough love and perseverance. I've learned that every man on the planet – and woman too – has his or her own unique flavour, and it's just a matter of nibbling at a few to see what best suits your taste. To shut your eyes and give the prawn's brains a go. To stir the goulash and see what lies beneath the surface. To slice open the pomegranate to reach the succulent seeds within.

But as much as I'm all the richer for such lessons, there's still something missing. Or, more to the point, someone. Stefano – my delicious Italian *doppio espresso* – had me totally infatuated, and even though it was over before it began, I still had hope we could have made a go of it. And even though I finally got a whisper in the wind that he 'might' still be married – although ironically from a not-so-old girlfriend of his – I occasionally find myself daydreaming about staring blissfully into his intense blue eyes as we sit on the stoop of our vine-clad Tuscan cottage. Still, I know when I'm beat – although he's still taunting me with emails that are threatening to drive me completely insane.

Ciao Bambi,
I'm sending you some kisses. Virtual. I know you like them. (The soul that can speak through the eyes, can also kiss with a gaze.)

Baci,
Stefano

Darling,
You say that our time together was like a fantasy - but people that know me are aware that they can expect everything - the unimaginable. And this date can be one of the few cases where reality exceeds imagination.
Molti baci (you need to practise your Italian and—... the Italian),
Stefano xxooxx

It's all a bit too much for me to deal with really, but when I advise my sweet tormentor that I'm thinking of swapping my allegiance for *doppio espresso* to a local billy tea, in order to preserve my mental health, his reply has me chewing my knuckles to the bone.

Ciao Bambi,
But there is no surrogate for espresso - an everlasting mind and body pleasure. May be see you soon. The world is so small and for sure our path will cross again. I was even thinking to come to Melbourne for the next week's Formula One event.
S xx

Of course Stefano never comes. And I was probably tempting fate by getting a cute new haircut – more pixie bob, than convict crop – so I wouldn't scare him off a second time.

And so my dreams of What Might Have Been slowly fade away with the last days of summer, with a slight autumnal chill settling in to my soul. And as the excitement of my trip is replaced with the mundanities of suburbia, I realise I need to get on with my life, and not worry so much about finding a man with whom to share it. After all, as the writer Allen Saunders once said – a quote later adapted by John Lennon – 'Life is what happens to us while we are making other plans', and there's a whole lot of other great stuff I can do to fulfil myself.

As the weeks turn into months, I find a certain inner peace. The quiet knowledge that everything will turn out fine, and that indeed the universe is unfolding as it should. And in time, when I'm ready for a new relationship, there'll be a million exciting new options to explore.

And no, he doesn't need to be my father to make the grade.

Sure, I'd still like to find someone with Dad's confidence, capability, honesty, intelligence, generosity of spirit, and the ability to fix a broken china ornament with two matchsticks and a squeeze of super-glue. But I'm happy now to meet someone halfway, because I've learned that the majority of men are just as vulnerable, clumsy, insecure and lost as me. That they're mere mortals, and not a captain at the helm of a ship to whom I need to look up in reverence, like that five-year-old I used to be.

I'm the impatient type though. As autumn settles in with steely skied conviction, and it's been nearly a year since I first started this whole crazy international manhunt, I find myself thinking again about finding The One. Or heck – even three-quarters of him. In which case, should I give Mark another chance? I'm still a bit in love with him, and it would be so much easier to stay with the devil I know than the devil I don't. And simply accept the fact that he's not the marrying type. But after a few weeks of repeatedly meeting him for coffee to see if the spark could be reignited, the oven warmed up for that sunken soufflé to rise again, I realise we've inflicted too much damage on each other – or I on him – and our relationship can never be the same. So I'm just going to have to start over. To move on from Mark. To forget Stefano. And Harry, Eduard and Olivier. To throw the checklist wide open, and who knows, I might find someone so unusual, so different, so delicious, it will quite change my palate.

And although I have as much confidence successfully dating in my late forties as I would surfing at Bondi Beach on a paper plate, I'm damn well going to give it a go. What have I got to lose? Well … apart from a bit of pride perhaps. But I don't want to spend the rest of my life as some lonely, bitter old woman who has no-one to tell me I've got long hairs growing out of my chin. Which means I have no choice but to get over my fear of failure and rejection, and just go for it. Or to quote one little known Australian proverb, 'Take the bull by the horns and hang on bloody tight.'

Or something like that.

But there's still a slight problem. How do I go about it? Finding a lifelong mate is clearly much more complicated than having friends set me up with someone they may barely know. So with no eligible single men lurking about in my social circles, an intense dislike of tacky pub pick-ups, and unwilling to take the advice of an internet site on where to find men – including 'comedy classes, donating blood, charity events, science-fiction conventions, and car shows' – I'm feeling a bit stuck.

Indeed, I'm beginning to accept that at my age, the only way I'll get to meet someone half compatible is through online dating, where at least everyone is looking for much the same thing. Which is hopefully love – give or take a few shameless philanderers. But I have a paralysing horror of cyberspace introductions. It all seems so desperate. And clinical – with endless checklists to identify the sort of women the men are after, and vice versa: 'body type, smoking habits, have children, want children, eye colour, hair colour, political persuasion, drinking habits'. To me, such tight guidelines are tantamount to an unskilled cook shopping for the ingredients to a rabbit casserole, and if there's even one thing missing, they throw a hissy fit and ditch it all together. Whereas the New Me would be happy to go without the damned cloves if everything else looked tasty.

But online dating still seems to be the only feasible option, so after two weeks of procrastinating, and wondering whether it would be much easier to become a nun, I finally join RSVP, an Australian online dating service promising to 'help people find the joy of dating'. I presume as opposed to 'the horror of dating'.

I soon discover that the problem with online

introductions is that not only do I have to say what I want in a man, but also to write quite a detailed personal profile on myself. Now, I'm good at writing children's books, but writing a profile is far more confronting. It's like rolling over onto your back and exposing your belly to total strangers. And it's tricky too, as it needs to describe my extrovert character without sounding too overbearing. My sensitivity without sounding too self-deprecating. I can't be too capable, or too pathetic. Too energetic, or too lethargic. So what do I write without sounding like I'm bipolar? I waiver for a few days between inventing a fantasy character – and with a name like Bambi I'm already halfway there – or being totally truthful. But being truthful in the past never got me anywhere. Most men don't really want to hear that I'm independent and have a mind of my own, know the meaning of 'sexual dimorphism', and wear cling wrap to parties. And worse still, have just travelled around the world dating seventy-five men – if they weren't insecure before, then that would surely be the final straw. But after much soul-searching, I finally decide that I simply need to trust that the right man will read my profile, and think I sound interesting enough to contact me. I just need to believe there's a man out there who's not scared to try out the zesty mint liqueur. After all, if I want honesty from any man I might ultimately date, then shouldn't I start off being honest too?

So I name myself 'Missadventure', and suggest that meeting me would 'be an adventurous journey rather than a mishap', and include a photo of myself travelling through Tunisia wearing a dramatic olive head-wrap and sitting atop a scruffy camel. Then I bravely launch myself into cyberspace along with another hundred million hapless souls looking for love, even sending an online kiss – which is akin to saying 'I like you' – to a tall English chap with a nice smile, living in Melbourne, to test the water.

Then I wait.

And wait some more.

Two weeks later, the Pom sends me a reply: 'I was flattered by your kiss but I have already started seeing someone.' Which of course means, 'Thanks, but you are not my type, and btw, how could you even think I would like you? Now naff off.'

I'm gutted. I finally put my pride on the line, and he shrugs me off like a bothersome fly. Not that I'm about to give up. I like a challenge. And perhaps I came across in my profile as a teensy bit ballsy, so I add a photo of me looking reasonably demure in a black party dress. Although I make sure to crop it to exclude an ex-boyfriend standing beside me, who's wearing a large red satin turban and thick black eyeliner.

I did always rather like the flamboyant ones.

Over the next three weeks I send off fifteen kisses to men I quite fancy, and receive ninety-five kisses from men whom I assume fancy me. Not that it means the latter think I'm a Sex Goddess, but are perhaps just using the scattergun approach, and hoping one or two kisses of the hundred they send might hit the mark. Still, I check them all out – online – then edit out the ones with seven kids on time-share, or who enjoy 'heavy-metal bands and punk fusion', or who I suspect share absolutely nothing in common with me apart from being lonely. Which brings it down to a paltry three there's any point meeting face-to-face. However, even those rendezvous end up badly. When to break the ice, I ask one gentleman – and I use the term lightly – what sort of animal he is, he responds 'a sperm whale', and raises one bushy eyebrow suggestively. The date lasts three and a half minutes more – just enough time for me to pay for my coffee – and I'm out of there, wondering what I'd ever done in my past life to deserve such humiliation in this one.

Just as I'm about to throw in the towel, having decided I'd rather be single than endure any more torture, a little face pops up on Cupid Match, which is RSVP's auto-matched way of nudging people together with similar interests. At first I ignore him, because although ML500 looks quite nice, he's got a really stupid byline – 'Let's put the fun back in funeral' – which frankly I find more offensive than amusing, and conclude he must be a bit of an idiot. But a few days later he pops up again, so I read his profile, and discover he's funny, adventurous, well-travelled and articulate. Upon checking out his photo more closely, I'm delighted that he's very tall, and at fifty-two years old is not yet a member of the twilight zone, even appearing to have his own teeth and hair. Brilliant.

Despite the funeral comment, I send ML500 a kiss, figuring I have nothing to lose. Indeed, I've decided that if he doesn't work out, I'll cancel my subscription, and call it quits.

Who needs a man anyway?

The very next morning I receive an email from ML500, which is so engaging and witty that if there was any ice to break, he's done it, and we're soon sailing on smooth tropical waters. Over the next week we correspond, and speak on the phone, twice a day, and I find myself constantly laughing out loud at his quirky humour – 'Do I cook? Absolutely! I'm quite a gourmet – my chicken schnitzel sandwiches are to die for.' I'm inspired by his get-up-and-go attitude, which includes him having once been the vice-captain of the Australian elephant polo team in Singapore. He's also an avid traveller, having lived in Bali for three years, then in Buenos Aries for thirteen months, where he was co-owner of a Raw Food restaurant. And as for the future, he has a dream to sail around the world.

Just my kind of man.

After a couple of weeks I suggest we meet for coffee to see if there's a physical – as well as a mental – connection. He doesn't have to be good-looking, but there's no use continuing if there's no chemistry happening. And chemistry's important – if there's no jam in the centre of a lamington, there's nothing to keep it stuck together.

ML500, who's now introduced himself as Greg, agrees, texting that he wants to meet 'sooner rather than later, and either burst the bubble, or dance with the stars'.

Now, if you're going to win a girl over, that's the way to start, so I excitedly set a date for coffee, and carefully check out his online photos again, so I'll know for whom I'm looking. One snapshot shows him clad in a blue singlet and board-shorts in Bali, his long lanky body draped over a café bench. The other shows a handsome face illuminated by the most amazing sparkling blue eyes, and a cheeky-boy grin that clearly matches a wicked sense of humour. I note the ears that stick out a good few centimetres beyond his closely cropped hair, and decide they're rather cute, whereas in the not-too-distant past such a prominent feature might have had me running for the door, or reaching for the sticking plaster to pin them back.

Thank goodness I'm not that same person, and I hope I never ever bump into her again.

Four days later I'm waiting for Greg in Amici, a funky café on fashionable Chapel Street in Melbourne. Despite Greg being my seventy-ninth date since splitting from Mark – including the three earlier RSVP dates – I'm still nervous, so I make sure I'm facing the door, so the first thing he sees of me isn't my angular Cruella de Vil profile. I want so much for Greg to like me straight away, unlike Ali in Switzerland, Claus in Denmark and Ben in England, whose disappointment upon first clapping eyes on me showed clearly on their faces, like I was a slightly lopsided cake they'd previously been looking forward to picking up from the bakery.

I shouldn't have worried though, as when Greg walks in and spots me, he heaves an audible sigh of relief, and almost sinks to his knees as if giving thanks.

And yes – I'm equally as grateful. Greg is beanpole tall, extremely well-toned, blessed with handsome features and elegant salt-and-pepper hair, and his eyes are an even brighter aquamarine than the photos he'd posted online. But most importantly, he has a smile stretching across his face like the entrance to Luna Park. I like men who smile, and Greg's is broad and open and honest, and immediately puts me at ease. We talk solidly for the next three hours, about anything and everything and whatever fits in between. During this time, I move my car twice to avoid getting a parking fine, with Greg cheerfully declaring he's happy to risk getting a ticket, just in case he comes back after feeding the meter only to find that I've fled. But there's no chance of that. No chance at all.

I'm not going to quiz Greg the same way I interrogated all my poor dates on my journey around the world. This date is different, and besides, we both live in Melbourne, and I'm not about to hop on a plane for Siberia tomorrow, so there's no need to rush things. Well, apart from asking him my animal question, just in case he turns out to be a snake or a bush rat. In which case I'll call it a day before I get bitten.

'Monkey,' he says confidently, 'because they're active and they're fun, and they're pretty clever. And besides, I was born under the sign of the monkey in Chinese astrology.'

This tells me two critical things. One – if he's a monkey, he's bound to have a cheerful disposition. And two – being interested in astrology suggests he's in touch with his spiritual side.

He's looking better by the minute.

We eventually parts ways – a little reluctantly – but still without committing to a second date. I think we're both being careful not to blow it, because this dating game is a finely choreographed dance, and too many misplaced steps can trip you right up. But before I'm even back in my car, he sends a text.

I have to say you are the most gorgeous breath of fresh air I have met since I don't know when. Maybe ever. I am gobsmacked. There is a God after all. When can I see you again?

I feel much the same, and as I drive home slowly, a bit light-headed, I'm crossing my fingers that this is a relationship with legs – extremely long ones at that – and I'm determined to give it my very best shot.

The next three weeks are a whirlwind of coffee-dates and dinners, emails and text messages, and I soon realise that I may have met my match. And yes – maybe even The One. Greg sees life as a fast-paced adventure, not something to be limped through. He loves the feel of salt on his skin, wind through his hair, and sunshine on his face. He holds my hand to cross the road, makes me laugh so hard I nearly wet my pants, meets my friends and family with enthusiasm and generosity of spirit. I love what he wears – not so much the colourful sweatshirts and the slightly frayed Country Road cargo shorts, but the heart on his sleeve, and the joy of life in his smile.

And perhaps best of all, Greg 'gets' me. He isn't scared of who I am. Indeed, he seems to relish it. He gives my 'inner dag' free reign, and my imagination wings to fly. He likes my creativity, my cheekiness, and even the fact I've travelled the world dating dozens of strangers. He thinks I'm beautiful, smart, eloquent, 'occasionally' funny, and even concedes that I'm better at Scrabble than him. Which indeed I am, but how many men would actually ever admit to that?

And so we evolve, growing closer with every passing day. It seems that Greg has found in me the gaudily wrapped chocolate that had been left in the box. He was brave enough to open it and see what it tasted like, upon which he wanted more. Lots more. And in turn I'm now pretty confident that he's The One. The irony of which doesn't escape me, given he was sitting in my backyard all along, so I needn't have travelled the world meeting gigolos and potential serial killers to find him. Even so, I'm still not being presumptuous that it's necessarily going to last. We're both free spirits, and hanging onto free spirits can be like grabbing at the fragrant steam from a pot of chicken broth.

But we get to three months, then four, then six, spending blissful days jumping waves on windswept beaches, watching *Batman* at the drive-in, swimming with giant groupers in the Whitsundays, snuggling up to watch videos on Friday nights, and making such passionate love that I'm happily exhausted for days. All of which were things I'd dreamt of doing over all those lonely weekends home alone before he came along. Indeed, even back to when I was tempted to ask the genie in the bottle to help out.

Then, before a year has passed – a year that's right up there as the happiest, funniest, most romantic and adventurous of my life – Greg requests a 'private chat' with my father. It takes a few days to organise, and by the time we drive over to the family home, Greg is almost beside himself, although still not giving anything away. I'm pretty sure I know what he's up to, but I don't want to assume anything, so I take Mum into the kitchen to leave Greg and Dad alone, thrilled by the old-fashioned ritual of 'secret men's business'.

My father is gravely ill – his body riddled with cancer that will shortly take away his fine, proud life. But although he's just a shadow of his former self, he still has the grace and bearing – and undeniable authority – of a senior naval officer, so as I hover near the kitchen door, I'm hoping Greg isn't going to faint. I strain my ears to hear the conversation, and after some small talk, my own dear Gregory Horton Berryman takes a deep breath and begins.

'Sir, it's still a little early for me, but given the current situation with your health, I'd like to ask you now, that when the time is right, and if your daughter continues to behave herself, may I please have your permission to marry her?'

My mother is gripping my hand nervously at the kitchen table, not quite believing that this day would ever come for her wild and wayward daughter.

I don't hear Dad's answer, as his voice is weak now, and doesn't cut stenoriously through the house as it used to, but suddenly Greg bursts into the kitchen with his face alight. 'He said yes!' he almost whoops with delight. And I suspect some relief. I start to cry, not so much because of Greg being the only man to ask for my hand in marriage – well, as good as – but because I'm so happy that my father is still alive for his permission to be asked. That he can now die in peace knowing I'm going to be okay, and be loved, and that he doesn't need to worry about me being alone anymore.

And so comes the end of my journey. And like the shepherd boy in *The Alchemist*, it truly has been a passage turned full-circle. I'd travelled the world looking for love, failed miserably, then discovered it had been waiting for me back home all along, like a heartwarming dessert at the end of a 22-course banquet. A dessert of apple and rhubarb crumble to be more specific. It suits Greg perfectly. The apple for his sweetness, the rhubarb for his occasional tartness and bite, a pinch of cinnamon for a spicy kick, and the macadamia and coconut crumble on top, because he's unquestionably a bit nutty! And it's cooked to perfection – not too hot and not too cold – providing me with a nourishing finale to my odyssey that I hope will fill me up for many years to come.

Yes indeed. It seems an Australian was finally able to pique my tastebuds.

I am facing the future with optimism. The hunger sated, the cravings tamed, the belly satisfied, the soul nourished, and a renewed thirst for adventure in the years ahead.

Ah-men.

Full Menu

Australia

1 Matt: kangaroo steak – free-range and organic, sweet, slightly gamey, not too heavy or rich

2 Bear: fish 'n' chips – fresh, natural, uncomplicated, perfectly salted, surprisingly sweet

Brazil

3 Chico: caipirinha (lime cocktail) – a silky mix of sweet and sour. Vibrant, refreshing and very intoxicating

4 Paulo: churrasco eye-fillet steak – red-blooded, prime cut, lean, served rare, but too rich and gamey for my taste

5 Carlos: caramel cappuccino – smooth and sweet, with a satisfying richness of flavour once you start sipping

Cuba

6 Fernando: mojito (lime & mint cocktail) – colourful, vibrant, invigorating, cheeky, and potentially dangerous

7 Ariel: hot chocolate – so sweet it will give you cavities!

8 Alberto: ajiaco (soup with vegetables and pork) – smooth, tasty, nourishing yet humble, and with a great depth of flavours that keep rising to the surface

Netherlands

9 Bram: Dutch blue cheese – rich, with a creamy aftertaste, and delicious bursts of flavour running through it

10 Harry: venison and angel hair pasta with apple sauce –
mild and sweet at first but with each bite the rich and
heartwarming flavours and textures intensify

11 Jos: capucijner mit speck (pea soup with smoked
bacon) – heavy initially, but adding piccalilli (pickles)
makes it delightfully piquant

12 Eduard: appeldrie-hoek (baked apple pastry) –
looks appetising and sweet, but its brittle crust and slightly
stodgy filling leaves you feeling dissatisfied

Germany

13 Christian: käsekuchen (cheesecake) – light and sweet at first,
but as you eat, the flavours deepen; safe, dependable, homely

14 Jens: Jägermeister (herbal digestive) – smooth, mellow
and rich on first sip, but halfway down it burns like fire,
before leaving you with a naughty after-glow

France

15 Olivier: 1999 canon-fronsac red wine – full of character,
well-balanced, smooth and delightfully intoxicating

16 Chou-chou: pommes dauphine (mashed potato puffs in
savoury choux pastry) – a friendly, earthy flavour

17 Jimmy: cognac – hints of fresh vanilla and
rich caramel, and very, very smooth

18 Pierre: sweet apple cider – lively, refreshing and very sweet

19 David: Cointreau (orange-flavoured liqueur) – easy on the
tastebuds, sweet, intense, deep and totally delicious

20 Sebastian: roquefort cheese with pears – starts off mild, then the sharp, biting taste of the green mould in the cheese comes out; rich and tangy, but very good

21 Alaine: steak tartare (raw minced beef and onions) – tasty and textural, but a little gloopy for my liking!

22 Francois: plaisirs d'automne red wine – being well-matured, it has a rich intensity of flavor, yet is soft and supple

Monaco

23 Jorge: poulpes à la genovese (octopus with tomato, onion, capers) – sweet first-up, but ends up very oily and rubbery, with grabby little suckers

24 Frank: artichoke – lots of effort for not much return; too much vinegar, and just as you start to cope with the prickly leaves, the choke will get you – most unpalatable

25 Thierry: waffle – dry, all air and no substance

26 Jean-Luc: escargot – slimy, and hard to tell its true flavour under the heavy garlic sauce

27 Enrico: strawberries and warm balsamic vinegar – sweet and elegant, great depth of flavour

Italy

28 Pasquale: tartufo (ice-cream dessert) – outer layer of smooth dark chocolate that hides a rich, creamy, vanilla interior with a secret centre

29 Francesco: mozzarella di bufala Campana – smooth, with a mild, refined taste and interesting textures

30 Raffael: menta (mint) gelato – sweet, colourful, melt-in-your-mouth goodness, with a refreshing fizz

31 Massimo: Campari and orange aperitif, sweet and tangy, with a slightly bitter twist

32 Stefano: doppio espresso – hot, intense, refined, robust, sweet, velvety smooth and full of flavour; brewed to perfection, and utterly decadent – instantly addictive

Vatican City

33 Gabriel: angel hair pasta with shrimps, garlic and virgin olive oil – warm, mellow, sweet; a heavenly flavour

Switzerland

34 Ali: bouillabaisse with extra cayenne pepper – complex, exotic, smooth and elegant, rich and luxuriant, loads of flavour, with a God-almighty spicy kick!

Liechtenstein

35 Martin: käsknöpfle (grated noodles and fried cheeses) – appears bland, but surprises with its rich flavour

36 Ernst: parsley cream soup – initially subtle in flavour, then develops a warm and deeply complex character; a dish with tremendous personality

37 Michael: spinach and veal ravioli – starts off restrained, but once the ravioli wrapper is removed, all the colours and flavours are revealed

38 Tibo: wild salmon and wasabi foam – rich and deep in flavour; but watch out for the wasabi – it bites!

Hungary

39 Andras: paprikás csirke (chicken in a paprika sauce) – richly
flavoured with a sweet base and a spicy kick

40 Attila: gulyasleves (goulash) – as you stir, the flavours
and textures come to the surface; rich and refined, sweet
and spicy, wholesome and oddly comforting

Denmark

41 Claus: salmiakki (salted licorice) – astringent, salty
and a little mouth-puckering at first, but the
flavour eventually softens and is very moreish

42 Niels: brunede kartofler (caramelised potatoes) –
doesn't pretend to be anything fancy, but has great
depth of flavour, and is very, very sweet

Russia

43 Artashes: blinis with different fillings – simple
yet sophisticated, with style and substance; every
mouthful is a delightful surprise

44 Sergei: pelmeni (dumplings) in mushroom broth –
nourishing and tasty; simple, honest and unpretentious

45 Andras: preserved cranberries – you think they'll be
sweet, but they have an unexpected sourness

Scotland

46 Hamish: Scottish salmon – the skin can be a little crispy,
but when you dig deeper it is sweet and succulent

47 Lorne: Brammle Scotch whisky liqueur (bramble
berries steeped in whisky) – tantalisingly delicious,
sweet and mellow; gives your cheeks an instant glow

48 Alistair: Scotch rib eye – red-blooded and meaty but too rubbery to get through easily, and a wee bit over-marinaded

Ireland

49 Brendan: Irish oak-smoked salmon and capers – elegant, refined, flavoursome

50 Sheamus: Baileys Irish Cream liqueur – deliciously smooth and rich

51 Mick: chicken and leek boxty (potato pancake) – filling, down-to-earth and wholesome

52 David: Kerrygold Irish buttered popcorn – irrepressibly cheerful – it really pops!

53 Eoghan: poisonous green potato – looks harmless but when potatoes are exposed to light, they produce a toxic substance called solanine, which can cause stomach cramps, fever, paralysis and even death; extremely unpalatable

54 Kevin: Brussels sprouts – overcooked and grey of pallor, but still quite tasty

55 Johnny: pear cider – irresistibly smooth, sweet, refreshing, with great depth of flavour

56 Michael: Guinness – frothy on top, but beneath the surface it's deep, dark and mysterious; complex and flavoursome, but perhaps a little bitter

Portugal

57 Fernando: pastel de nata (custard tart) – a chewy base, but its centre is all heavy sweetness and creamy lusciousness, with deeply complex nuances and great textures

58 Phillipe: chocos com tinta (cuttlefish in ink) – too much black ink and watch out for those grabby little tentacles!

59 George: Sagres beer – refreshing, crisp, bright and cheerful

60 Pedro: old tawny port – old, rich, heavy, dark and very complex

61 Fernando: Casal Garcia sweet port – light and bubbly, sweet and open, fresh, young, easy to toss back; quite delightful!

62 Carlos: sardinha assada (grilled sardines) – oily, rich and decidedly fishy; handle carefully to avoid choking on the bones

Wales

63 Robin: cennin hufennog (creamed leek) – appears bland but becomes sweeter with each layer; rich, elegant and surprisingly nourishing

64 Rhys: Welsh beef tenderloin – rich, rare and full of flavour, but way too gamey for my liking – too much testosterone?

England

65 Sebastian: rolled roast pork – heartwarming, rich, nicely textured, uniquely savoury and sweet at the same time

66 Stuart: runner bean – tall and thin, hyperactive, sweet, and constantly climbing the wall!

67 James: mushy peas – colourful, earthy, flavoursome, wholesome and mushy

68 Ben: hot English mustard – sharp, complex and tasty, but so blistering it can blow your head off; best left in the jar

69 Nick: rice pudding with jam – comfort food: unpretentious, heartwarming and very sweet

United Arab Emirates

70 Nasser: kibbeh nayyah (spiced raw meat patties) –
red-blooded, spicy, colourful and rich, but far too slimy for me

71 Abu: pomegranate – big and round, with juicy,
crunchy, little bursts of sweet and sour

Oman

72 Fahad: dates – very sweet, rich, and easy to
digest; but watch the pip!

Japan

73 Naoki: green wonton filled with minced pork and
water chestnuts – a friendly and cheerful colour, and
once unwrapped the even bolder flavours reveal themselves

74 Vori: nikuman (steamed pork bun) – plump, pale
and a bit puffed up, but with quite a tasty centre

75 Shin: miso soup – looks simple and light, but when
stirred up, hidden things float to the surface

Australia

Dish of the Day

Greg: apple and rhubarb crumble – sweet with occasional
tartness and bite, a pinch of cinnamon for a spicy kick,
and macadamia coconut crumble on top for a bit of
nuttiness; cooked to perfection – not too hot, and
not too cold, and very nourishing